U-Boat Aces

Titles in the 'Fortunes of War' series

FORTUNES OF WAR

U-Boat Aces

BY GEOFFREY P JONES

CERBERUS

First published by William Kimber & Co Ltd in 1988

PUBLISHED IN THE UNITED KINGDOM BY;

Cerberus Publishing Limited

Penn House

Leigh Woods

Bristol BS8 3PF, United Kingdom

Tel: ++44 (0) 117 974 7175

Fax: ++44 (0) 117 973 0890

e-mail: cerberusbooks@aol.com

www.cerberbus-publishing.com

British Library Cataloguing in Publication Data.
A catalogue record for this book is available from the British Library.

ISBN 1 84145 035 9

PRINTED AND BOUND IN MALTA.

Contents

Acknowledgements

Firstly, I must thank my brother Ted for the seven maps and diagrams he has provided for this book – he was in England for the first time in 14 years, on long-service leave, from Perth Western Australia. I consider his map of *Ark Royal*'s wartime voyages excellent and it illustrated the old saying 'a picture is worth a thousand words'. Colin Davison, editor of the Western Morning New's, was kind enough to allow me to quote from the newspapers of September 1939. Negatives of photographs from the *Western Morning News* that I would have liked to use were destroyed when Plymouth was later blitzed. Gus Britton of the Royal Navy Submarine Museum and Jak Matlmann-Showell were always available at the end of a telephone line when I had queries. Karl Wahnig (ex-U-802) made suggestions and Heinz Guske (ex-U-764) helped with translation. Material for the book was researched in many places, but the prime English sources were the Imperial War Museum, the Colindale Newspaper library, the Public Record Office and the Royal Navy Submarine Museum – so, many thanks to their helpful staffs. Other people who helped, including many first person stories, are mentioned in the text of the book.

Many previously unpublished copyright photographs are included in the book. Paul Kemp of the WM's picture library and Hörst Bredow of the Bundesarchiv kindly helped select official photographs. Other individuals and organisations who supplied Partnerships Ltd, Fox Photos, Douglas Gowland, Mrs J Gwyer, Dr Uwe Jenisch, P & O Steamships Ltd, with the remainder from the author's collection.

Introduction

Members of the *Barham* Survivors Association know that their ship was torpedoed by *Freiherr* Hans Diecrich von Tiesenhausen; they also know what happened to U-331. Do the survivors of *Ark Royal* know which U-boat commander sank their carrier? The difference between the loss of one man and hundreds obviously concentrates the mind and interest.

Survivors from the carrier *Courageous* tell of seeing their U-boat attacker sunk, and this was reported in the newspapers – was it true? Relatives and friends of those killed in the escort carrier *Avenger* did not know how their men died. Survivors from *Orcades* want to know why their liner was directed into the path of a waiting U-boat.

Empress of Britain, Barham, Warwick Castle, Courageous, Avenger, Strathallan, Eagle and *Ark Royal* were all sunk while being escorted: what happened to the U-boats that sank them? *Viceroy of India, Orcades* and *Duchess of Atholl* were all unescorted when sunk despite their huge troop carrying capacity.

In every one of the incidents their U-boat attacker escaped – surely the commanders must have been aces? If they were, what else did they sink and what was the eventual fate of them and their boats. It is these questions that I have attempted to answer in this book. I have spent a long time researching, and written other books in the meantime, while endeavouring to piece all the obtainable facts together. The reader will obviously realise that as it was impossible to get a sight of the last log from a sunken U-boat, other means had to be found. It was not possible to obtain detailed information from certain theatres of war and this problem had to be surmounted. One can never be sure one has collated all the facts, but I think I have squeezed every known source in the preparation of this book. It covers the sinkings of the large ships of around 20,000-tons and more and a representative escort carrier. Each U-boat crew was different but those moulded together by the successful U-boat commanders must have been something special. Eighty percent of U-boat men did nor survive the war yet twenty-three of the thirty most successful commanders did. Perhaps the sinking of so many large targets may not leave the British reader feeling too comfortable, but this should be balanced by the U-boat losses shown – fifty consecutively launched U-boats from one yard and twenty-five from another. Many U-boats were sunk without even firing a torpedo, but this book is about the others – those who survived – commanded by U-boat aces.

Where times are given they are local times unless otherwise stated.

GPJ
Abbey Wood
1988

CHAPTER ONE

TWO WEEKS OF WAR

After a midnight meeting of the cabinet the British Ambassador in Berlin gave the German government notice at 0900 on Sunday, 3 September 1939, that unless they agreed within two hours to withdraw their troops from Poland, which they had invaded two days earlier, Great Britain would declare war.

At 1115 that morning the Prime Minister, Neville Chamberlain, broadcast from Downing Street the announcement that Great Britain was at war with Germany. The broadcast was followed almost immediately by an air-raid warning, which proved to be a false alarm.

That evening *Kapitänleutnant* Fritz-Julius Lemp, commander of U-30, torpedoed the Donaldson liner *Athenia*, west of the Hebrides, in the mistaken belief that it was a troopship. In fact it was carrying passengers, including women and children, to America. The U-boats had struck the first war blow.

Other U-boats were also at sea, for U-12, U-13, U-15, U-16, U-17, U-20, U-21, U-23, U-24, U-56, U-58 and U-59 had sailed at 0400 on 25 August from their North German bases as instructed by the Flag Officer U-boats.

The U-boat most concerned in this chapter, U-29, had left Wilhelmshaven on 19 August, commanded by *Kapitänleutnant* Otto Schuhart. The commander, who as a 20-year-old, qualified in the officers' class of 1929, had been with the U-boat for five months. The boat, which was to survive until the last week of the war, was one of six Type VIIA boats built at the AG Weser yard at Bremen and launched in August 1936. The other four Type VIIA boats were built at the *Germania Werft* at Kiel. The boats carried eleven torpedoes for their five tubes, four forward and one aft. The aft tube, fitted above the stern, made the Type VIIA boats easily identifiable and distinguished them from the more illustrious other Type VII boats.

The first Royal Navy ship to be sunk in the war, the aircraft carrier HMS *Courageous*, was laid down in the Kaiser's war. A Devonport ship, the carrier displaced 22,500-tons. Originally built by the firm of Armstrong as a cruiser, begun in May 1915 and completed in January 1917, *Courageous* was one of the emergency war programme vessels. Her original cruiser design was formulated by Lord Fisher in 1915 with a view to operations in the Baltic, which explains her maximum draft of between 22 and 28-feet empty and full load.

On trials she met heavy weather and was driven into a head sea, straining her hull forward. Doubling plates were added there, and subsequent trials showed that the defect had been overcome. She was taken in hand for conversion into an aircraft carrier at Devonport in June 1924, and the work was completed on 5 May, 1928; her conversion had cost over two million pounds. She was one of the fastest warships in the world, and had crossed the Atlantic in a record time of less than four days.

The enormous upper deck of *Courageous*, 786-feet long, was clear except for the funnel and control tower, which lay well aft and off the centre-line on the port side. The funnel and control tower were known as the island. The deck had long lines upon it, marked in white, with divisions at every foot to show aircraft just where they had landed; and it was fitted with sunken electric lights for night landing. All round the ship ran a stout netting, where the landing crews waited, and in which an aircraft that had overshot the deck might be pulled up. The after part of this great deck could be lowered in one piece, like a gigantic lift, to the covered deck below, a vast area filled with aircraft, torpedoes and gear. Round the outside of this lower deck were placed the sixteen 4.7-inch guns which were the carrier's defence against both surface and aerial attack.

Courageous was not the easiest carrier to work from. The airflow over the stern might come at a pilot like a waterfall and the hot gases from the funnel whisk him up just when he wanted to sink down.

In 1938 *Courageous* had another refit and a light tripod mast was fitted on her superstructure. As her machinery was as in 'C' class cruisers, the carrier had achieved 32-knots in service.

The Devonport-based carrier, under the charge of Captain W T Makeig-Jones, could hold twenty-four torpedo-carrying aircraft. HM ships *Eagle*, *Hermes*, *Furious*, *Glorious* and *Ark Royal* were the other large aircraft carriers on the Royal Navy's strength at the outbreak of war. HMS *Argus* was a flat-top.

At the beginning of 1939 there were 80,000 officers and men on the strength of the Naval reserve and 15,000 of these were brought to readiness by mid-June and the bulk of the rest by the end of July. The wartime complement of the recently refitted *Courageous* had its quota of reservists and pensioners who had been called back to the colours.

To deal with U-boats it was considered that the surface vessels and aircraft allocated to trade protection could best be divided into anti-U-boat hunting units, and disposed at strategic points round the British Isles.

By 31 August all Home Fleet ships had taken up, or were going to, their war stations, ammunitioned, and ready to proceed. At Portland were *Courageous* and *Hermes* with the battleships *Resolution* and *Revenge*, cruisers *Ceres*, *Caradoc* and *Cairo* and nine destroyers of the 18th Destroyer Flotilla.

Three years earlier King Edward VIII had visited *Courageous* while she was at Portland and sung 'Tipperary' in the centre of two thousand naval ratings at an entertainment on board; two years later his brother, King George VI, having led the Home Fleet to sea from Weymouth, attended a concert given by men of the Fleet in the hangar of *Courageous*, and expressed his thanks for a 'good show'. At the beginning of the month the King had again been piped aboard *Courageous* while she was in Weymouth Bay at Portland on the occasion of the inspection of the Reserve Fleet.

On the day that Hitler invaded Poland, *Courageous*, having recommissioned, was still at Portland, but was now with the Home Fleet. Before dawn on Saturday 2 September *Courageous* escorted by the destroyer HMS *Sturdy* sailed for Plymouth in accordance with instructions received from the Admiralty. She was thus lying in Plymouth Sound when the Prime Minister made his war declaration.

It was not heard by many of the crew's relations and friends who thronged the Hoe, looking down at the carrier, when news of the ship's arrival had passed from mouth to mouth. On board *Courageous* the declaration was heard in silence but this was soon shattered as the bugler sounded 'Action stations' and the commander ordered 'Man the side'. At the same time, from shore, the wailing of the air-raid sirens could be heard. The sailors were looking for U-boats! Very soon it was decided the carrier would be safer in port and it proceeded to berth in Devonport dockyard.

Local leave was granted to the off-duty watch that evening and the men scrambled ashore after handing in their station cards. Some caught the bus to their homes on the estates at St Budeaux, while others were satisfied to invade their favourite tavern. They were not to drink for long as a white-gaitered party of sailors wearing armbands with NP, (naval patrol, but colloquially known as 'nasty people') was sent round to all the watering holes to order the crew back on board.

Miraculously, all the men were back on board when *Courageous* sailed on the tide in the dark hours. Just like Sir Francis Drake, three-and-a-half centuries earlier the men had been plucked from their play at Plymouth to sail and fight the foe.

Courageous had been ordered to join the Channel Force with HMS *Ramillies*, presumably in the light of an air reconnaissance report of Sunday afternoon on the activity of *Kriegsmarine* ships in the Schilling Roads. Later the carrier's orders were altered, possibly in view of the sinking of *Athenia*. The carrier, with three destroyers, was sent to hunt U-boats. *Courageous* carried no fighters for protection, for no enemy aircraft could reach the war position to the south-west of Ireland; her twenty-four biplanes were all for attacking U-boats while the asdic-fitted destroyer escort would protect the carrier from underwater attack.

The early Monday morning risers, walking their dogs on the grassy Hoe, soon saw that their home port carrier was no longer in dock. Many other things changed too; children had their already long summer holiday extended as they filled sandbags to protect their lower school windows. The County Cricket championship which was drawing to a close and the Football League programme which was just beginning had their fixtures cancelled. Theatres and cinemas closed, it was not considered safe for people to congregate anywhere. A black-out was in force and many pedestrians were injured as cars were only allowed to drive on sidelights. To help ease black-out conditions and save electricity and fuel, summer time was extended by six weeks. Women aged 18 to 50 were urged to join the WRNS to release men for sea service. While the pensioners and reservists were getting used to their 'Ticklers' again on board civilians ashore were paying 1/4d for twenty-five Players cigarettes.

Some of those called back to serve in *Courageous* were over fifty years of age and had fought all through the Kaiser's war. Their experience was not used to train young sailors, they were sent to fight.

Out at sea *Courageous* was placed under the orders of the Commander-in-Chief Western Approaches, and it was suggested by the Admiralty that it should be employed well out in the Atlantic for hunting U-boats and the protection of trade. *Courageous* was escorted by HM destoyers *Kempenfelt*, *Ardent* and *Echo* and was to continue at sea for as long as fuel permitted. Included in the operational orders was the information that convoys to North America were running from Liverpool and the Thames estuary and that from the 11th other convoys would be running from the Bristol Channel ports to those on the French Atlantic coast.

Just prior to the war a Government section was formed to plan and organise the defensive arming of the whole British Merchant Navy in co-operation with the Ministers and the ship-owners, anti-U-boat and anti-aircraft guns were collected and distributed. The dockyards prepared the ships for their fitting and naval reservists and Merchant Navy crews were trained in their use. The guns, for the most part, were naval weapons which had been removed from scrapped warships.

Meanwhile U-29 had reached its patrol area and just after midday on 8 September torpedoed and sunk the London registered *Regent Tiger*. At over 10,000 tons the tanker was the largest merchant ship sunk so far. The next victim for Otto Schuhart presented itself in much the same area five days later. This was an 800-ton steam tug *Neptunia* which only a few days earlier had been in Falmouth for repairs. It was mid-afternoon when U-29 surfaced and sent a shot soaring over the tugs bows. *Neptunia* was signalled to 'Abandon ship' and the twenty-one-man crew did so. A torpedo was fired, probably set too deep and then the guns crew sent twenty-six to thirty shells into the tug before it sank. Later the crew described the event:

> It happened about four o'clock on Wednesday afternoon. We were steaming at full speed when suddenly a shot fell in front of us. It came from behind us, and on looking round we saw a U-boat had come to the surface. It signalled to us to abandon ship, and we had no option but to do so.
>
> We got out the lifeboat and the dinghy and the lifeboat towed the smaller one. The commander of the U-boat fired from 20 to 30 shells at the Neptunia.
>
> After about an hour the commander came alongside and asked us if we had any bread and water, and we replied "Yes". He also asked us if we had any cigarettes and matches, and we told him we had not. He gave us cigarettes and matches, and two bottles of brandy - one for each boat. Unfortunately one bottle thrown to the second boat was missed and it fell into the water.
>
> He told us he was sorry, but they were at war, and added, "It is your turn now and it may be my turn next week".

The commander, they said, appeared to be about forty years of age. Those on deck wore no uniform and they appeared a motley crowd. One man was wearing a tweed cap and jacket. The commander said, 'I am sorry I can't tow you near to a ship. There are two destroyers about and I have to put off.' He added that they would meet an American ship directly. 'The U-boat cleared off, and we waved to each other like football teams,' they stated.

The commander was 'a proper toff, they asserted. 'He could not have done more for us in the circumstances. Of course, we were on the high seas. That is our job.'

One crewman said, 'I lost £20 worth of gear, but if I met the commander tomorrow I would stand him a drink.'

They stated they had travelled for 28 to 30-hours, and then met the coaster *Brinkburn*, which took them on board and brought them to Falmouth. At first the coaster's crew thought they were a submarine. They calculated that they had gone 130-miles before being picked up.

In addition to the gifts mentioned, they were also given some bandages for the wireless operator, who had broken his arm when lowering the boat, and a box of red flares.

There was nothing to indicate which U-boat it was as all markings had been painted out.

The day after the tug was despatched Otto Schuhart sighted another target. In the afternoon, a second tanker *British Influence* of 8,431-tons was hit and sunk with a torpedo and artillery attack. One of the survivors said he was on watch in the tanker when, at about noon, he saw a U-boat surface. He continued:

> An order was given by the U-boat commander to lower the boats. The U-boat had by this time come alongside. The commander asked the crew if they had sufficient food, tobacco and clothing. He then said he was going to sink the ship.
>
> The U-boat later came alongside the lifeboats and the commander said a rescue ship was on the way. He fired three rockets in the air to attract the rescue ship. When the ship did not seem to be appearing the U-boat commander told the crew to stay where they w"ere and he would go and get it. After some time the U-boat returned with the Norwegian ship Ida Bakko. When the crew of the British Influence were on board the Norwegian vessel they gave three cheers for the U-boat crew. The Germans replied by giving a similar three cheers for the British Influence crew.

The U-boat, U-29, then submerged.

At almost the same time as the last sinking *Courageous* and its escort were steaming into Plymouth Sound to refuel. There were no successes to report although it was thought that a U-boat could have been damaged by a Swordfish attack on the 10th. Also on the 10th the carrier suffered its first casualty when a Swordfish failed to return. It was a cloudy day and the aircraft was heard flying above the carrier but failed to see it and obviously crashed when the fuel ran out. There was at this time no radio contact between ship and aircraft, just W/T signals and the carrier dare not break wireless silence as it would attract the attention of listening U-boats.

When the carrier arrived at Plymouth some of the crew who obtained local leave scanned the newspapers to see what had been happening on shore while they had been away. They read that convicts who had nearly completed their sentences were being prematurely released from Dartmoor, that Registrars were literally working overtime conducting wartime Registry Office weddings and that the restrictions on public gatherings had been relaxed providing places of entertainment closed at 2200. Billy Cotton had been unable to appear at the Palace Theatre as five of his band had been called up!

Courageous left Plymouth again after less than 48-hours in port. Hundreds of people watched her depart at 1030 on the Saturday morning; she proceeded to the westward, to the Atlantic, to an operational area of south-west Ireland. The carrier HMS *Hermes* was carrying out a similar anti-U-boat patrol to the south of her and had put to sea 36 hours earlier.

The captains of both carriers had attended a meeting ashore at the Area Combined Headquarters on Thursday the 14th, where the latest appreciation on the British dispositions and U-boats was made available to them. It was made quite clear to both commanding officers that they were not tied in any way by the appreciation. They were given a free hand as regards the conduct of their operations. The object was given as the destruction of enemy U-boats and it was impressed on the commanding officer of *Courageous* that once contact had been made with a U-boat it should be hunted until it was destroyed.

When *Courageous* sailed, her escort comprised HM destroyers *Inglefield*, *Intrepid*, *Ivanhoe* and *Impulsive*. Nothing happened until 2035, when *Impulsive* dropped two depth charges on a contact and *Inglefield* left the screen to assist, leaving the other two destroyers to reform the screen. This contact was not confirmed by *Inglefield*, but both ships continued to search until 2150 when the contact was abandoned as 'non-sub'. It was not thought desirable to rejoin the carrier during the night, so the detached destroyers remained ten miles to the southward, rejoining at 0700 on the 17th when all four destroyers again formed a close anti-U-boat screen for *Courageous*. A patrol of three aircraft had been flown off on clearing Plymouth, being maintained during daylight hours to a distance of fifteen miles on either side of the ship.

The war was two weeks old.

The first intimation of the presence of U-boats was received at 1545, when a signal from a British steamer was intercepted stating that she was being attacked with gunfire by a U-boat in a position which put her about 130-miles to the westward; *Kafiristan* was sunk by U-53. *Inglefield* and *Intrepid* were immediately detached to hunt the U-boat if it submerged, and a striking force of four aircraft was flown off to attack the U-boat. A Swordfish from *Courageous* attacked U-53 causing it to dive. The other two destroyers remained as a screen to the carrier, which at 1630 flew on the three patrolling aircraft that had been recalled, and at 1645 she proceeded at 23-knots to close the reported position of U-53 and so lessen the distance the striking force had to return. This was necessary on account of the incomplete state of training of the observers who frequently failed to find the carrier.

On this occasion two of the four did lose themselves and had to be given D/F bearings to get back. From this time onwards no anti-U-boat air patrol was maintained, as it was deemed undesirable to have too many aircraft with only partially-trained observers in the air at one time even though visibility was good. At 1800, speed was increased to 25-knots and zig-zagging was discontinued to make good more distance to the westward, but at this speed the destroyers could not use their asdic sets effectively. Forty minutes later, speed was further increased to 26½-knots to get to the rendezvous for the returning aircraft in time, and at this speed the destroyers were obliged to house their asdic domes.

The first aircraft returned at 1900, and from this time until 1945, the carrier was manoeuvred for flying them on, speed being reduced to 18-knots at 1915 when the destroyers again lowered their asdic domes and set anti-U-boat watch.

The aircraft still in the air did not know that U-53 had been attacked and had submerged - they continued flying until they reached their prudent limit of endurance. In fact one pilot, Lieutenant A C B Lamb, flying in a Swordfish with his observer and telegraphist/air-gunner, only just made it back on board. The fuel gauge was showing zero as the biplane, turning into the wind, approached *Courageous*. The carrier's batman was desperately trying to wave the aircraft off, but the pilot, who had risked the crosswind, did not have enough fuel to circle round while the carrier turned into the correct position, the tank of the radial engine was almost empty. The final approach was made successfully and the aircraft hooked the arrester wire. The Swordfish had landed safely and all the aircraft were now aboard.

Zig-zagging was resumed as soon as the last aircraft had been flown on, the speed being maintained at 18 knots. At 1958 *Courageous* was hit by two torpedoes on the port side just abaft the bridge. A third torpedo missed.

The torpedoes had been fired from U-29. The U-boat was still in the same patrol area in which it had accounted for its first three victims, waiting in the shipping lanes of the Western Approaches. In the late afternoon a passenger liner was sighted through the periscope. A Swordfish, obviously from *Courageous* searching for *Kafiristan* and U-53, was observed at the same time and it appeared to the German commander that the ship in his sights was a worthwhile target as it had an aircraft escort.

Just as the attack had been set up, the ship altered course. The submerged U-boat could not match its speed so the commander decided to wait until the ship was out of sight so that he could surface and at maximum surface speed manoeuvre in front of the ship for a text book attack. Before surfacing an all round sweep with the periscope revealed a smudge on the horizon. A bead was taken and gradually the unmistakable shape of an aircraft carrier revealed itself. Everything now slotted into place, the explanation as to how a biplane with limited endurance was so far from land. All ideas of attacking the passenger ship were dropped, the man-of-war was the new target.

It took two hours for the U-boat to approach within striking range and then Otto Schuhart had a piece of luck. As the carrier turned into wind to fly-on the last aircraft her 786-foot length presented a huge target for the U-boat to aim at and three torpedoes were quickly on their way.

No torpedo tracks were seen by either *Courageous* or the escorting screen before the ship was hit. Immediately after *Courageous* was torpedoed *Ivanhoe* made three attacks, with charges set at 100-feet on contacts but these attacks were eventually considered unsuccessful. On board the carrier two heavy explosions were felt in rapid succession. All the lights went out at once and the ship almost immediately took a heavy list to port. The ship had already been darkened although the sun had not yet quite set when this was done and all dead lights and most of the screen doors were therefore closed. One torpedo hit the port to the heavy list of the ship and the fact that there were no lights or broadcaster working, the remainder could not be closed. Shortly after the explosions the captain had given the order to flood the starboard bulge. A party proceeded to 'Z' seacock in order to attempt to flood the bulge; the cotter pin was removed but in spite of a wheel spanner the valve could not be turned. It was assumed that the rod gearing was distorted and jammed by the explosion.

All boats except seaboats were turned in and secured. Owing to the heavy list which the ship took to port at once and which finally reached about 35 to 40-degrees, it was not possible to lower any boats except the starboard cutter. This boat suffered some damage on being lowered and subsequently became completely waterlogged. The fourth motor boat on the port side right aft was, however, traversed out and some ratings were able to unhook the falls as soon as she became waterborne owing to the list of the ship. It was only found possible to cast loose about three of the Carley floats on the starboard side, and these were lowered. Gratings and loose woodwork were also thrown over the side to help men in the water.

Both aircraft hangars were evacuated by the few officers and ratings who were there at the time the torpedoes hit. Personnel in the lower hangar had some difficulty in forcing a way through the fire curtains which were jammed down after the explosions.

Several officers aft on the quarterdeck of *Courageous* said that they saw a periscope fine on the port quarter showing up against the reflected glow in the water from the western sky. Some of them loaded a starboard 4.7-inch gun but owing to the list of the carrier it could not be trained. Several officers and ratings saw the stern of the U-boat come up out of the water after the first depth charge attack.

The captain had ordered the international code signal 'Stand by me' to be hoisted ten minutes after the hit when some bulkheads were heard to collapse. *Courageous* sank at approximately 2015.

While *Ivanhoe*, which was stationed on the side whence the attack had come, concentrated all energies on attempting to destroy the U-boat, *Impulsive* was ordered to pick up survivors. Rescue work, at great risk to themselves, was also carried out by three merchant ships in the vicinity: these were the British *Dido* and two neutrals *Collingsworth* and *Veendam*.

Captain (D) in *Inglefield* arrived at the place of sinking at 2335. He saw two ships brilliantly lit; these were the Dutch *Veendam* and the American *Collingsworth*. He steamed round to find out what men-of-war there were on the scene and found *Kelly*, *Caradoc*, *Ceres* and *Ivanhoe*, all darkened. He was informed by Lord Louis Mountbatten from *Kelly* that *Impulsive* had returned to Plymouth with survivors.

Kelly was embarking survivors from the American ship by boat. *Caradoc* was lying astern of *Veendam* and had sent an officer on board to ask if there were any survivors to be transferred. A signal was received from *Dido* telling *Inglefield* that she had 300 survivors on board, most of them unclothed, and that they had no food or blankets for them. On learning that *Veendam* had no survivors on board, *Caradoc* was ordered to close *Dido* to transfer the survivors aboard while the destroyers *Intrepid* and *Ivanhoe* patrolled round while the transfer was made. Before this transfer could be made the cruiser was ordered away and *Inglefield* went alongside *Dido* at 0115 and transferred the survivors, twenty-three officers and 195 ratings – these included six stretcher cases. Most of the men were half naked, but all were in good heart.

Dido, which had been stopped on the scene for some six hours, was then given a destroyer escort on her voyage to Liverpool.

At daylight, the scene of the sinking was thoroughly searched for more survivors. A large number of Carley floats, aircraft dinghies and general wreckage was found, also several bodies, but no survivors. At 1000 *Inglefield* and *Ivanhoe* set course for Plymouth at 28 knots.

The *Veendam*'s captain, A Filippo, made a long log entry for Sunday 17 September, 1939, using European time. Here is an extract in his words:

> At about 2000 we saw the aircraft carrier and two destroyers which had come in sight during the late afternoon, heading east-south-east. At about 2020 the aircraft carrier developed a heavy smokescreen and at the same time we heard a few heavy explosions and observed a heavy vibration in our ship and observed at the same time a waterspout near the most westerly destroyer. At about 2030 we saw at about four points on the port bow that one of the men-of-war signalled with a strong morselight 'sinking'.
>
> Immediately we gave our alarm signal to go for the lifeboats and lowered our three motor boats and a lifeboat into the water and started right away to look over the oilspot caused by the sinking of the aircraft carrier which had gone down stern first listing to starboard just a few minutes before. Our lifeboats came into a heavy layer of fuel oil and found a lot of all kinds of floating material but no trace of any living human being. In the meantime we brought other lifeboats outside in case more would be needed. We saw on the oilfield a number of rafts with small lights on them. As far as we could see from our ship as well as from our boats on the water there was not a living soul around. In the meantime the night fell and we observed numerous small lights around which we found out later were from rescuing boats sent out by the destroyers and other ships.
>
> One seaman was brought on board our ship by one of our motor boats and given in care of our ship's medical officer, who worked over this seaman for a long while but in vain. We kept searching with one of our motor boats and with our ship manoeuvring around in the oilcovered place putting as much of our lights over side as we had on board.
>
> At about 0030 one of the officers of the other warships came on board to ask whether we had any survivors. We told him about the one seaman who had passed away and handed him the watch and keys of the seaman. Some time later one of the warships came close by and we were thanked by the commander on the warship. We took all our boats in board and proceeded on our voyage at 0130.
>
> Next morning while putting the body in its coffin we found the name of the seaman on one of his socks.

The official statement on the sinking of *Courageous* was issued on the Monday afternoon. It read:

> HMS Courageous, *one of Britain's earliest aircraft carriers has been sunk by a German U-boat. Her survivors were picked up by destroyers and merchant ships. It is believed that the U-boat, which was heavily attacked, was destroyed.*
>
> *The full complement of* Courageous *is about 1,200 officers and men, but as she was carrying a reduced number of aircraft at the time, it is presumed that she had a somewhat smaller crew. The Ministry announced that the next-of-kin of ratings believed lost would be informed from the depots, and those of the officers from the Admiralty C W Branch.*

There was shocked disbelief in Devonport, the depot for *Courageous*. Just a few days before, the men had been at home happy and well, and now this. Crowds congregated to see which ships were arriving back, and more importantly, whom they were carrying.

There were pathetic scenes outside the Naval hospital as one grey ambulance after another entered the gates with their loads of injured men. Children gazed wide-eyed, not really appreciating the situation, and women onlookers voiced sympathetic expressions of opinion as anxious relatives hurried into the hospital grounds in search of news. White-faced women, their eyes brimming with tears, were carrying in their hands envelopes bearing the familiar letters 'On His Majesty's Service', words which had a particular significance for them at this time.

One young woman said to be a bride of only a few weeks, aroused universal sympathy when she arrived on the arm of a stalwart sergeant in khaki. She almost fainted as she entered the hospital gates, her face deathly white, and when she came out a little later she was crying bitterly, whether from relief or grief no one knew. A girl not yet out of her teens, who had heard of the disaster while at work, was seeking news of a beloved brother. 'There are only the two of us,' she said, breaking down. Her father, too, was in the Navy, she said.

'Have you got anyone in here?' was the general question. Many of those who crowded round the hospital gate were there to get information of their relatives or friends, but some of the immediate relatives waited anxiously at home for news from the Admiralty.

'Do they know how many survivors there are?' and 'Where did it happen?' These were the snatches of conversation which the *Western Morning News* reporter caught from the waiting women. 'It has been like this since one o'clock,' said one woman and an old seafaring man said, 'The Admiralty will let you know as soon as they can.'

The walking wounded were released from hospital. One of these, a fifty year-old chief engine-room artificer, had already served twenty-one years in the Royal Navy and was recalled as a Reservist just before the hostilities had begun. In the Kaiser's war he was in the cruiser *Nottingham* when she was torpedoed in the North Sea in 1917. He was then in the water six and a half hours before he was picked up. He was bathing an injured foot when he was interviewed by a local reporter. He had a badly-bruised big toe which he received when he was clambering aboard the destroyer which rescued him. He said:

I was in the water one and a half hours before I was picked up this time. The explosion and the sinking of the old Courageous happened so quickly that even now I can hardly believe it. Just before it happened I had been down in the mess, and I had decided to go on deck to have a smoke. I was halfway up the hatch when the ship was struck. I was blown up the rest of the way and landed sprawling on the deck.

The ship immediately began to take a heavy list, and within a very short time the order was given to abandon ship. I saw a rope dangling down. It was a drop of about forty feet into the sea, and I slid down the rope and struck out away from the ship.

One incident occurred about this time which I shall never forget. A group of men clustered on the fore-part of the ship raised a tremendous cheer. They had seen the U-boat which struck us blown up by one of our destroyers.

The sea was full of bobbing heads around me. I was fully clothed, and although in my young days I was a pretty strong swimmer the weight of my clothes began to tell. There was nothing for it but to undress completely in the water. I can recall now unlacing my boots. I was nearly in my birthday suit when I was picked up.

There was a destroyer about half-a-mile away and two liners, one an American vessel. I struck out and swam gradually towards the destroyer. It was then beginning to get dusk, and from a Carley float near by which had about fifty or sixty people on it one could hear snatches of 'Keep the home fires burning'.

As I got near to a destroyer the slight swell kept pushing me away from it until I was picked up by one of the destroyer's whalers. The destroyer's crew were awfully good. They wrapped us in blankets and any odd pieces of clothing they could find. They threw over cork lifebelts, oars, and bits of wood for us to clutch on. One member of the crew, a strong swimmer, repeatedly dived overboard and rescued men.

The destroyer I was in picked up 362 men. There was hardly room to move in the ship. Three of the men, including a stoker who was terribly burned, but who had somehow managed to keep alive in the water, died during the night.

The survivor, from Penzance said there must have been a large number of the crew between decks who were trapped when the carrier suddenly listed.

Another reservist described how" he was on the flying deck; the ship, he said, heeled over, and he and his companions were thrown on to her side, which was almost flush with the water. 'While I was undressing,' he said, 'I caught a last glimpse of the captain, who called out, "Take your time, boys. There is no hurry." As I jumped off I saw him raise his hand in salute to the flag, and down we went.'

Now, in complete contrast to the two Reservists is the story of a five-foot-tall fifteen year-old Royal Marine bugler from Plymouth. He had been a member of the crew for two months. He explained that he could only swim a little but he managed to struggle about fifty yards to a float, on which there were about fifty other survivors. He said they paddled the float away from the ship and at the same time sang 'Hi Ho, Hi Ho', the marching song from the film of *Snow White*. After being afloat for nearly an hour they were picked up by a destroyer.

Another Penzance survivor, a pensioner who served in the Kaiser's war without injury, told a *Western Morning News* representative that when the explosion occurred he was in the boiler-room hanging some clothes to dry. There was a terrific flash and then darkness. He managed to climb over the flight deck to the starboard side. On the way he heard the command to abandon ship. He knew it was suicide to dive off the ship, and he believed several men lost their lives through trying it. He met several others, and they tried to push a Carley float into the sea, but were unable to move it owing to the angle at which the ship was heeling. Then they dropped a 70-foot rope over the side and lowered themselves into the water.

To conclude the story of the men who were involved in that terrible Sunday night tragedy here are two accounts from officers, beginning with that of the captain's secretary:

> *When the explosion occurred I was having my supper. Immediately following the explosions, which seemed to lift the ship, within a second all the lights went out and crockery and other articles in the wardroom went slipping about as the ship heeled over.*
>
> *I got out of the wardroom and made my way up to the upper deck to the seaplane platform, on top of the quarterdeck. There were a lot of people there already waiting for instructions. I do not think the people realized that she was going down as fast as she finally did. When it was realized that Courageous was going down they were told to get into the water. Orders had been given by the captain to abandon ship. Those who had the chance had lifebelts, a number of boats were lowered, and the Carley floats were launched. Most of the men had jobs to do before abandoning their ship as I had myself. They all carried out their duties and there was no disorder or panic of any kind whatever.*

The last account is from a very perceptive lieutenant-commander; part of his story reads:

Owing to the list there was no contact with the bridge at all, and all orders had to be shouted. Difficulties were added to by the continuous sounding of a very powerful siren-like hooter in our ship which the explosion had started, and which we could not stop.

I told the men near me to get their clothes off, as the order had been given to abandon ship. Fortunately it was a fine evening and there was no sea. The weather was also fairly warm.

Owing to the rapid and terrible list of Courageous *only one of our boats was actually launched, and that was due to the bravery of an able-seaman swimming right under the side of the carrier and releasing a motor boat which had not got jammed, it was a very brave act.*

One cannot help taking one's hat off to the U-boat commander. It was pretty certain that he knew he would be scuppered after he had fired at us. But I think the sinking of Courageous *was absolute luck. My personal view is that the U-boat was waiting for a ship that came to our rescue. We were going on opposite courses, and she was right ahead of us.*

As we now know, U-29 had been stalking another ship when *Courageous* was sighted.

Courageous, turning into the wind, had given Otto Schuhart the opportunity he was seeking; it was most fortuitous. Luck continued to run for the U-boat commander. It will be remembered that *Courageous* had a very shallow draft being designed for Baltic operations. However, she was just one day out from port and fully loaded with fuel oil and aviation fuel and was therefore sailing low in the water. Had she been returning from patrol the torpedoes might have missed, going under the carrier. It will be remembered that U-29 had missed *Neptunia*, probably setting the torpedoes too deep, and also that none of the torpedo tracks had been seen from the carrier or its escort which suggests they were not surface skimmers; this confirms that there was a tendency in the U-boat for deep settings and the probability is that, say, a week later, with *Courageous* over six feet higher in the water the torpedoes could have missed.

Otto Schuhart's luck did not stop there. After U-29 broke surface straight after the attack the commander immediately ordered it down to 300-feet; the destroyer's depth charges were set to explode at 100-feet, so the U-boat escaped.

Winston Churchill, First Lord of the Admiralty, made a Commons statement on Wednesday, 20 September. He said *Courageous* had on board 1,202 officers and men and there were 687 survivors. He continued:

The loss of this valuable ship to the Navy is not one I would wish to minimise. Since the outbreak of war HMS Courageous *had rendered conspicuous service in the protection of merchant shipping against U-boat attack, and her operations against individual U-boats have not been without success.*

Mr Churchill referred to the gallantry of the ship's company, and expressed the sympathy of the Government with those bereaved.

In reply to a question, the First Lord said *Courageous* was accompanied by her full escort of destroyers. In reply to a second questioner who asked: 'Will the First Lord explain how it came about that the U-boat was able to get within striking distances of *Courageous* in view of the fact that the Admiralty had frequently assured the House that it could deal with the U-boat menace, and that it was impossible for a U-boat to get within striking distance?' Mr Churchill said: 'The question is not one which can be dealt with by way of a supplementary answer, but I see no reason to doubt the soundness of the broad views which the Admiralty expressed before the war as to the means of coping with this peculiar form of menace.'

There were cheers in the House of Commons at Mr Churchill's reply but in Germany they claimed a wonderful success and further confirmation of the fact that the English defence forces were not as effective as they advertised themselves to be.

The Members of Parliament were after Winston Churchill again the next week, He was asked: 'Whether, after full consideration, he was satisfied that the protection given to the aircraft carrier *Courageous* was sufficient and if not, could he give an assurance that in future instructions would be given that aircraft carriers when proceeding through waters where U-boats might be expected would have the same protective screen of destroyers as was given to battleships.'

Mr Winston Churchill: 'I cannot undertake to hamper the judgement of experienced sea officers by any general ruling as to the degree of risk they should accept. This must depend upon the need or opportunity of the moment and the resources available.'

The circumstances attending the loss of *Courageous* were investigated by a Board of Enquiry, from whose report it appears that the carrier at once took a heavy list to port. Fruitless attempts were made to correct the list by flooding the starboard bilges, but the valves had jammed. All ventilation and many of the watertight doors were open, which permitted an almost free run of water throughout the ship as the list increased and was a factor to the rapid sinking. The ring main was not split at the time, which was a contributory cause of all lights and communications failing throughout the ship. The carrier had only recently commissioned and her ship's company were inexperienced in working in total internal darkness; there was inevitably much confusion and, in some cases, a lack of initiative on the part of the officers.

In the light of events there is no doubt that the employment of large aircraft carriers for hunting U-boats was a mistake. At the same time, it is only fair to comment that it was no more than a temporary measure intended to cover the period before the full convoy system came into operation. The risk to a hunting carrier was by no means ignored, and the opinions of the Naval Staff all emphasized the vital necessity for a full-time, effective anti-U-boat screen, especially as a carrier was obliged to maintain a steady course during the periods when aircraft were being flown off and on.

Now to return to U-29 at sea. The attack on *Courageous* had been made from 3,000 yards and, as has been already recorded, the late evening sun had been seen glinting on the periscope. Many survivors were also convinced that U-29 had been sunk. This was not so. *Ivanhoe* carried out three depth charge attacks on the U-boat at 2000, 2017 and 2028, but all were unsuccessful as the commander had taken his boat down to 300-feet. The depth charges which had been pre-set to explode at 100-feet shook the U-boat but this was all.

This was the end of a very successful first wartime patrol by U-29. The U-boat would have needed to return to base at this time anyway as fuel and provisions were running low. The northabout route was taken and the successful U-boat reached Wilhelmshaven to much acclaim on Tuesday, 26 September.

The whole German nation were overjoyed by this success, Hitler visited the North German port and from Karl Dönitz's unpretentious wooden headquarters the Führer and his entourage sped by car to the U-boat's berth.

The weather-stained U-29 and its crew were inspected by Hitler accompanied by his Naval adjutant, von Puttkamer. At the officers' mess the Führer, Admiral Erich Raeder, Commander-in-Chief *Kriegsmarine*, and *Kapitän zur See* Karl Dönitz, Commander U-boats, spoke to Otto Schuhart and his IWO about their attacks. The adjutant commented: 'Hitler carried back to Berlin an excellent impression of the leadership of the U-boat arm as well as of the liveliness and spirit of the crews.'

Once all the ceremonies were over the crew were allowed to proceed on leave, the second war patrol would not commence until mid-November, However, on 14 October, Günther Prien sank the British battleship HMS *Royal Oak* in Scapa Flow. His daring foray and escape in U-47 again put the U-boat arm in the world's headlines.

A veil can be pulled over U-29's second war cruise to the Atlantic from

14 November to 16 December. Although other U-boats were enjoying successes in the area U-29 had no sinkings to report.

Christmas and New Year were spent in port as U-29 did not commence its third patrol until 11 February. This time there was a new role for the U-boat to perform: minelaying. Eight mines were laid off Bull Point in the Bristol Channel and on the very day they were laid, 3 March, one of them sank the 710-ton British ship *Cato*. The U-boat was now free to continue with its patrol and in the darkness of the next morning a bigger British steamer, *Thirston*, of 3,000-tons, was torpedoed and sunk 32 miles west of Trevose Head. Just after midday U-29 attacked two more British ships in the Western Approaches.

In the early afternoon U-29 torpedoed the 6,717-ton British ship *Pacific Reliance*. However, the crew of the motorship thought they had struck a mine, even although the force of the explosion had caused the ship to break in two. The coastal steamer *Macville* rescued the fifty-three crew members and brought them to Cornwall.

Then an SOS was sent from the London tanker *San Florentine*, of 12,842-tons, saying she had been torpedoed nineteen miles north of the Longships lighthouse off Land's End. Certainly two torpedoes had been fired at her from U-29 and light explosions were heard in the U-boat. The German intelligence service, B-Dienst, had been amongst others who had picked up the SOS and U-29 was credited with the sinking. However, the tanker was not struck at all. Obviously the wireless operator had sent a signal saying they were *being* attacked and it was misinterpreted as *been* attacked.

The explosions heard in U-29 must have been end of run detonations. These were the last torpedoes fired on the patrol.

The U-boat arrived back, and secured to the jetty at Wilhelmshaven, on Tuesday, 12 March. Only one day earlier U-31 had been sunk by an aircraft attack in the Schilling Roads, so the lookouts had every incentive to keep a sharp look out.

The crew were not allowed too much leave on this occasion; another new role was envisaged for U-29. Kart Dönitz had to withdraw most of his boats for Operation *Weserübung*, the planned invasion of Denmark and Norway. The Flag Officer U-boats was especially keen as the occupation of ports in Norway would allow him more bases and the U-boats would be able to remain at sea for longer periods. The operation, which commenced on 9 April, was a vast undertaking; suffice it to say that U-29 only occupied a minor role, that of a transporter.

Dönitz sent his U-boats to lie in wait off the Norwegian coast and in the

North Sea. Off the fiord entrances groups of U-boats', sent to protect the German landings had waited to follow the ships into the fiords; five at Narvik, two at Trondheim, five at Bergen and two at Stavanger. Thirteen U-boats lay in three groups off the Shetlands Islands and Orkney. Another four, in two groups, lay off the south of Norway. Altogether there were nine U-boat groups, four other U-boats not attached to a group and six other U-boats, including U-29 being used as transporters.

It was not until 17 April that U-29 sailed, arriving at Trondheim on the 23rd. The U-boat remained for four days, during which time it refuelled before sailing back to Germany.

A great deal happened before U-29 put to sea almost a month later; following Denmark and Norway, Holland, Belgium and Luxembourg had been overrun and France invaded. The Dunkirk evacuation began on 26 May and U-29 sailed the next day. The U-boat was to travel further afield than ever before; its orders were to patrol off the South-Western Approaches and off Portugal. The U-boat refuelled in the neutral Spanish port of Vigo on 20/21 June; it was not until July that the Biscay ports were used.

The U-boat sailed west, into the Atlantic, when it left the Spanish port and it was here that the first victim of the cruise was trapped on 26 June. The 5,000-ton Greek steamer *Dimitris* required both a torpedo and gun attack before sinking. A torpedo was saved a week later when the Panamanian steamer *Santa Margarita*, also of 5,000-tons, was sunk by gunfire to the north-west of the last victim. Tracking still further out in the Atlantic another victim was torpedoed just before midnight. The ship was the 9,000-ton British tanker *Athellaird* whose silhouette stood high and clear against the night sky.

Tuesday, 2 July, had been a good day for the U-boat arm because as well as Otto Schuhart's brace, Günther Prien in U-47 sank the Blue Star liner *Arandora Star*. The torpedomen on the U-boat had worked hard preparing the torpedo which had been kept until last as it was thought to be faulty. Little did they realise that the torpedo would kill many of their countrymen as when it was fired the 15,500-ton liner, battling through the waters to the west of Ireland, was carrying 1,500 German and Italian internees to Canada. The crew numbered approximately 500 and about a thousand survivors were rescued and brought back to Scotland, but 143 Germans and 470 Italians perished in the cold Atlantic waters that morning.

The two U-boat commanders Schuhart and Prien, each with a capital ship success under their belt, returned to their home ports, U-29 arriving at Wilhelmshaven on 11 July. There the crew were somewhat surprised to learn that their base had been one of the targets that sixty-four RAF aircraft had bombed two nights earlier.

It was more than seven weeks before U-29 was called on to make its sixth patrol. During this time there were several air raid warnings sounded at Wilhelmshaven as RAF aircraft attacked North German towns. *Admiral Scheer* was also at Wilhelmshaven and on the night of 20/21 July the RAF lost five raiders to flak while attacking the pocket battleship.

On 2 September U-29 left Germany for the last time as an operational U-boat. Three days later it put in to Bergen, now in the hands of the *Kriegsmarine*, and stayed at the Norwegian base for six days before making for its patrol area in the Atlantic.

In the middle of August Hitler had declared a total blockade of the British Isles and at much the same time the first large scale attacks on convoys began. Now, towards the end of September, U-29 was to become involved.

On the 25th, to the west of Ireland, an outward-bound convoy was attacked. Wilhelm Ambrosius in U-43 scored the first success and half-an-hour later, at 1400, U-29 torpedoed and sank the British steamer *Eurymedon* of over 6,000-tons. Other successes against convoy OB217 were registered by Hans Jenisch in U-32 and Victor Oehrn in U-37.

A week later Otto Schuhart was met by an escort in the Bay of Biscay and taken into Lorient. Karl Dönitz had also moved his headquarters to the French base and during October his force reached a level of proficiency which it was never to recover during the war.

The siren sounded at the French base on the night of 27/28 October, RAF minelaying aircraft were nearby and U-29 had to be escorted out to sea when it left for the fine natural harbour of Brest on 31 October. The U-boat only stayed in the Brittany base for two days, RAF Hampdens laid mines outside Brest during the night of 1/2 November, but it was on this morning that U-29 left for its last war patrol, to the Atlantic.

The seventh, and last, war patrol drew a blank and after four weeks the Type VIIA boat put into Bergen. The boat, and its commander, had completed their active war service. Otto Schuhart stayed with the boat for two months, until January 1941, when it joined the 24th Flotilla for training purposes.

The U-boat then had a succession of commanders, many of whom went on to make names for themselves in other U-boats. The first was *Oberleutnant* Georg Lassen, from January to September 1941, although on 1 June the 24th Flotilla proceeded to Hopla Fiord, near Trondheim, owing to the danger of the Russian war, but returned to Memel in September. Later, for his achievements with U-160, Georg Lassen was awarded the Knight's Cross with Oak Leaves. *Oberleutnant* Heinrich Hasenchar was then in command until May 1942 when *Oberleutnant* Karl-Heinz Marback took over before going on to U-953. The U-boat was temporarily withdrawn from service from June to November 1942. *Oberleutnant* Rudolf Zorn, later of U-302 and U-650, commanded U-29 from November through until August 1943. *Oberleutnant* Eduard Aust, later of U-679, was commander until November 1943, although in September it had transferred to the 21st U-boat Flotilla at Pillau.

The last commander was *Oberleutnant* Graf von und zu Arco-Zinueberg, who was with U-29 until 17 April 1944 when it was officially withdrawn from service. The U-boat that sunk the aircraft carrier *Courageous* was then transferred to the 4th ULD as a shooting range boat for torpedoes until August 1944. It met its final inglorious end in *Kupefermühienbucht*, Flensburg, where it was scuttled in May 1945, four days before the war in Europe ended.

When *Kapitänleutnant* Otto Schuhart left U-29, he joined the 21st U-boat Flotilla, based on Pillau. This was a school-boat flotilla directly controlled by the 1st U-boat Training Division.

Otto Schuhart had his headquarters in the depot-ship *Pretoria*, the ship also accommodated officers, chief petty officers and petty officers of the division. Ratings were accommodated in *Robert Ley*.

The fêted commander of U-29, holder of the Knight's Cross, sank eleven ships totalling 78,800 GRT. This was not enough tonnage, however, for his inclusion among the top thirty U-boat commanders, although undoubtedly he was a U-boat ace.

CHAPTER TWO

HANS, THE GIANT KILLER

Just before the depression of the late twenties there were always new ships being ordered from British shipyards. In 1927 John Brown's yard on Clydeside built the luxurious liner *Empress of Britain* for the Canadian Pacific line. The giant ship dwarfed the terraced houses around the yard as its massive size took shape. When launched it had a displacement of 42,350 tons.

Shipwrights and interior designers abounded on board in the latter stages of the fitting out, seeing that the creations of top talented artists were carried out – much use was made of wood panelling. An innovation for the wealthy passengers was the introduction of a worldwide radio telephone service routed through the wireless room. Passenger cabins had their own telephone through which calls could be connected to the shore.

The ship was designed for the North Atlantic run between Quebec and Southampton and at its trials off Scotland over the measured mile it steamed at 25.5-knots, blistering the paintwork on its three giant funnels. The luxury liner also competed in the round-the-world cruise market and became the largest ship ever to squeeze through the Panama Canal, and was also the largest ship, at this time, to traverse the Suez Canal.

Before World War Two was declared the liner had completed eight world cruises and had made as many round cruises to the Caribbean/Bermuda area. The liner had also completed its century of trans-Atlantic crossings.

The *Empress of Britain* had brought back King George VI and Queen Elizabeth from their tour of the United States and Canada earlier in 1939.

As the war clouds gathered over Europe many prudent North Americans booked their one-way passages for the scheduled departure date from Southampton on 2 September. In fact, so many passengers were seeking accommodation that temporary berths were erected and when the ship sailed, over 1,300 passengers were carried safely across the Atlantic. Such was not to be the fate of those who left Liverpool one day later, as the Donaldson liner *Athenia* was sunk by Fritz Lemp in U-30 off the Hebrides. He mistook the steamer for a troopship and sank it without warning.

Another U-boat, U-32, left Wilhelmshaven on Monday 4 September, by this time the *Empress of Britain* was well clear of land, cutting a swathe through the North Atlantic at 22-knots, a speed that the captain knew that no marauding U-boat could match.

The news that war had been declared was received in stony silence by the passengers. A transcript of King George VI's message to the Empire was printed in the ships newspaper as was the news that Winston Churchill was back at the Admiralty, a post he had held coincidentally at the outbreak of the Kaiser's War. Extra attention was focussed on boat drill aboard the liner.

The Type VIIA U-boat, U-32, had been built at the AG Weser yard at Bremen a decade after the *Empress of Britain*. It was the sixth such boat built at the yard and the last of the type to be launched. Four others had earlier been launched from the *Germania Werft* at Kiel. The boats, constructed under the limitation of the London Naval Treaty, displaced 626/745 tons although they were commonly referred to by British sources as 500-tonners. The boat was laid down on 1 April 1936, launched on the following 25 February, and completed on 15 April 1937.

Kapitänleutnant Werner Lott was appointed as the first commander of the U-boat. After trials in the Baltic, testing both the boat and its crew, U-32 was declared operational. The following year, at the time of the Spanish Civil War, the ocean-going U-boat carried out two patrols in Spanish Waters from 5 February until 8 May and for three weeks in October. So that its German identity would not be confused it had a red, white and black vertical stripe painted on its conning-tower; also, pre-war the number 32 was clearly marked in white paint on the conning-tower. Unlike the *Luftwaffe*, the *Kriegsmarine* did not get involved in the Spanish domestic conflict. Much priceless experience of warlike conditions was gained by German and British boats in the area.

Eight months after returning to Wilhelmshaven, following its Spanish sojourn, U-32 took part in tactical exercises in the Baltic. In July and

August 1939 U-32 was used as a temporary replacement for U-36 at the U-boat training base at Neustadt. Accordingly the U-boat was not available when U-28, U-29, U-33 and U-34, all of the 2nd U-boat Flotilla, left Wilhelmshaven on 19 August. *Korvettenkapitän* Paul Büchel took over command of the U-boat at this time as its first commander was transferred to U-35. The 1WO for the first war cruise was *Oberleutnant* Hans Jenisch. As a nineteen-year-old he was in the training class of 1933, being promoted to *Leutnant zur See* in October 1936. He served aboard *Deutschland* before joining the U-boat branch in 1937. He qualified as a torpedo officer the following year and was promoted to *Oberleutnant* and appointed to the 2nd U-boat Flotilla. He then joined U-32.

The U-boat left Wilhelmshaven on 4 September carrying mines and torpedoes on its first patrol. Its route took U-32 through the English Channel and on 17 September it laid twelve mines off Scareweather light vessel and just after noon on the next day a tramp steamer, the 4,863 ton London registered *Kensington Court* hove in to view. It was unarmed bound for Birkenhead from the Argentine with a cargo of wheat.

Büchel attacked on the surface without warning, deciding to give his 3.5-inch guns' crew some practice. The steamer's Geordie master, Captain J Schofield from South Shields, said, 'We sent out an SOS when the U-boat approached and attacked without warning.' He turned his vessel's stern to the U-boat, which kept firing from the range of about a mile. The master continues:

> After it had fired about five shots it came very close to the ship's stern, and I decided it was time to stop the ship. I gave three blasts on the whistle, and the crew took to the boats.
>
> One of the boats was lost. Shortly after we got away in the port boat there was a big explosion in the starboard well. We did not know whether it was a torpedo or shell. We started rowing away, and soon afterwards sighted a Sunderland. I said; 'This has come in reply to our SOS.' Everybody was pleased, and we all started to cheer. Still, we did not think it was possible for them to rescue us that way. We thought they would give a signal to a warship or something like that. When the first 'plane alighted on the water and someone signalled to us from the wing, we began to realise that they were going to take us on board.
>
> There was a second 'plane there. We told the officer that there were thirty-four of us, and he said he would take about twenty and the other 'plane would take the rest.
>
> While we were getting on board a third 'plane came over and flew round. We wondered how they would get us on board, because the sea was choppy, but a door in the side of the flying boat opened and a small collapsible boat was pushed out.
>
> It was all very remarkable to us. It was the modern method of rescue, and we had never

had any experience like it. When we got on board they gave us cups of tea and cigarettes.

Having despatched its first victim, U-32 crept away, submerging as soon as a flying boat was seen. As the U-boat carried on with its Atlantic patrol north, up past the west coast of Ireland and Scotland, the telegraphist signalled news of its first victory back to base. A few days later Admiral Dönitz sent a signal to all boats:

> *Armed force should be used against all merchant ships using their wireless when ordered to stop. They are subject to seizure or sinking without exception.*

The U-boat passed between the Faeroes and the Shetland Isles until, on 28 September, it had reached a point off the southern coast of Norway. In the middle of the afternoon a small Norwegian steamer, *Jern*, was seen some 65-miles north-west of Skudenes. At this time Norway was neutral but the sight of a German U-boat was enough for the captain of the 825-ton vessel to scuttle his charge.

The U-boat continued down through the Skagerrak, reaching its base at Wilhelmshaven two days later. Here the commander was awarded the Iron Cross 2nd class. The U-boat was sent to Kiel for repair to a torpedo tube and it was subsequently discovered that it required a refit that would take a month to complete. However, in the meantime, even although the U-boat was out of action, the mines that it had laid earlier were doing their dirty work. On 5 October the 8,000-ton British steamer *Marwarri* was mined and damaged three-and-a-half miles from the Scareweather light vessel and the following evening the 9,482-ton British steamer *Lochgoil* was also mined in the vicinity but did not sink. The U-boat was expected to commence its second war cruise at the end of October but its engines were not working properly and in addition it was found necessary to fit twelve new cylinders. Advantage was taken of this enforced time in port to send Hans Jenisch, the 1WO, to Warnemünde for his commander's course.

After the completion of the refit U-32 carried out trials in the Baltic where surface and submerged speeds were tested. It was while U-32 was on its trials that the disastrous raid, known as the 'Battle of Heligoland Bight' took place on 18 December. A force of twenty-four Wellington bombers left England, in daylight, to attack 'naval targets' at Wilhelmshaven. Instructions were given not to attack at less than 10,000-feet, thereby avoiding the flak. All but two of the bombers reached the target area and attacked, in good visibility, from 13,000-feet. However, the unescorted bombers had been picked up by radar on the way out and a force of Me 109 and Me 110's were waiting for them off Cuxhaven on the return journey. Ten of the Wellingtons were immediately shot down, two others ditched on the way home and three more crash-landed and were written off. The percentage loss was one of the worst to be suffered by Bomber Command. Two *Luftwaffe* fighters were shot down.

The work on U-32 and subsequent trials occupied a considerable time and the U-boat was not ready to resume its war career until after Christmas.

The sailing date was set for 28 December. Hans Jenisch had just completed his commander's course, and he was to resume his career as 1WO in U-32. He had married while on his course.

There were one or two new faces on board as U-32 left Wilhelmshaven, the naval base that had housed the High Seas Fleet at the end of the Kaiser's War. The U-boat carried mines and a number of torpedoes fitted with magnetic pistols. The U-boat proceeded north, through the Skagerrak and in the darkness of New Year's Eve the small Norwegian steamer *Luna* was torpedoed and sank between Norway and Scotland. The U-boat then passed north of the Shetlands but the crew were unable to lay mines in the intended area owing to the presence of patrolling British warships. The U-boat commander proceeded on course for some five hours finally deciding to lay his mines off Ailsa Craig.

During the patrol the U-boat had been sighted and attacked, unsuccessfully, by aircraft. The attacks brought to mind the loss of U-35. When they were last ashore the crew heard that their former commander, Werner Lott, had been captured when U-35 was depth-charged by three destroyers off the Shetlands at the end of November – his wartime successes had been the sinking of four small vessels. The U-boat returned safely to Wilhelmshaven on Sunday, 21 January.

Before the third patrol Hans Jenisch, the 1WO, took over command from Paul Büchel. There was some talk at the time that the Admiral commanding U-boats was dissatisfied at having the mines laid in the wrong place and so replaced the commander.

Whatever the reason, the choice of a new commander turned out to be an inspired one. Hans Jenisch was 26 years old, a native of East Prussia, and newly married. He was able to spend some time at home as the third war cruise was not due to commence until 26 February.

The U-boat, which had spent exactly five weeks in port, again carried both mines and torpedoes as well as a new commander and 1WO as it was conned out into the Schilling Roads. Up through the Skagerrak and then through the Fair Island channel U-32 made its way until, in the early hours of 2 March, it slowed down as the new commander had his first target in sight. It was a 4,000 ton Norwegian steamer *Belpamela*. Three torpedoes exploded a few yards from the side of the vessel and it was damaged, this was at a time when several U-boat commanders were experiencing faulty torpedoes. There was no mistake when another Norwegian steamer was sighted seven hours later. This time the U-boat was on the surface with the guns crew closed up and they did not take long to finish off the 2,818-ton *Lagaholm*.

The new U-boat commander did what not many others did during the war – he daringly conned U-32 down through the North Channel, into the Irish Sea, to lay eight mines off Liverpool Bay. These brought a later dividend when a 5,000 ton British steamer, *Counsellor*, was sunk after it struck one of them.

Once again U-32 was sighted and attacked several times from the air, but with the war only eight months old Coastal Command had neither the suitable aircraft nor the weapons with which they would later reap outstanding rewards against the underwater attackers.

When U-32 put into Wilhelmshaven on Saturday 23 March, feverish activity was apparent all around. The forthcoming sea invasion of Norway was being prepared. Every available U-boat was utilised, including the oldest 250-ton school training boats. The U-boats were divided into nine groups for the invasion of Norway and Denmark on 9 April. However, along with U-28, U-29, U-43, U-101 and UA, U-32 was given the mundane task of being a transporter. It was not until Operation *Weserübung* was well in hand that U-32 was used.

The U-boat left Wilhelmshaven for Trondheim on 27 April with a cargo of ammunition and an 88-mm gun. It carried neither mines nor torpedoes. As there were several Royal Navy vessels operating off Norway, the U-boat proceeded north keeping close to the coast once it had passed Kristiansand on its way to Trondheim.

An unsuccessful depth charge attack was made by destroyers on 2 May. On 5 May, the U-boat reached Trondheim, where the 1,000 ton ex-Turkish submarine known as *UA* was also alongside; it too had taken a cargo of ammunition from Germany.

The homeward journey was eventful as, three days after leaving Trondheim, U-32 was attacked three times by destroyers; on one day it was attacked twice, on each occasion by two destroyers, and on the following day an attack was carried out by three destroyers. Depth charges were dropped but no damage was done.

No ships were sunk on this cruise, the only barren one of U-32's career. The U-boat arrived back in Wilhelmshaven on 13 May, with an engine missing badly on one cylinder, but the dockyards and repair shops were so crowded that it was ordered to proceed through the canal to Kiel, where repairs were effected within three days.

The repaired U-boat returned to its base at the earliest possible opportunity as Britain was at its lowest ebb: it was the time of Dunkirk. When U-32 left Wilhelmshaven for a patrol to the south of Ireland on 3 June it carried five torpedoes in the tubes and six reloads, no mines were taken.

Passing north of the Shetlands into the Atlantic, U-32 proceeded down the west coast of Ireland to the Western Approaches. Three small ships were sunk on the evening of 18 June. The Norwegian *Altair* was torpedoed and two Spanish fishing smacks were sunk by gunfire. Twenty-four hours later the 5,334-ton Jugoslavian steamer *Labud* was torpedoed and sunk south-west of Fastnet. Two days later the U-boat was among convoy HX49 homeward-bound from North America. The crew could hear explosions; they did not know that Günther Prien with U-47 and Fritz Lemp in U-30 were also present. Their U-boat joined in the action at 0036 on the 22nd torpedoing the 9,000-ton Norwegian tanker *Eli Knudsen*, which sank.

Hans Jenisch returned to Wilhelmshaven on Monday, 1 July, after a patrol of exactly four weeks. A subsequent refit on U-32 included diesel repairs. Over six weeks were spent in Germany and all the crew were given leave.

When the U-boat sailed out of Wilhelmshaven on Thursday 15 August for its sixth war cruise none of the crew could have guessed it would be the last time they would set out from a German port. Again, carrying eleven torpedoes U-32 passed north of the Shetlands to the Atlantic. Only after they were well out to sea were the men told that the cruise was to end in France and not in Germany. This caused mixed reactions.

Following the occupation of France its Atlantic coast was now available to accommodate U-boats and Admiral Dönitz wasted no time in selecting Lorient for his headquarters. The first boat to take advantage of the harbour facilities was Fritz Lemp's U-30 on 7 July. The use of these bases gave U-boats an extra fortnight on patrol as they did not have to make the long passage out and home round Scotland. The *Luftwaffe* occupied bases at Vannes, and Merignac near Bordeaux.

The operational area for U-32 on this sixth cruise was off the Hebrides and it had patrolled for ten days without success until on 30 August it intercepted a homeward-bound convoy. In the early hours between 0220 and 0234 three ships were torpedoed and sunk: the British steamers *Mill Hill* and *Chelsea*, both between 4,000 and 5,000-tons and the Norwegian vessel *Norne* of nearly 4,000-tons. Two days later, on the evening of 1 September, the new British cruiser *Fiji*, launched from John Brown's Clydeside yard just three months before the war, was torpedoed and damaged. With another cruiser *Fiji* was scheduled to escort troopships out for the Dakar operation.

This was the final success of the cruise but U-32 met a lifeboat from the *Belgian Ville de Mons* which had been torpedoed by U-47 on 2 September about 150-miles west of the Hebrides. Hans Jenisch gave water to the men in the boat and a course to steer to the nearest landfall.

This action confirmed the opinion that the other officers aboard had of the commander as well-mannered and polite. They also thought he was difficult or impossible to influence, but very determined. He was well liked by his men although they did not like his 1WO successor, Hans Jenisch was sailing in unfamiliar waters as he crossed the Bay of Biscay to enter Lorient for the first time on 8 September. It was appropriate that Lorient was selected as the French base for U-32, as it was shortly to be known as 'the base of the aces'.

Hans Jenisch was certainly aspiring to that status. Many of the men were surprised at their destination, for they thought the boat would dock at Brest. Nevertheless they were pleased to get ashore and the first priority was to have a bath to remove the 'submarine stink'. The 1WO, 2WO, a petty officer and a rating were awarded the Iron Cross first class and ten other members of the crew received the Iron Cross second class.

Unfortunately for most of them they could not parade their new medals to the folks at home as at this time the U-boats were on a quick turnaround. Admiral Dönitz's insistence on the quickest possible turnaround in port was the cause of some resentment. The commanders admitted that their nerves were being affected by continuous cruising and the strain of the Atlantic war was already telling, although it was only twelve months since the fighting started.

At Lorient some of the experienced personnel were taken off to crew new boats that would otherwise have been manned by newcomers to the service. This was obviously a correct decision and their places in U-32 were filled from the pool of U-boat personnel at Lorient. These were later described as 'inexperienced youths with little or no training who have been drafted without option'.

After a rest of only ten days, the seventh war cruise commenced on 18 September. U-32 left Lorient and was accompanied by a minesweeper as far as the entrance to the harbour; leaving Ile de Croix to port, it proceeded to its operational area 'some hundreds of miles out in the Atlantic'. It was to prove a most rewarding patrol.

The journey through the Bay of Biscay gave new members of the crew a little time to shake down and find their sea legs. They had to learn fast as U-32 was set to attack HX72 which was already taking a mauling from a wolf pack. Kretschmer in U-99, Prien in U-47, Bleichrodt in the most successful U-boat of the war U-48 and Schepke in U-100 had all achieved sinkings before U-32, with the ace designate Hans Jenisch, arrived.

The U-boat was to the south of the others in what was to be one of the first wolf-packs attacks. By the evening of 21 September four ships of the convoy had already been sunk and the other thirty-seven were strung out in nine columns with two sloops ahead and a Flower Class corvette on either side. A veteran destroyer, *Shikari*, was rescuing survivors from the sunken ships. In the two hours either side of midnight U-100 sank four more ships and U-48 damaged another.

The convoy was approximately 320-miles west of Malin Head when U-32 joined in the action. Hans Jenisch says there was no moon and it was very dark at the time he attacked. A torpedo was fired at *Collegian*, a 7,886 ton Liverpool registered steamer, which sent out an SOS after the torpedo attack. Some time later U-32 returned on the surface so the ship's captain put the stern towards the U-boat, stopped zig-zagging and opened fire. The U-boat returned the fire using two guns to fire off 25-rounds. It was said that the nearest shot landed 200-yards away from the steamer. At the same time the *Collegian* fired just ten rounds and claimed the last shot was very close to U-32.

After this inconclusive engagement the U-boat dived, Hans Jenisch says because of the intervention of sea escorts and because he thought he saw a Sunderland. This was confirmed by Michael Irwin who, as a twenty-year-old, was officer of the watch in Lowestoft. The sloop, which was fifteen miles away, saw the flashes from this gunfire, and proceeded to the position. A signal was also received from *Collegian* saying she was being shelled. Forty minutes later a further signal from the steamer said she could see the U-boat astern. It was light when Lowestoft reached the presumed vicinity of the attack and a search was commenced with HMS *Heartsease*, a Flower Class corvette, and later with *Skate*, a destroyer that was built in the Kaiser's war, and *Shikari*, returning from its mercy mission. The sea escorts saw the arrival of the first air escort, in the shape of a flying boat; this was obviously the Sunderland that Hans Jenisch thought he saw.

After a search of fifty minutes Lowestoft obtained a contact at 1,400-yards' range. Course was altered towards, but the contact was lost while closing. The position was crossed, and after turning, firm clear contact was regained at 1,300 yards' range. Lowestoft attacked, and thinking that the U-boat had dived deep, the depth of water being 500-fathoms, released six depth charges set to 250, 350 and 500-feet. After the attack contact could not be regained. A search was carried out with Heartsease, but nothing further could be detected. This was not surprising as the tactics that the U-boat adopted were to dive to only 60-metres initially and then to proceed at depth, heading west, that is, away from the convoy.

The attack by U-32 was the last on the convoy which had lost eleven ships sunk and two damaged. It was no wonder that the inadequate escort failed to sink any of the attacking U-boats as all the five were to be in the list of the top thirty when the final U-boat table was published and three of the commanders were in the top dozen listed successful U-boat commanders. Perhaps it was the understatement of the Atlantic war when the escort commander reported on arrival in port: 'It is my opinion that the convoy was attacked by more than one U-boat.' How many torpedoes did he think a U-boat could carry?

The next ship was attacked by U-32 three days later, but away from the convoy. It was light when the British steamer *Mabriton*, of 6,694-tons, was torpedoed and sunk on 25 September.

Early the next morning U-32 caught up with an outward bound convoy that had been successfully attacked by U-29 and U-43. In the darkness a torpedo thumped into the side of *Corrientes*, a 6,863-ton British steamer, but she remained afloat until given the coup-de-grace by U-37 two days later. It was daylight, six hours after the first attack, when the Norwegian motorship *Tancred* was torpedoed. This 6,000-ton vessel sank. In the early afternoon of the same day the British steamer *Darcoila* was sunk and there were no survivors. A British report, rather strangely, said, 'The SS *Darcoila* of 4,804-tons, which left Milford Haven on 20 September has not been heard of again.'

By now five of the eleven torpedoes carried had been fired. In the late afternoon of 28 September another British ship *Empire Ocelot* of 5,759-tons, bound from Liverpool to the USA in ballast, was torpedoed when about 700-miles west of the coast of County Mayo. She was struck in the boiler-room almost amidships by a torpedo estimated to have been travelling very fast, about six feet below the surface. There was a moderate swell at the time, but the ship stopped and the crew took to the boats. Shortly afterwards the survivors saw U-32 go alongside for a moment, but not for
long enough for anyone to board the steamer, and fired about eight shells at the sinking ship. The empty torpedo tube was soon reloaded and the

next victim was torpedoed in the early morning nine hours later. This was *Bassa*, another steamer of much the same size as the last victim; this British ship did not need artillery fire to finish her off.

The Dutch SS *Hanlerwijk* of 3,278-tons was missed by a torpedo fired by U-32 at 1130 on 30 September. The U-boat then followed the steamer and sank her by gunfire eight hours later.

When the *Hanlerwijk* was sinking the U-boat approached her at periscope depth, as the Germans wanted to try to read the name of the ship; but the setting sun, low down on the horizon, was shining into the periscope and Hans Jenisch misjudged the distance, with the result that the U-boat came into collision with the sinking ship. Although U-32's bow was damaged the torpedo tubes were not affected.

The German High Command announced on 1 October that Hans Jenisch had sunk six armed enemy merchant ships, totalling 34,760 GRT.

Kayeson became the ninth and last victim of this seventh war cruise when it was torpedoed and sank in the early evening of 2 October. The 4,606-ton British steamer was well out in the Atlantic, just to the south of the position where U-32 had torpedoed the three outward bound ships six days earlier. This was a very auspicious start for the first patrol out of Lorient. It was to this French base that Hans Jenisch returned on 6 October. The whole crew of the boat were feted on arrival and the award of three Iron Crosses second class to ratings had been promulgated on 3 October and it was announced a week later that Hans Jenisch had been decorated with the Knight's Insignia of the Iron Cross. As well as the sinking of the ships the citation noted that he had carried out difficult mine laying operations 'in the immediate vicinity' of the English coast. Shortly after returning to Lorient half the crew of the U-boat set off for leave in Germany, most travelling together by train. Admiral Dönitz organised a special train for his men which became known as the *BdU Zug*. It expressed the fortunate crew members via Nantes, Le Mans, Paris and passed through Luxembourg, the whole journey to Wilhelmshaven taking two and a half days. Some officers flew to Germany.

The *Kriegsmarine* had established good relations with the *Luftwaffe* at Vannes when they had earlier also taken part in Operation *Weserübung*, the invasion of Denmark and Norway, and were now bombing Britain by night. The airmen had air transport available for leave and the aircraft returning to their home stations at Kothen and Lüneburg often had room available for U-boat officers going to North Germany from Lorient.

For those not taking home leave there were many delights in the French base. Clothes and wine were sold to them at reduced prices in special shops and there was fraternising with some of the French girls.

Hans Jenisch spent his 27th birthday, on 19 October, at his home at Gerdauen – it was to be his last time there for several years. Those who stayed at Lorient the whole time that U-32 was in port experienced four air raid alerts. On the night of 16/17 October Bordeaux was bombed and on other occasions the sirens wailed out when an aircraft laying mines off the coast had been picked up by radar. Those that were caught in town during the alerts sheltered in cellars.

Once again there were minor changes of personnel when the U-boat was in port and a new potential commander was carried as a supernumerary to gain experience. The officers were pleased to see him as it would help out with watchkeeping, but the crew certainly were not; they considered it unlucky to carry a 'passenger' and they were to be proved right.

When all the crew had mustered again on U-32 they were told that the U-boat would be returning to Germany at the conclusion of the next cruise so they spent all their money on luxurious French goods to take back to their loved ones in their homeland, lingerie and perfume being the most popular items.

While at the base U-32 had been serviced in the open air as the construction of the bunkers that were later to protect the U-boats had not commenced at this time.

When U-32 cast off from its mooring for its eighth war cruise on 24 October nobody could possibly have guessed it would be its most successful and its last. A minesweeper accompanied the U-boat down the River Scorfe to the entrance of Lorient harbour for the last time. On board were eleven torpedoes, nine air and two electric. Five were in the tubes and of the six spares, four were housed in the bilges under the deck plates and two were wrapped in canvas above the deck plate in the forward compartments. The crew took their few possessions with them; they had said their farewells to the friends they had made in the French port.

Out in the Bay of Biscay U-32 proceeded to its operational area off the North Western Approaches. Bad weather was encountered about the second or third day out and the cruise became uncomfortable and dull.

Another ship was experiencing these unpleasant conditions as it sped through the water at 22-knots. This was the *Empress of Britain* which we left just after the outbreak of war when it disembarked its passengers in Quebec. The liner was then requisitioned as a troopship and its livery was painted grey. It then made for Halifax Nova Scotia and commenced its new role on 10 December. The liner sailed in the first big Atlantic convoy, its destination the Clyde, home of its makers.

Five more return Atlantic crossings were made in the first half of 1940 and then, on 6 August, the giant liner set out for the Middle East, for Suez by way of the Cape. The return journey started nearly seven weeks later.

The Canadian Pacific liner called in at Capetown. It left Table Bay, under Government charter, on 12 October for Liverpool with a complement of 419 crew and 223 passengers, which included servicemen and their families. Also carried were 700-tons of Government stores.

The ship was equipped with a 6-inch anti-U-boat gun, a 3-inch anti-aircraft gun and four machine-guns manned by servicemen.

The *Empress of Britain* was routed independently and had experienced good weather for the first two weeks, until she reached a position west of Ireland during the darkness of 25/26 October when heavy cloud and rain was encountered.

At the *Luftwaffe* base of Merignac, near Bordeaux, the meteorologists had correctly forecast the weather and a report was given to *Oberleutnant* Bernhard Jope who was due to fly the first patrol of the day, to an area north-west of Ireland. His aircraft was a large four-engined Condor, the Fw 200, a variant of the pre-war passenger transport.

Just after 0300 the engines of Jope's Condor roared into life as it took off for an armed reconnaissance. Some five hours later, after flying over endless sea, often through cloud, a huge ship was sighted below, to port. Immediately the aircraft made ready to attack. Jope circled and dropped down to approximately 500-feet.

A run was made along the line of the ship from the stern and two bombs were dropped, one was a near miss but the other struck just forward of the third funnel. This hit set the upperworks amidships ablaze and the smoke obscured the view of the anti-aircraft gunner. However, the Lewis gunners opened up.

It was only when the bomb hit the liner that the folly of leaving the ornate decoration aboard when the wartime conversion took place, was realised. The wood panelling was soon alight and in the space of the ship-wide compartments smoke billowed up.

Further runs were flown over the blazing ship and it was machine-gunned; another bomb wrecked the after steering position and the anti-aircraft gun was put out of action. The Condor pilot was sure the ship was doomed as it was ablaze from end to end with black smoke covering the upper works and spurts of red flame issued up through uncovered hatches. As *Oberleutnant* Jope turned for base let us go below for the report that the master of the *Empress of Britain* made at the time. Captain C H Sapsworth

CVO described the attack:

> At 0815 I was in the wheelhouse when I heard the men say they had sighted an aeroplane on our port quarter. It was then about a mile away, circling astern of us, and we thought it was a friendly machine as it did not take up a bombing position, i personally have had many experiences, particularly in the Channel, when our own aircraft have flown over us, the whole length of the ship, at a low altitude, without giving the prescribed recognition signal of crossing our bows a mile ahead, giving us some anxious moments in consequence.

> The aircraft lost height and proceeded to fly along the starboard, but when it was abreast of the after gun it turned sharply and flew diagonally across the stern at a height of about 700-feet, releasing two bombs, one of which fell just forward of the third funnel, the other one being a near miss on the port side, at the same time firing a red and white Very light. All this took place within a minute of sighting it, so that there was little time to get the guns to bear, but before the bomb hit the ship the after gun was in action; they were all experienced Naval gunners on the after gun. At the same time all four Lewis guns opened fire.

> The enemy flew ahead, circled the bow, and manoeuvred to make another attack from aft. I increased speed to 24-knots and by using the helm endeavoured to keep the after gun to bear all the time. He made the second attack in exactly the same way as before, dropped two bombs, both of which were direct hits in the same position almost as the first one. By this time the ship was well alight amidships from the first bomb and now the whole ship was filled with dense black smoke. We then saw the plane flying well ahead and shaping up to attack from forward. I think he had had enough of the after gun which the gunnel – was letting go whenever possible in a most satisfactory manner. The Lewis gunners were also firing when it was possible, but I think the shells from the HA gun were set for 3,000 -feet and the enemy kept well inside that range, flying between 500-feet and 700-feet over the ship.

> He approached from ahead and as he flew over the foremast he machine-gunned the bridge, having already opened fire on the men who were aft, during his first two attacks. As he flew from stem to stern he released another two bombs, one of which fell on the top deck, the other being a near miss. He carried out two more attacks, making five in all, both from forward, each time dropping two more bombs, machine-gunning as he approached and using his rear gun as he flew off. We found bullet holes right across the fore side of the bridge, but I personally did not see any marks from cannon shells, although the Naval gunners reported that he had used a cannon.

> After the fifth attack the enemy flew off, about 30-minutes from when we had first sighted him. The wind at the time was north-east force 3 freshening later to 4-5, 7-10ths cloud, fairly low, but good visibility.

> As soon as the first bomb had fallen on the ship the air-raid alarm was sounded which, in our ship, meant everybody to go below decks except those on duty. Unfortunately, the ship was so filled with dense black smoke that everyone amidships had to be taken either

forward or aft. After approximately 20-minutes of this I sounded the 'abandon ship stations' signal as I could see that many of our life-boats were already on fire and I wanted to get the boats in the embarkation position as soon as possible in case it became necessary to abandon ship. At this time I had not definitely decided on doing so. When this signal is given all passengers should come up to the promenade deck where we have proper embarkation doors to every boat through the bulwarks, but now, owing to both promenade decks being on fire, this could not be carried out.

I now decided to stop the ship - we had been proceeding at 24-knots - hoping to let her run off her way and at the same time manoeuvre her to avoid the plane which was still attacking. I distinctly saw several of our tracer bullets hitting the plane, our machine-gunners did excellent work, but it had no effect on the enemy.

The ship was thoroughly alight from the fore end of the bridge to the after funnel and I could see we should have to abandon her. Some of the boats had already been put in the water to save them from burning, I looked over the side and saw some of them hanging on by ropes under the stern and I realised it would be very dangerous to put the engines astern. In any case, on going to the engine-room telegraph I found it had been carried away, one system of telephones was burnt and useless, and there was just one telephone communication left with the engine-room. I got through after some difficulty and gave the order to the engineers to shut down boilers and proceed to boat stations. About 300 people were already in the boats, mostly in those astern, the ship still having about 8-knots way on her.

While this had been going on, at the air-raid alarm two large fire parties, one forward and one aft, had got all their fire fighting appliances and attempted to fight the fire from either end; but unfortunately the water supply from the engine-room had been broken by the bomb explosions and we only got a small trickle of water forward, and none at all aft. The men did what they could with extinguishers, but the fire was already hopelessly beyond control. Fifty minutes from the first attack, at about 0910, the bridge began to burn and it became impossible to get forward or aft on the ship so that wherever people were at this time, there they had to remain. I sent everyone off the bridge, as it became untenable, and I also had to come down to the boat deck which was already on fire. Two officers and myself were the only people left amidships, as far as I could see for the dense smoke. Then I saw two other officers, who had been lowering boats, standing on a ladder ready to swim for it. We followed their example, and the last boat, which was hanging on to the port side, managed to pull along and take us on board. There was a slight sea and swell, but no considerable rise and fall, and the ship was still doing about four knots. There was a party of about thirty men still on the fore part of the saloon deck and before leaving I sang out to them to try and come amidships as there was still one boat which would pick them up, but they said they could not get there owing to the fire. I told them to throw the life rafts over the side, there were about thirty of them on that deck, and this they did; we spent the next two hours picking up some twenty people including several women. A good many of the boats had been lowered in such a hurry to avoid the fire that there were only three or four people in them; two motor boats also got away but one was so badly holed by bullets that the engine was flooded, and the other got away without an engineer. After some delay an engineer was transferred from another boat, he eventually got the engine going and picked up several empty boats which he towed back to the ship and took off the remaining people who were mustered on the fore deck, everyone from the after part having left by this time.

About 1400 the smoke of destroyers was seen approaching, and all survivors were rescued by 1600 and taken to Gourock where we landed at 0830 on the next morning. Sunday 27 October.

I think most of the forty-five people who are missing were killed by the explosion: we actually found nine bodies, and five or six others were drowned through taking to the water too soon. There was never the slightest sign of panic amongst the crew, nor the passengers, and I should particularly like to recommend the machine-gunners on the bridge who did marvellous work. They comprised eight soldiers specially attached to the ship, and they never stopped firing for a moment, not even to take cover from the machine-gunning. One soldier shot away ten trays, and then asked me for someone to fill his tray so that he could work more quickly, so I sent one of my bridge-boys to help him.

When attacked, the liner had been about fifty miles north-west of the north-west coast of Ireland and this was the position given by *Oberleutnant* Jope. Machine-gun fire from the liner had slightly damaged the nose of his aircraft.

As a matter of routine news of the attack had been passed on to U-boat headquarters at Lorient. The *Kriegsmarine* authorities then sent out a W/T signal to the U-boat commanders, advising them that the damaged ship was a troop transport. A later German reconnaissance flight showed that *Empress of Britain* was under tow. It also reported that the fire appeared to be under control. As the master had said in his report, destroyers rescued the survivors and then tugs were sent to try to bring the damaged liner nearer shore. Two more destroyers were despatched to guard the ship under tow.

The W/T signal from Lorient was picked up in the wireless office of U-32 but not acted upon immediately as Hans Jenisch thought that as U-31 was probably nearer, Wilfried Prellberg, its commander, would act on it and attack the liner. When the message was repeated on the Sunday, adding that the ship was crippled and under tow, Hans Jenisch some sixty miles from the estimated position, decided to take action. By noon the smoking liner was in sight dead ahead. Other masts were seen, those of the escorting destroyers; they were the old 'S' class *Sardonyx*, launched in 1919, and the 'Shakespeare' class *Broke*, launched a year later. Visibility was good and it could be seen that the liner was under tow, making about four knots.

A Sunderland was keeping watch over the slow moving liner and its presence kept the U-boat down. When the light was fading U-32 surfaced but the liner was no longer in sight. The U-boat submerged and the hydrophones picked up the sounds of propellers twenty miles distant. Resurfacing, in the darkness, U-32 headed for the position. Hans Jenisch placed his U-boat almost exactly in the course of the large ship, and the risk he ran was very great. The two escorting destroyers preceding the *Empress of Britain* passed zig-zagging, one on either beam of the U-boat. The Germans thought that their boat must be seen at any moment. Then two tugs passed towing the damaged ship, and Hans Jenisch, with characteristic intentness of purpose and cool judgment, waited until the last moment before increasing the speed of his engines and then, at a favourable moment, fired three torpedoes almost simultaneously from a range of 600 metres.

The U-boat was on the port side of the *Empress of Britain*. One of the torpedoes hit on the port side abreast the foremost funnel, and another hit the engine room further aft. The third exploded prematurely.

The U-boat turned away and made off, still on the surface, at emergency full speed. The *Empress of Britain* was enveloped in a large cloud of steam and when this thinned, some four minutes later, the torpedoed ship had already sunk.

Hans Jenisch was the only U-boat commander to sink one of the 'giant' liners that had been requisitioned for war service. He had now accounted for over 100,000 GRT of Allied shipping.

The crew of the U-boat were elated, none more so than the engineering officer, who had been promoted from the lower deck and had only recently joined U-32. The prospective commander aboard U-32 for experience before getting his own command had served in the destroyers *Richard Beitzer* and *Theodore Riedel* and the cruiser *Blücher*, which he had left just one week before it was sunk with heavy loss of life in the Norwegian campaign. He was not to be so fortunate this time.

As U-32 escaped to the west after torpedoing the *Empress of Britain* the tugs towing the liner quickly cast off their tow ropes, but British sources say that the liner took ten minutes to sink, not the four reported from the U-boat.

When at a safe distance, the news of the sinking was transmitted to U-boat headquarters. This good news could not immediately be given to Admiral Dönitz; he had flown from Paris to Berlin with Günther Prien who was due to be invested with the Oak Leaves by the Führer. After landing at Templehof airport they drove to the Kaiserhof Hotel for dinner.

Here the Admiral was paged for a telephone call. He returned to his table beaming; 'Jenisch has sunk the *Empress of Britain*,' he exclaimed, continuing, 'I can just imagine my Jenisch creeping up on her with his tongue half out of his mouth.' The news made the meal all the more enjoyable, washed down as it was by a Moselle wine.

Meanwhile, out at sea and in more salubrious surroundings, the successful U-boat went in search of further prey.

The next intended victim was *Balzac* a British ship of 5,372-tons and a convoy straggler which was sighted in the forenoon of 30 October. Hans Jenisch was extremely suspicious of the ship steaming alone zig-zagging. He thought it might be a 'Q' ship – a U-boat trap. However, at 1240 he fired a torpedo, but this missed the ship and exploded on her starboard side fifty yards abeam of her mainmast. The explosion caused a large disturbance in the water and a blue haze was observed. As *Balzac* did not know the cause of this she reported that she was being shelled. *Balzac*'s report was received by HM destroyers *Harvester* and *Highlander*, both new destroyers that were being built for the Brazilian Navy and put into service with the Royal Navy on the outbreak of war. At this time *Harvester* was searching for the commodore of convoy SC8 but on receipt of the signal proceeded to look for the steamer, approaching the position from the southward at 25-knots *Harvester* was in a position 45-miles from *Balzac*, swept from the northward and the two destroyers met at 1610 and signals were exchanged.

An hour-and-a-half later *Balzac* was sighted on the port bow by *Harvester*, who closed and interrogated her about the U-boat attack earlier in the day. *Highlander*, when about ten miles distant, steering to intercept the convoy, was informed.

In the meantime Hans Jenisch, after missing *Balzac*, became increasingly puzzled by the behaviour of the merchantman, and followed her submerged. Between 1300 and 1400 hours the radio officer of *Balzac* heard a pulsing sound on his receiver and the master, concluding that this might be due to the presence of a U-boat, altered course several times and ran into rain squalls. The guns' crew and all look-outs were standing by. The submerged U-boat continued to follow the ship and came to periscope depth, but dived at once upon sighting destroyers; hydrophone watch was set but nothing was heard.

Later U-32 came once more to periscope depth, again saw destroyers and submerged. It then pursued *Balzac* at full submerged speed. After some deliberation the operators at the listening apparatus reported to the commander that they thought that they heard suspicious sounds. The commander sent back the laconic reply: 'Rot, that is our own noise, we are travelling at full speed.'

Hans Jenisch, intent as ever on his purpose, was apparently neglecting the proximity of hostile warships and continued to follow *Balzac*.

At 1812, *Harvester*, about 1,000 yards on *Balzac*'s port bow, obtained asdic contact on the port bow at very short range. Before the contact had been classified the periscope of a U-boat projecting about two feet out of the water was sighted to starboard.

For some time *Harvester*'s hydrophone effect had been indistinguishable from *Balzac*'s in the U-boat, so when Hans Jenisch raised his periscope and saw *Harvester* very close indeed he at once ordered a crash dive; U-32 was then about eighty yards on *Harvester*'s port beam.

After signalling SSS, submarine in sight, the captain ordered full astern port, full ahead starboard with his rudder hard-a-port, with the intention of ramming, the range of the periscope being such that this manoeuvre appeared possible. As the destroyer turned, it was appreciated that the U-boat was going fast and thus came inside the destroyer's turning circle. Engines were therefore reversed, full ahead port, full ahead starboard, to swing the stern over the U-boat.

At the moment when the U-boat crash dived, engine movements had stopped *Harvester*. Full ahead was ordered and a pattern of six charges with deep settings was dropped. The pattern would have had an effect on U-32 had it turned to port, but in fact it turned to starboard.

After its crash dive U-32 did some rapid manoeuvres, including reversing engines, in its efforts to escape, the destroyers could be heard almost overhead. Depth-charge explosions were heard and thought to be fairly close, but no serious damage was caused.

Harvester was turned at 1,000 yards and contact regained by *Highlander*, who was closing and was given the range and bearing. *Balzac*, being in the way and preventing an immediate attack, was informed that she was steaming into danger and was given a course to steer.

Harvester then lost contact, possibly due to the target being end on, another contact was obtained but was classified as 'non-sub'. Meanwhile *Highlander* obtained a good contact and passed over it at slow speed, giving range and bearings, and also dropped a calcium flare.

At 1848 *Highlander*, while turning, signalled that she would attack if *Harvester* obtained contact. Shortly afterwards *Harvester* did obtain contact at about just over a mile, being at that time at right angles to *Highlander*'s track. However, before she could confirm and report the contact, a signal was received from *Highlander* to 'attack', whereupon *Harvester* moved in at

18-knots, but as the other vessel was seen to be doing the same thing *Harvester* reversed engines, but held the contact until *Highlander* dropped a fourteen charge pattern.

The position of the charge agreed with *Harvester*'s contact, which became confused with echoes from the detonation of the charges, and was lost.

Harvester turned parallel to *Highlander* and continued on a course of 120-degrees to sweep the area in case the attack had been unsuccessful.

After *Highlander*'s fourteen charge pattern had been fired at 1853, the range was opened to 1,600 yards by plot and the destroyer turned to starboard. At this moment a track was seen on her port bow. Visibility was bad, as there was a dark rain squall and daylight was fading, but course was altered towards this track which gradually resolved itself into two tracks, eventually thought to be torpedoes. At this moment large air bubbles were seen and asdic contact was gained.

Down below the 14 charge pattern had come as a highly unpleasant surprise and caused considerable damage to the U-boat. The lighting system failed and all electrical instruments were put out of action; valves refused to function, a junction of the compressed air leads was fractured, causing excess pressure in the U-boat. Some small leaks were started, also the after ballast tanks were crushed in on both sides and put out of action. The depth gauge was smashed and the electric switch gear which broke away was seen hanging by its wire connections. The crew were sent forward and orders were given to blow all tanks. An attempt was then made to surface by using the hydroplanes, but the motors would not function.

At 1908, fifteen minutes after the depth charges had been fired U-32 finally surfaced with its stern well down. The commander thought that he might be able to dive again and shouted orders to the engineer officer, but there was no more compressed air. The idea of firing torpedoes at the attacking destroyers had also to be abandoned, owing to the complete lack of compressed air.

Hans Jenisch then gave the order to abandon ship: the crew escaped through the conning-tower and jumped into the sea. The engineer officer opened the necessary valves to make sure U-32 would sink.

Highlander informed *Harvester* that U-32 had surfaced and opened fire with her 4.7-inch guns at point blank range. It was almost dark, but one shot was seen to hit the conning-tower. Fire was opened with the machine-guns in a further attempt to prevent the Germans from scuttling their boat, but several of them were seen to be abandoning it. Owing to the darkness it was impossible to tell how many had jumped overboard, and the possibility of ramming was considered in case the U-boat was shamming. However, it was soon apparent that the U-boat was finished, as its bow, high in the air, was caught in the beam of *Harvester*'s searchlight and it was seen to sink stern first.

Harvester closed the position ready to drop a 14 charge pattern, but shouts from the water showed that the majority of the crew were out and she therefore reversed engines and stopped in the middle of the swimming men. *Harvester* rescued twenty-nine survivors and *Highlander* four. Nine men lost their lives including the 2WO.

The German prisoners did not disclose any information to their captors that might have been useful but a British summary of their attitude is interesting for the insight it gives to German thinking at this time: 'Maintaining that Germany is at present only marking time until after the consolidation of a series of political victories and corrective adjustments in the Balkans and elsewhere, they think, at any moment deemed suitable, a German attack on Great Britain would be overwhelmingly successful, and profess to be amazed at the British failure to see the inevitability of our utter defeat at any moment convenient to Hitler.'

When, after the war, all necessary adjustments had been made Hans Jenisch, who had been commander of U-32 for only nine months, was credited with sinking fourteen ships totalling 100,592 GRT. This placed the commander at number 32 of the all time list of successful U-boat commanders. The U-boat, it will be remembered, had also sunk five ships before Hans Jenisch was appointed in command.

CHAPTER THREE

ARK ROYAL AND U-BOATS

The *Ark Royal* was the third ship to bear the name. There had been ships before, and aircraft carriers since that have borne the name with pride, but the one everyone remembers is the *Ark Royal* with which Britain went to war in 1939. She had a shorter life than any other of the name, as finally she was sunk by U-81, but not before being claimed sunk many times by Doctor Goebbels' propagandists.

This *Ark Royal* was the first to be designed exclusively as an aircraft carrier. She was the last carrier to be launched before the war and was the embodiment of all past experience of carrier construction. She could accommodate sixty aircraft in her hangars, had two aircraft lifts, accelerators for catapulting, an emergency crash barrier and arrester wires which could be lowered hydraulically to facilitate deck landing.

The carrier was built by Cammell Laird at Birkenhead and launched in April 1937. After fitting out, the carrier, with her 800-foot long flight deck, raised steam for the first time and headed for the open waters for trials.

The crew were drafted from the Portsmouth division, *Ark Royal* was a Pompey ship and after trials in the Clyde, Fleet Air Arm aircraft flew on. The major role of the carrier was as an aerodrome at sea.

Many of the pilots that joined *Ark Royal* had served in the older carrier *Courageous* and they soon appreciated the improved facilities. Following suggestions, eight feet was added to the funnel to take gases away from the landing deck; this made life much easier for the pilots landing on.

The carrier made its first appearance at its home base towards the end of 1938 when it secured at the South Railway Jetty at Portsmouth Harbour. The flight deck towered 70-feet above the waterline and with the island and funnel above this the 22,000-ton carrier looked enormous and attracted admiring glances from commuters crossing on the Gosport Ferry.

The new carrier joined the fleet for the 1939 Spring cruise to Gibraltar and the Mediterranean. While homeward bound a fire broke out in a hangar and all of one of the squadron's aircraft were destroyed. It was a good, but expensive, work-out for the damage control party. A tough test for the carrier was crossing the Bay of Biscay in a force nine gale.

After Easter leave the carrier proceeded along the coast to Portland, the crew taking part in the regatta, and then on to Torquay. Here the South Devon boatmen welcomed the Navy, taking locals and visitors alike for a 'trip round the *Ark Royal*'. The carrier returned to Portsmouth and summer leave was granted, war clouds were on the horizon. Many reservists and pensioners were called back to the colours and *Ark Royal* received its quota. As they tramped over the cobbled roadways of the dockyard, past Nelson's *Victory* in her dry-dock, struggling with bags and hammocks, they gazed for the first time at the huge carrier that was to be their new home. *Ark Royal* sailed north to Invergordon and then on to Scapa Flow. Here the carrier joined with other ships of the Home Fleet.

The carrier was at sea when hostilities commenced. Captain Power announced the news on the tannoy. Immediately the carrier's aircraft became the eyes for the fleet until 6 September, when they all returned to Scapa Flow.

The next day, fully refuelled, the carrier was back at sea with the fleet for a sortie off the Norwegian coast. *Ark Royal* returned on the 10th.

In order to search the area to the westward of the Orkneys, through which merchant ships taking a northerly route would pass, and in view of the intended sailing of the Home Fleet from Scapa Flow to Loch Ewe, the carrier, escorted by four destroyers of the 8th Destroyer Flotilla, left Scapa at 2030 on 11 September and proceeded to the westward to hunt U-boats; one had been reported as having sunk a ship about 100-miles north of Rockall.

Early on the 12th, *Ark Royal*'s aircraft attacked a U-boat and forced it to submerge, and two of the escorting destroyers were detached to hunt. Before noon the weather, which had been good, deteriorated and put a stop to flying; further air search became possible later in the day, but no results were obtained.

Search was continued the next day, again a U-boat was sighted and attacked, though with no better success that the previous day.

At daylight on the 14th, three more destroyers joined and aircraft were flown off on a searching patrol, but nothing was seen. While the immediate area round the force was covered, information was received soon after noon that the British ship *Fanad Head* had been torpedoed about 200-miles to the south-westward. All aircraft were accordingly recalled and four destroyers were despatched to investigate. *Kapitänleutnant* Fritz Lemp in U-30, which had sunk *Athenia*, had struck again.

At 1432 *Ark Royal* turned into the wind to fly off three Blackburn Skua light dive bombers, while the destroyers maintained their course and speed. The carrier then turned back after the aircraft had flown off and was then about four miles astern of the screen. At 1507, when *Ark Royal* was about two miles astern of the screen, U-39 fired two torpedoes at her, both of which missed astern and exploded in the wake. *Ark Royal*'s speed had been estimated at 22-knots by the German commander when in fact she was doing 26-knots. *Kapitänleutnant* Gerhard Glattes, in U-39, had passed about 3,000 yards from the nearest destroyer, and, hearing the explosions, was under the impression that he had scored a hit. However, his was not to be the glory that was reserved for Otto Schuhart three days later when he sunk the first British man-of-war, *Courageous*.

The destroyers immediately turned back, spread 2,000-yards apart, and started to search to the north-westward of *Ark Royal*. Speed was reduced to 15-knots and both *Faulknor* and *Foxhound* obtained contact. *Foxhound* attacked at once and dropped two charges set at 250 and 300-feet.

The U-boat had dived deep when it saw the destroyers coming, and at the time of the first attack, at 1525, was at about 230-feet. The attack put the lights out and damaged the main battery. The main electric motors were also put out of action due to short-circuiting caused by flooding.

Faulknor followed immediately with another attack, and a full pattern of depth charges was fired. This caused more leaks in the U-boat. *Firedrake* carried out another attack at 1546 with depth charges set to 250 and 500-feet. This did more damage to U-39 and water started pouring in. This attack caused the mortal damage and U-39 was by now quite out of control and was filling with chlorine gas. The commander ordered his charge to surface and it broke surface at 1546. All three destroyers immediately opened up but fire was checked when it was seen that the crew were abandoning their boat through the conning-tower, wearing life-belts. All the forty-three crew members were rescued by the British.

In the meantime the Skuas that had flown off from *Ark Royal* just before the attack on the carrier had proceeded on diverging tracks. Two of them were destroyed by their own bombs. The bombs were dropped from too low an altitude and the force of the explosion blew their tails off, killing their gunners. Both pilots however, were rescued by U-30, the U-boat they were attacking. At about 1600 the U-boat was sighted and attacked with four 20-lb bombs by the remaining Skua. The aircraft climbed again and attacked with its 100-lb bomb. The U-Boat disappeared but was seen at 1625 again off the *Fanad Head*'s starboard quarter. The aircraft dived again firing from its port gun, expending 1,150 rounds in one continuous burst. The pattern was seen all round the conning-tower and several members of U-30's crew were injured and later landed in Iceland for treatment.

Meanwhile this remaining Skua returned to *Ark Royal* to tell of its account of the attack on U-30 and to listen to what had happened to the carrier from U-39 while it had been aloft.

All was soon ship-shape on the carrier and when it was realised that U-30 was still at large a force of six Fairey Swordfish aircraft was sent to search for it. They found that Fritz Lemp had needed a torpedo to sink the ship that had refused to sink by gunfire. The U-boat was on the surface and was attacked by the biplane bombers who claimed to have sunk it. They had not and U-30 survived to put a torpedo into the port side of HMS *Barham* three month later. However, as will be seen in the next chapter, the battleship did not sink on this occasion.

Ark Royal returned to Scapa Flow with the fleet and the U-boat prisoners were landed from *Faulknor*.

After a few more short patrols with the fleet *Ark Royal* once more put to sea again on 25 September. This time it was not a hunt for U-boats but for the British submarine *Spearfish* which had been badly damaged by a depth charge attack. After the submarine surfaced, the wireless operator had repaired the W/T transmitter and at dawn a signal had been sent asking for an escort, since the crippled submarine was within easy range of *Luftwaffe* aircraft.

Twice during the day *Spearfish* sighted aircraft, which fortunately had not seen the submarine, which was unable to submerge. At 0400 on the 26th the destroyers *Somali*, and *Eskimo* meet the submarine and at 0900 the submarine sighted *Ark Royal* and the battle fleet. Several Do 18's were seen during the forenoon and a sub-flight of Skuas from the carrier brought one down – the first British aerial success of the war. The crew were rescued and became prisoners-of-war.

The other Dorniers would obviously report their loss and the crews of the sixteen 4.5-inch anti-aircraft guns protecting the carrier were extra vigilant during the forenoon. However, the watch had changed before the inevitable attack came during the afternoon, from a Heinkel.

'Where is the *Ark Royal*?' mocked Lord Haw-Haw from the German radio English language broadcast on that evening of 26 September. The traitor William Joyce was to have the opportunity of asking this question many more times in the next two years and this question is still remembered as well as his opening announcement of 'Germany calling, Germany calling'.

It was the Heinkel incident earlier in the day that prompted Joyce's question. When attacked, the carrier's captain had taken avoiding action and a bomb fell 15-feet away. *Ark Royal* was shaken, anything portable was deposited on the deck, but no material damage was sustained.

Arriving back at base the German pilot reported that he had attacked an aircraft carrier in the North Sea and that a bomb had hit, or near-missed, the target. The German propaganda machine swung into action, the pilot was decorated and promoted, and against his will, a book was produced under his name entitled *How I sank the Ark Royal*.

At the beginning of October *Ark Royal*, with escort, sailed south to West Africa and stayed in the South Atlantic until the German battleship *Graf Spee*, which had been marauding in the area, scuttled itself off the River Plate in mid-December. *Ark Royal* returned to Liverpool two months later.

There then followed a month in the Mediterranean before she returned to help protect convoys and give air support to British troops involved in the Norwegian campaign; here *Ark Royal* was in almost continuous action until 14 June.

Three days after arriving back at Scapa Flow, *Ark Royal* was at sea again – Italy had joined the war on the side of the Axis and *Ark Royal* was to go to Gibraltar. With HMS *Hood* and a destroyer escort the carrier sailed well out into the Atlantic to the west of the Bay of Biscay and here, on 22 June, they were seen from U-46. Engelbert Endrass, the commander, thought the carrier was *Illustrious* and fired a three torpedo salvo. Unfortunately for the U-boat none of the torpedoes caused any damage.

Ark Royal arrived in time for the distasteful Oran incident, in which French battleships were sunk by the British to avoid their falling into German hands. Here her aircraft spotted for the Fleet. The remainder of the summer and autumn was spent on duty in the Mediterranean and off West Africa for the Dakar fiasco.

After a refit in Liverpool *Ark Royal* returned to the Mediterranean and after Taranto *Ark Royal*'s aircraft helped protect the convoys through to

Malta. In early 1941 the German battle-cruisers were at sea and *Ark Royal* was with Force H at Gibraltar. Back in the Mediterranean *Ark Royal*'s fighters were in battle with the *Regia Aeronautica* aircraft and the bombers were found targets to attack.

On 22 February, at Vegesack, North Germany the U-boat, U-81, which was to sink *Ark Royal* was launched. On 20 May *Bismarck*, Germany's most powerful battleship, steamed into the North Sea. Three days later the *Kriegsmarine* ship, with *Prinz Eugen*, was sighted between Iceland and Greenland. *Hood* and *Prince of Wales* gave chase. The next morning *Hood* was sunk and *Prince of Wales* damaged. *Ark Royal*, with Force H, headed north from Gibraltar to intercept the *Bismarck*. At mid-morning next day *Bismarck*, damaged by a torpedo hit from a Swordfish launched from *Victorious*, was sighted sailing alone nearly 700-miles from Brest. The damaged battleship had to be stopped before it reached the protection of *Luftwaffe* aircraft, and port. In the early evening fifteen Swordfish torpedo-carrying aircraft took off from *Ark Royal*. The biplanes attacked *Bismarck* against all odds and a torpedo dropped by one of them jammed the rudder of the battleship which could then only circle out of control. The next day British ships finished off *Bismarck* and *Ark Royal* returned to Gibraltar.

The carrier made runs to Malta flying off Hurricanes for the beleaguered island and its aircraft also acted as an air umbrella to assist convoys to get through.

Admiral Dönitz was pressed into sending more U-boats to join the 29th Flotilla in the Mediterranean and, in November, *Ark Royal* was to meet one of the new arrivals, U-81.

The Type VIIC boat had been launched less than nine months earlier from the Bremer Vulkan yard. *Oberleutnant* Friedrich Guggenberger, of the 1934 class, was the first commander of U-81. By mid-July the boat had completed all the Baltic Sea training and was in Kiel awaiting its first war cruise. Leaving on the 17th, U-81, sailed north, up through the Kattegat and Skagerrak, hugged the Norwegian coast and put into the beautiful base at the Norwegian port of Trondheim on 1 August, The U-boat carried out one short patrol from the 13th Flotilla base, which took it to the Kola area. The next patrol commenced on 27 August and took U-81 to join with a pack of U-boats south of Greenland. Their target was a slow homeward bound convoy of sixty-four merchant ships which were escorted by only one destroyer and three corvettes. By 9 September, with the convoy already round Cape Farewell, the pack struck – U-81 opening the account with a moonlight sinking of the 5,591-ton London registered *Empire Springbuck* with two torpedoes. The ship was a convoy straggler and blew up when the torpedoes hit its high explosive cargo.

During the night U-85, U-432 and U-652 all made attacks and at dawn U-81 sank its second victim, another British ship, the 3,252-ton *Sally Maersk* with two torpedo hits. Three ships had been lined up in the sights and five torpedoes fired, but only one ship sank. Others in the pack, including U-82, U-433, U-207, U-202, U-84, U-98 and U-372, registered successes and by the time fog came down on the afternoon of the 11th eighteen ships of convoy SC42 had been sunk. At the conclusion of the patrol U-81 put in to Brest, on 19 September. Thus, in less than three months, U-81 had berthed in three different U-boat bases in three different countries. The boat's crew only spent six weeks in France before being sent to another operational area, the Mediterranean.

Much to Admiral Dönitz's annoyance, Hitler had offered Mussolini twenty U-boats to help him keep open the lines of communication in the Mediterranean to assist the Italian forces fighting in North Africa. In October alone over 60-percent of the shipping despatched from Italy to Libya was sunk in transit. The Type VIIC boats were most suited to the Mediterranean conditions, and U-81 was one of those sent.

The boat left the Biscay base on 4 November and a week later it was ready to attempt the passage through the heavily defended Straits of Gibraltar at night. Each U-boat commander had his own ideas of entering the Mediterranean and most chose to pass on the fast-flowing, incoming tide. Guggenberger, now promoted to *Kapitänleutnant*, was no exception. He chose to pass through on the night of the 11/12th on the surface and kept close to the European side, so close in fact that he was picked up by a beam from the lighthouse that juts out from Tarifa at the most southerly point of Spain. The U-boat passed two fishing vessels and two destroyers but remained undetected, much to the relief of all.

Once through the narrow strip of water, U-81 and also U-205 were ordered to locate and attack heavy units of the Mediterranean Fleet, heading back to Gibraltar after supplying Malta with fighters. Italian air reconnaissance had been active and made contact with the ships at 0930 on 11 November and at 1500 the next afternoon the fleet did not know whether they had been spotted later. The force included the battleship *Malaya* and *Ark Royal*. On the 13th, mastheads indentified as belonging to warships were sighted and U-81 moved into position.

Back a day now with Force H: After flying off aircraft for Malta, and, with the operation completed, the ships set course to the westward at 1130 on the 12th. The disposition of the force was *Malaya*, *Ark Royal*, and the small fleet carrier *Argus* in single line ahead, screened by the modern cruiser *Hermione* and destroyers. One Swordfish was maintained on anti-U-boat patrol until dusk but nothing was sighted. Six Swordfish were flown off at 0645 to carry out a dawn search, to a depth of 70-miles. Nothing was sighted, however, and the search was landed on at 0850. Outer and inner anti-U-boat patrols were flown and maintained throughout the day.

Various exercises were carried out by the fleet. The wind being almost ahead, no appreciable ground was lost by flying operations and *Ark Royal* remained within the screen. At 1415 *Hermione* parted company to take up a position to starboard and act as a target for a throw-off shoot by *Malaya*. Destroyers adjusted positions accordingly.

Destroyers on the screen reported asdic contacts at 0955, 1157 and 1518. In each case Force H made an emergency turn of ninety degrees until clear of the contact or until it had been reported as 'non-sub'.

The contact obtained at 0955 was classified as a U-boat. A counter attack was made with a pattern of five depth charges set to 50-feet, but was not considered by the destroyer making it to have been accurate. Contact could not be regained.

Malaya's throw-off shoot was completed at 1515 and fourteen minutes later Force H resumed course after the emergency turn to evade the asdic contact reported at 1518. *Hermione* proceeded ahead to Gibraltar. *Ark Royal* had aircraft to fly off and land on and was given permission to manoeuvre as necessary to do this but to keep well within the screen.

At 1529 *Ark Royal* altered course into the wind; and when six Swordfish and two Fulmars had been flown off and five Swordfish had been flown on, the carrier was four cables to starboard of the line. Before flying on the remaining aircraft *Ark Royal* turned to port to regain her position between *Malaya* and *Argus*.

At 1538, when nearly in station *Ark Royal* again altered course into the wind. Force H had been ordered to carry out a zig-zag and the first turn was made at 1540, The starboard wing destroyer had, however, anticipated this and turned with *Ark Royal* at 1538 in order to give her cover. While the ships were altering course, the starboard wing destroyer detected hydrophone effect. As this coincided with the approximate bearing of the next destroyer on the screen and faded out, it was disregarded and not reported. The operator on watch subsequently stated that the hydrophone effect on this occasion was louder than any he had heard previously.

At 1541, after landing on one aircraft and in a position four cables from *Malaya*, *Ark Royal* was hit by a torpedo on her starboard side immediately below the island. No track of the torpedo was seen, either by anyone in the carrier or by any of the aircraft, which were circling overhead.

Ark Royal was just thirty miles short of her destination, Gibraltar, when she was struck. Those crew members on duty for the first dog-watch were taking tea and they, together with the rest of the crew, were shaken when the carrier was hit amidships. The torpedo hit the starboard boiler room. Immediately all hands rushed to their action stations as the great ship heeled over to starboard. No broadcast orders were given as the power had temporarily failed.

The explosion occurred under the bottom on the starboard side abreast the island structure causing a hole approximately 130-feet by 30-feet which was reported to have blown in the bottom plating. The air spaces, oil tanks and watertight compartments on the starboard side, together with machinery spaces and other main compartments in the vicinity of the explosion flooded rapidly. The carrier immediately heeled 10-degrees to starboard. Flooding of the main switchboard room and telephone exchange caused the failure of all lighting, electrical power and telephones. No major damage occurred to main or auxiliary machinery. The telegraphs from the bridge to the machinery control room were jammed, and the heel had increased to 17-degrees before the engines could be stopped. Counterflooding was carried out and reduced the heel to 14-degrees.

A call had gone out to Gibraltar for tugs, and the destroyer *Legion* was skilfully brought alongside half-an-hour after the explosion and the majority of the ship's company were disembarked. One seaman had been killed but all the remainder of the crew were saved, Electric power, feed water and pumps were supplied to the carrier by an escorting destroyer and the carrier was taken in tow at two knots. Steam was raised in the port boiler and lighting was restored. The starboard engine room flooded slowly, and the heel increased again to 17-degrees. Flooding of the boiler uptakes caused a major fire in the port boiler air casing, which led to the evacuation of the boiler room and to total loss of power.

Initially, when one of a four torpedo spread had struck the carrier, after a run of 7-minutes 43-seconds, the rest of the warships were more concerned with attending to the carrier and the crew in U-81 thought they had got away with it. Then came the asdic 'ping' as the destroyers found the U-boat, at 460-feet. More than 180 depth charges rained down in the next three hours, but the U-boat escaped to join the 29th Flotilla.

Back in *Ark Royal* orders were given to abandon ship when the heel had increased to 27-degrees. Twelve hours after being hit, all personnel had been withdrawn, and the heel had increased to 35-degrees. The carrier capsized and sank two hours later.

The sinking of the carrier whose name had survived from the British flagship of the Spanish *Armada* campaign had at last taken place. This time the Germans really had sunk the famous carrier.

But was it all so calculated as it sounds? *Oberleutnant* Johann O Kreig was the 2WO and signals officer aboard U-81 at the time and tells his version of the story from the time the U-boat left its French base:

In November 1941, we sailed from Brest, initially on a westerly heading. Having reached open waters and carried out our first exercises, deep-diving test, practice-alarms and damage-control, our commander, Kapitänleutnant Friedrich Guggenberger, revealed both destination and objectives to the boat's crew.

Franz-Georg Reschke, in U-205, and our boat had been ordered to the Mediterranean with the object of attacking enemy naval forces, whose activities had been seriously curtailing the shipments of supplies for the German Afrika Korps.

The other U-boat was set to pass Gibraltar about two days ahead of us, whilst it was our intention to follow during the night of 11/12 November.

Our crew had been hoping we might go to the Caribbean, where negligible defences offered a high rate of success amongst the large tankers and shipping in general. Our present orders, therefore, did not generate a great deal of enthusiasm.

But there was no time for losing oneself in idle thought. Hard training was the order of the day during our southward journey, for both boat and crew had to be in top condition for the tasks ahead.

We approached the Straits from the south, hugging the Moroccan coast in the hope of attracting as little attention as possible. Crossing the Straits, we aimed directly at Gibraltar, pretending to make port there.

I had been watch-officer at dusk and remained at my post throughout. There were too many vessels, lights and beacons to be kept under observations, and changing the watch might have been ill-advised.

Having closed with the Rock as much as we dare, we swung away on an easterly tack. Our extremely powerful binoculars enabled us to make out the shore-batteries; indeed, we could even detect the striking of matches now and again, when the guard there was, presumably, having a smoke.

Units of the Royal Navy as well as other vessels seemed to be very reluctant venturing close in-shore. This did serve us well, for we could proceed on the surface and arrived in the Mediterranean just before dawn without having been spotted. Sometimes one's luck does hold!

Having successfully penetrated the Straits and reached the Mediterranean, we disappeared from the surface, intent on concealing our presence - and we were not averse to a brief period of rest either. On Thursday, the 13th, we blew the tanks and made for the surface. A radio-signal, received shortly thereafter, informed us that:

A task-force, comprising the battleship Malaya, *the aircraft-carriers* Ark Royal *and*

Furious, plus one cruiser and several destroyers, have been attacking German and Italian shipping off Sicily and are now returning to Gibraltar at a speed of about 18-knots. ETA about 1600 CET.

Our position appeared to be a little too far north of the enemy's estimated mean-course. In order to come south and get somewhat closer to Gibraltar, we steamed at fullest speed in the hope of reaching the best possible point for interception.

At about 1430, the sighting of an aircraft in the south-east forced us to go below. Petty Officer Telegraphist Lorenz, working the sound-receiver, picked up propeller noises both in the same direction and further to the east; the former somewhat faint and dullish, the latter more distinct.

Our commander concluded that the slowly increasing volume of those dullish sounds would be produced by the big units of the battle-fleet, and - as the bearing held steady - he was in a good position for an attack.

About an hour later, an all-round-sweep by periscope revealed several mast-heads in the south-south-east; whereas a cruiser and two destroyers were coming in from the east – dead on collision-course!

What should we do? Attack the cruiser, or go for the big-game? The commander decided: let's take on the main-force!

Dead silence within! The screws of the two destroyers and the somewhat lower sounds of the cruiser are quite audible during their approach; even without any assistance from the sound-receiver. The commander's use of the periscope – however sparing - compels us to keep our fingers crossed, lest we should be spotted.

Then the orders ring out loud and clear: 'Fan-shot, tubes one to four! Enemy on starboard bow, position 70, speed 18, spread 200, distance 4,000!'

The commander appears to be incredibly calm. 'Tubes one to four standing by,' comes the report.

Once more the periscope goes up.

'Fan-shot ready!'

'Fan is ready!'

'Fan-FIRE!'

One by one, four deadly 'fish' clear the tubes, and the loss of their combined weight necessitates appropriate counter-measures. But, in spite of speedy adjustment of the hydroplanes and the order 'all hands forward', this difficult manoeuvre does not fully succeed!

First the conning-tower breaks surface, but then – the counter-measures taking effect – we sink away fast; almost like a crash dive.

We are convinced the look-outs of both cruiser and the destroyers must have spotted our conning-tower on the surface, a few hundred yards is no distance at all, and any moment now we must expect a depth-charge attack by those destroyers.

Calmly the commander orders: 'Go down to 160-metres, fast!' Endless seconds pass *before reaching the almost certain safety of the depth ordered, but – apart from any sounds within the boat – there is silence beyond!*

Sparky's report of two detonations to the south is received with some incredulity. But then, quite suddenly – and more than ten minutes after our attack and the subsequent showing of our conning-tower detonations can indeed be heard in that direction.

The lull is over, the heat is on; a storm is let loose upstairs! The noise of the innumerable detonations all round almost completely obliterates the propeller sounds of the main force. Slowly, however, the picture clears somewhat. It seems, the fleet is making for Gibraltar as before, whereas the destroyers remain in the area. The latter appear to be searching for us, and they continue their search over several hours without making any contact.

The commander is disappointed, as is everybody else. Depressed we set to work; reloading the tubes without making any excessive noise, waiting for the next detonations, pricking-up our ears for any sounds made by the destroyers. It is an endless game of cat and mouse.

At last, many hours later, the destroyers call off the search. Silence reigns again up top. We make for the African coast, sink to the bottom – and play 'dead'.

Surfacing at noon the following day, we are greeted by a calm and peaceful sea; no enemy in sight.

Radio-signals arrive, and Sparky hands me a top-secret message, which may only be decoded by the Signal-Officer, me.

The slowly emerging text simply takes my breath away for it reads: 'Reuters report sinking of Ark Royal. *Reschke and Guggenberger report observations.'*

Taking the message, I race to the control-room, climb the ladder like a monkey, through the conning-tower to the bridge, and hand the signal to the commander. He reads it, shakes his head in disbelief and merely remarks: 'Man; this is equivalent to giving birth whilst still a virgin! My attack was aimed at the Malaya!!!

Having considered all the circumstances, we concluded that the sinking of Ark Royal *must be attributed to one of our torpedoes. Although she was not the target, the hit may be due to possible miscalculation of either speed or distance. Our boat was the only one operating in this area at that time; Reschke in U-205 can be ruled out, for he would have been some 300 miles to the east of our position!*

News of the sinking had travelled fast. As usual Reuters were quickly off the mark, which is how the *Kriegsmarine* chiefs heard of it. The New York evening papers headlined: *ARK ROYAL* SUNK and the Saturday British dailies carried headlines like the *Daily Express ARK ROYAL* WENT DOWN -LIKE A GENTLEMAN' and although many of the wartime papers were of only four pages many column inches were devoted to the life of the world's most famous carrier.

The sinking of the carrier started a grim period for the Mediterranean Fleet. Eleven days later U-331 sank the *Barham* and her two sisters battleships *Queen Elizabeth* and *Valiant* were badly damaged by charges from human torpedoes in Alexandria harbour on 18 December. On the same day the cruiser *Neptune* and the destroyer *Kandahar* were sunk in a minefield off Tripoli.

When the Americans entered the war early in December, Hans Speidel was shortly to join U-81. He had entered the *Kriegsmarine* in 1936 but two years later he transferred to the Naval Air Arm and later the *Luftwaffe*. He served in the western and eastern theatres of war, attacking targets in France, England and Russia. After the necessary re-training he was appointed 1WO aboard U-81 and took part in five Mediterranean operational patrols.

The next sinkings for U-81 did not occur until mid-April when the U-boat was in the eastern Mediterranean. A 1,150-ton French steam trawler and the 6,000-ton British tanker *Caspia* were torpedoed and sunk ten miles south of Beirut on the 16th and the blaze from the tanker could be seen from U-331 many miles away. Later the same day three sailing vessels were set ablaze. Another was fired the next day, two on the 22nd and another four days later. Each victim was in the 80-100-ton category. Of these sinkings, the new 1WO Hans Speidel remembers:

> We sank some Arabian dhows, plying from Cyprus, by gunfire. One of those, however, had initially been boarded by a small prize-crew and on their return they carried their 'prize' of two sacks of wonderful fine bread. After the dhow's crew had taken to their dinghy, we sank her by repeatedly ramming her very gently with our own bow; there was no need to use any demolition charges.
>
> The previously attacked tanker, burning fiercely and illuminating the area, made it very easy for us to spot those dhows' sails at night, for they stood out as white dots against the horizon.
>
> A further incident during this patrol occurred one afternoon. We were in position close to the coast, surfaced at 1600 and attacked both oil-tanks and pier of the large refinery near Haifa by gunfire. I believe any forces guarding those installations had been taken completely by surprise, for there was no defensive or retaliatory fire at all.
>
> This incident had been mentioned, two days later, during the daily broadcast of the 'Forces Report' on the radio.
>
> On the next patrol we were standing off the African coast in the area off Tobruk. Field Marshal *Rommel* commenced an extensive offensive on 20 May, 1942. We learnt by radio signal that one of our aircraft had been shot down and that the crew had taken refuge in their inflatable dinghy.
>
> Steaming with both engines full ahead, we were on our way, intent on finding the dinghy and rescuing the crew. Shortly thereafter, however, we received a further

HMS Courageous, *turning into wind, as Lieutenant Charles Lamb brings his Swordfish into be the last ever aircraft to land on the carrier.*

HMS Courageous *sinking: she was hit by two torpedoes 14 minutes after the Swordfish landed and sank in 17 minutes. Photographs taken from HMS* Impulsive.

HMS Kelly *commanded by Lord Louis Mountbatten rescued survivors from* Courageous.

Otto Schuhart (left), who in U-29 sank the first warship in the war, speaks with Fritz-Julis Lemp who in U-30 sank Athenia *on the first day of the war. The photograph was taken at a lock in Wilhelmshaven in the spring of 1940.*

Kensington Court *sinking after an attack from U-32. The crew in the lifeboats were rescued by Sunderland flying boats.*

S3 Collegian *damaged in a torpedo and gunfire attack by U-32.*

Kapitänleutnant *Hans Jenisch and U-32. The photograph of the commander was taken just before his last patrol while U-32 was photographed during the Spanish Civil War.*

Empress of Britain *anchored at Hong-Kong while on a world cruise.*

Empress of Britain *in wartime livery.*

Empress of Britain *on fire following the aircraft attack.*

Fritz-Julius Lemp, commander of U-30, takes a close look at the Fanad Head *before sinking her.*

HMS Ark Royal – *the world's most famous aircraft-carrier.*

Kapitänleutnant
*Fredrich Guggenberger
and U-81.*

Snapshots taken just after U–81 torpedoed Ark Royal.

Snapshots taken just after U-81 torpedoed Ark Royal.

HMS Barham *photographed pre-war off Alexandria.*

HMS Valiant *photographed pre-war near Malta.*

HMS Griffin

HMS Jervis

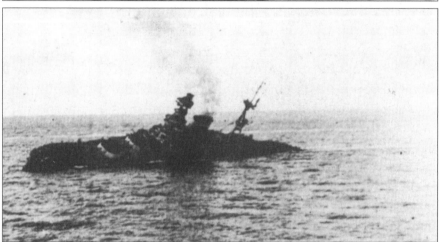

Sequence of events as Barham *is sighted and torpedoed.*

Barham *turns over and explodes, taking 868 crew members with her.*

Kapitänleutnant
*Freiherr Hans-Dietrich
von Tiesenhausen, with
U-331 at Salamis in
1942.*

The Lockheed Hudson of No 500 Squadron with which U-331 (below) was attacked.

wireless message, stating that U-652, under the command of Kapitänleutnant Georg-Werner Fraatz, had been heavily bombed and was unable to manoeuvre any further.

Following this message, we changed course and met U-652 some two hours later. Their rudder was jammed, their engines were out of action and the boat was quite unable to dive. We took it in tow with the intention of making for Piraeus in Greece.

Initially we made fair progress, but it very soon transpired that the distance to be traversed thus would defeat our salvage attempt – in particular when taking into account the ever present danger of attacks from the air. In order to meet such contingencies, we had planned to cut the tow immediately, allowing U-81 to dive to safety. Therefore, conditions permitting, U-652 would give the 'all-clear' by exploding three hand-grenades in the sea, whereupon U-81 would surface again, resuming the tow. Indeed, that is precisely what happened next, and we acted as planned. However, having resumed towing, we soon found U-652 could not be kept afloat by reason of uncontrollable flooding of the boat. In consequence, the whole crew was taken off to join our own and Kapitänleutnant Fraatz sank his boat by firing a torpedo from our stern tube.

One can imagine the cramped conditions this produced, squeezing two complete crews, a total of ninety-six men, into the already confined space of one boat! This fact alone, quite naturally, made very heavy demands upon everybody. The engineer officer, in particular, bore the heaviest burden, for all his previous calculations – weight, its distribution, trim etc. – had to be taken into consideration, in the event of a crash dive, for example, could no longer be applied and had to be re-calculated and/or adjusted to meet the now prevailing conditions/circumstances.

About an hour after the disposal of U-652, whilst the navigator had the watch on the bridge, the call came down 'Commander on the bridge, attack by enemy submarine'!

The commander, followed by myself, made for the bridge with extreme haste, and on arrival there we observed a fan-shot of four torpedoes racing towards our boat. Thank heavens for the bubble-trails of those torpedoes, for they enabled us to be on top of the situation by taking note of their position during every moment of the attack. Unfortunately, the navigator had ordered a turn to port, instead of pointing the bow into the fan by a starboard turn. This wrong manoeuvre exposed the boat to an increased danger of being hit. The crew below had no inkling of the events unfolding around them, but you may be assured that everyone on the bridge drew a deep breath, when the first two torpedoes passed both bow and stern at a distance of about three metres.

We did reach Greece in one piece and made fast in Piraeus, the reception party assembled could not believe their eyes when they noticed two crews emerging from one boat!

One originally scheduled task during our next patrol was to land a sabotage party drawn from the Brandenburg regiment, on the coast of Palestine; their objective being the demolition of the rail link to Haifa. However, this idea had never been put into effect, for the whole thing had been cancelled at the last minute prior to our departure and we never learned the reason for said cancellation.

During this patrol we reached Haifa one night and, penetrating to within sight of the oil terminals, sowed the area with mines.

While on those patrols in the Mediterranean a number of quite remarkable incidents occurred.

On one occasion, for example, we encountered a British destroyer in the Nile delta, whilst having a mere 40-metres of water under our keel. We made our escape bid by steaming 'full ahead' on the surface. Luck was with us, for at the moment the engine room reported slipping of the starboard clutch, the destroyer, fully visible to us, suddenly turned at a distance of a mere two miles and sped off.

The commander, Friedrich Guggenberger, having been blessed with excellent power of vision, could beat everyone of us at spotting the tips of any masts on the horizon. He had often acknowledged the advantages gained for the boat by my own experience and knowledge derived from my activities with the Luftwaffe, in particular with regard to the recognition of aircraft types.

One evening an oil-encrusted seagull had settled atop our diesel's exhaust. We took him below, cleaned him and quartered him in the forward torpedo compartment. His favoured food was the rind of cheese. He also made use of soapy water prepared for washing our socks.

One night, patrolling off Tobruk under a full moon, we were suddenly attacked by a Sunderland flying-boat. We dived, but received a number of depth charges. Our boat behaved in a manner as if it had been clamped down and held fast at both ends, bow and stern, whereas strong movements in a vertical plane, up and down, could be felt in the control room at the boat's centre.

We had named our seagull 'Jacob', and during the general pell-mell of this attack, which shattered gauges, I grabbed the microphone and in as loud and distinct a voice as possible asked: 'All stations! Question: How is Jacob?' It was amazing to note how the general tension suddenly ebbed away, everybody broke into a broad grin. We had been lucky; the damage was slight and we had weathered this storm quite well.

Returning to La Spezia, we announced our successes by flying the relevant pennons. In order to indicate the sinking of the dhow by ramming, which we had done in an earlier patrol, we had marked our bow by a large dash. Everybody, naturally, enquired as to the meaning of this sign.

Hans Speidel left the boat to take his commander's course and later commissioned U-643. Later the 2WO also left for the same course, having served a very full apprenticeship aboard the famous boat.

Operation *Torch*, the invasion of North Africa, commenced on 8 November, and almost exactly a year after the sinking of *Ark Royal*, U-81 was back in the same area. In the early hours of 10 November it attacked an escort vessel and a steamer. A red flash was seen from the escort and the British ship *Garlinge* was sunk. The London registered *Garlinge*, of 2,012-tons, was a collier and was sailing in convoy when sunk. The next success for U-81 came in mid-afternoon of the 13th when two ships were attacked and the British transport *Maron* of 6,487-tons was sunk in a convoy between Algiers and Gibraltar – it was a year to the day that *Ark Royal* had been torpedoed. However, other U-boats had not been as fortunate as U-81, four had been lost between 12 and 17 November in the area; they were U-660, U-605, U-595 and U-331.

This patrol, against the invasion fleet, was the last in U-81 for its commander Friedrich Guggenberger – he was already the holder of the Knight's Cross and was soon to be presented with the Oak Leaves.

The new commander of U-81 was 'Hanno' Krieg, who was delighted to take over command in the boat he knew and loved so well. He travelled down to Pola from Gotenhaven where he had been commander of the training boat U-142 and on Christmas Eve took charge of the boat he had started with as a 2WO on its first cruise.

On 5 February, not far from Tobruk, a mid-morning attack on a tanker was unsuccessful. Two explosions were heard but the torpedoes were faulty. Four days later a small boat was sunk by gunfire and the next evening the 6,671-ton Dutch ship *Saroena* was torpedoed. The next day four small boats, in convoy, were sunk by gunfire 40-miles west of Tripoli. A month later, off Palestine, two more sailing vessels were sunk by gunfire on 20 March and a small Egyptian boat was torpedoed nine days later.

By now the Allies were mopping up the Axis forces in North Africa and U-boats were laying mines off Casablanca and in May they extended their minelaying to the coast of Greece, Sicily and Sardinia. On 12 May, all organised Axis resistance in Tunisia ended.

At sea again U-S1 had four successes to report on 26 June. First, the 3,742-ton Greek steamer *Michalios* was torpedoed and sunk one mile west of Latakia and then three more sailing boats were sunk by gunfire.

On 10 July the Allies invaded Sicily, their first foothold in Europe. This meant plenty of work for the remaining U-boats. Since the Operation *Torch* campaign, U-224, U-443 and U-83 had been sunk in the Mediterranean and others attempting to enter had been sunk before they could arrive. Within days of the Sicilian invasion the port of Syracuse had been seized and ships there were the next target for U-81.

'Hanno' Krieg, who had guided U-81 through the Straits and had decoded the '*Ark Royal* sunk' signal and was now commander of the U-boat tells the story of this patrol:

> At the beginning of the Allied invasion of Sicily, U-81 happened to be in the docks at Salamis in Greece for some minor repairs.
>
> Although some 80-percent of the crew were suffering from diarrhoea with vomiting, accompanied by the inevitable high temperature, I nevertheless pressed for immediate departure. Such malady, caused by the bite of certain mosquitoes in the area, usually lasted for some five to ten days. In spite of the Medical Officer's disapproval, we set sail in order to catch and attack the invasion fleet in good time.
>
> My plan called for a slow advance to the target area around Sicily – hoping the crew would recover during this time – and to stay below as much as possible.
>
> We set a westerly course, between Crete and the mainland, but life on board became almost intolerable on account of the extremely adverse sanitary conditions. There was only one WC available for the crew of fifty-four, more than forty of which were suffering as previously indicated. However, and as I had hoped for, a few days later some half of the invalids had recovered and it was my opinion we could take the risk of doing battle.
>
> Although we had, of course, not lost the way, our exact position was by no means certain. Radio bearings in this area could not be relied on and the usual astro-navigation had been severely curtailed. We had been unable to 'shoot the stars' since leaving Crete in our wake, and dead-reckoning was the only aid available.
>
> A look through the periscope at dawn of 21 July revealed very much the same weather picture as before; it was just plain dull with a touch of fog. By about 1000, however, matters had improved somewhat, and looking west, I could make out a number of barrage balloons in the sky.
>
> As our estimated position was still some thirty miles off the target area, I assumed those balloons were being flown by merchant vessels as a defence against low flying aircraft. If this were correct, there had to be a convoy in that direction. Alas, we could detect no sounds to confirm my assumption.
>
> At 1015 I brought the periscope up once again – and I could not believe my eyes, for to the west I spotted the mountains of Sicily! Taking some bearings, we found our position to be just off the port of Syracuse. And the barrage balloons had no connection with any convoy at all; they were, in fact, part of the harbour defences.
>
> Having studied the charts minutely, I decided on going as close to the harbour as possible at periscope depth, though being left with a mere 2-3-metres of water between seabed and keel!
>
> We approached stealthily. Looking at the moorings, I noticed two large passenger liners, sporting two funnels each, now doing service as troopships. At the port's entrance a 'guard-

dog' was slowly steaming to and fro,

About three miles to the east of the harbour mouth a flag-bearing buoy was aimed at by a number of entering landing craft. 'Well', I thought, 'if that is the way to the target, why not take the same path?'

Rounding the buoy and entering the channel was taking a grave risk. Any passing large vessel would leave no room for evasive action; our keel was barely clearing the bottom and any manoeuvre to either side might possibly lead us straight into a minefield. Nevertheless, I pressed on and took the boat nearer to the basin.

By noon the 'guard-dog' ceased patrolling the entrance. At the same time we were being overtaken by a landing craft, at a distance of about 80-metres, and both craft entered the basin between two further large buoys.

Though using the echo-sounder might betray our presence, I opted for taking that risk just the same. The reading obtained: A hairy two metres of clearance below! Now or never! 'Stand-by all tubes! Single shot!' I ordered. The almost unbearable tension of the crew evaporated.

Four times I bellowed: 'FIRE!'

Then: 'Hard a-starboard, reverse course!'

Having turned sufficiently, I fired our last torpedo from the stern tube right into the centre of the basin's entrance, hoping it would meet a target within.

Just before completion of our turn, the first shot struck home, precisely in line with one of the large troopships. Detonations of numbers 2, 3 and 4 followed in quick succession.

I did not see the explosion-clouds with regard to the troop transporters, but one detonation appeared to be short of the target – an anti-torpedo net, perhaps?

As to the last 'fish'... I did not observe a detonation effect in the centre of the basin, but I had to pay the closest attention to our course on the way out and the passing of the entrance buoy. The speed was 'dead slow', lest any telltale swirl betray our passage and the periscope had to be handled with the utmost delicacy for the very same reason. Though a number of small boats excitedly scurried back and forth within the basin, it did not seem likely that even the mere idea of a U-boat, having had the brazen audacity of penetrating in shallow waters right up to the port's door had ever occurred to anyone there. Be that as it may; we had not been discovered, we reached the outer marker without problems and made for the protection of deeper waters.

These events, by the way, and the ensuing stress and strain during the last hours, certainly proved their therapeutic value with regard to the erstwhile invalids amongst the crew. Almost everybody had recovered - and the WC's indicator at last proclaimed: VACANT!

The 12,000-ton ship that had been attacked had in fact been saved by a torpedo net but the 7,472-ton British steamer *Empire Moon* was damaged.

Early the next month U-81 was again on the other side of the

Mediterranean, and in mid-morning of 6 August a target was attacked off Tobruk. Four detonations were heard but no results were seen.

Bad news for the Germans came on 8 September when Italy surrendered and on 13 October they declared war on their former ally. Although Marshal Tito's Yugoslav partisans had begun disarming Italian occupying troops, a German offensive against them meant that U-81 was reasonably safe at Pola although the town's anti-aircraft guns were no longer manned.

On 18 November U-81 was active in the area off the foot of Italy and the British steamer *Empire Dunstan* was torpedoed and sunk. This third *Empire* boat to be attacked was the last recorded success of 'Hanno' Krieg who later in the year was awarded the Knight's Cross.

The Allied Strategic Air Force Command was bombing all enemy ports along the coast and on 9 January Pola was among the targets. The unprotected port was an easy target for a USAAF raid. U-81 was put out of action and the nearby ex-Italian U-boat *Nautilo* was also hit. Fortunately for the *Kriegsmarine* the commander was not aboard at the time of the attack.

This inglorious end to the successful U-boat was not immediately known to the Allies and it was not until an Enigma decrypt of the German naval key Porpoise was available that they could claim the disablement of the U-boat that with a single torpedo had sunk the most famous aircraft carrier of all time.

Neither of the two commanders of U-81 was in the list of the Top Thirty of U-boat sinkings, but their records, together with the survival of the boat in an area where many were lost at sea, surely qualify them to be included in the list of U-boat aces.

CHAPTER FOUR

THE BOLD BARON

The first Type VIIC boat built at the privately owned *Nordsee Werke* at Emden was U-331, and its crew were to be very grateful to the yard for the high standard of workmanship.

There was only one commander of U-331 through its two years of life; he was *Freiherr*, (the English equivalent is Baron) Hans-Dietrich von Tiesenhausen. Born in Riga early in 1913 he moved with his parents to Brandenburg after the Kaiser's war. In 1934 von Tiesenhausen entered the *Kriegsmarine* and did a six month training course at Stralsund, after which he joined as a cadet the sailing training ship *Gorch Fock*. This was followed by a world cruise in the cruiser *Karlsruhe*, after which he proceeded to the Naval College at Flensburg as a midshipman. Following, came two more periods of sea-time in the cruisers *Nürnberg*, interspersed with return visits to the Flensburg College until he was commissioned on 1 April 1939. He was then appointed to be the Adjutant of the 5th Naval Ordnance Department, which post he filled at the outbreak of war.

Early in 1940 he volunteered for U-boats and was appointed to the U-boat training school at Neustadt. He served for a short time in U-93, then commanded by *Kapitänleutnant* Klaus Korth, before proceeding on his first operational patrol as 1WO to *Kapitänleutnant* Otto Kretschmer in U-99. He left U-99 towards the end of 1940, and after the usual training for the post of commanding officer, was given command of U-331.

After sailing from Kiel in July 1941, U-331 proceeded through the 'Rosengarten', a bank between Iceland and the Faeroes about 30 miles in radius, into the Atlantic. Its operational area was off Cape St Vincent, Spain. Here it joined the patrol line of boats and remained in position for some weeks, without, however, making frequent sightings. On only one occasion did it make an attack, firing a salvo of four torpedoes, all of which missed. On one occasion it met another U-boat which came alongside to exchange mail, and, in doing so, damaged U-33FS No 1 diving tank.

In mid-August 1941, U-331 made for Lorient where it was attached to the 2nd U-Boat Flotilla.

The U-boat began its second patrol at the end of September 1941. Leaving Lorient it proceeded across the Bay of Biscay partly submerged and partly surfaced with orders to enter the Mediterranean. The passage of the Straits of Gibraltar was made alone one night in early October and began late in the afternoon, submerged. It remained down until early the following morning, when it surfaced, only to submerge again as daylight broke and remained so until well clear of the Straits. It was not attacked at any time during the passage.

Proceeding straight to its area of operations in the Eastern Mediterranean, U-331 had travelled as far as to between Sollum and Alexandria when it was attacked by what it thought were Tank Landing Craft, and two of the crew were wounded, one fatally. He was buried at sea four hours later.

Immediately after this incident U-331 set course for its base, Salamis, where it was to be attached to the U-Boat Flotilla, commanded by *Kapitänleutnant* Fritz Frankenheim. It arrived at the end of October 1941.

The U-boat sailed from Salamis on its third patrol at 1000 on 12 November 1941. Before sailing the crew were surprised to see a party of seven soldiers come on board. This was a commando party which Tiesenhausen had been ordered to land at a given point on the North African coast.

At the beginning of August 1941, these seven men were sent to the Headquarters of the Lohrregiment Brandenburg at Berlin, and practised for a week laying demolition charges beneath a railway line. They drew tropical kit. On 28 August they left Berlin by air for Athens where they reported to *Hauptmann* Schiffheuer, an officer attached to Abwehr II at Athens. They attempted to leave Athens by air but their Do 24 crashed into the quay and the attempt was abandoned. They were instructed to embark on U-331 on 12 November.

The U-boat set a southerly course and four nights later was lying in a bay about fifteen miles westward from El Alamein, at a point where the railway line from Alexandria runs within a few miles of the sea. The seven soldiers were to blow up a length of line. A heavy sea made it impossible to land them that night and U-331 had to lie off the coast for 24-hours. It then approached to within one mile of land at a point between Ras Gibeica and Ras el Schagig, and put the demolition party into a rubber dinghy. Included in the party was Wolfgang Ebertz, a wireless operator from U-331.

The dinghy reached the shore safely and six of the party went off to lay the charges, leaving one soldier and the rating to guard the dinghy. After some hours these two were surprised by sentries, but they overpowered them. The demolition party completed their work and returned to the beach where they remained undetected until the following night. They saw U-331's green light, and having loaded up the dinghy, pushed off, only to capsize in the surf. The gear was thrown into the water, and, though they managed to save the Very pistols, the cartridges were wet and they could not make their presence known to von Tiesenhausen. The party therefore returned to the shore where they were all captured a few hours later. Ebertz was found to be wearing a British Army shirt marked with von Tiesenhausen's name. This then was the end of a mission that had been named 'Operation *Hai*'.

Meanwhile, out at sea U-331 waited all night for the party to make themselves known again the following night but at daybreak abandoned hope and proceeded towards Sollum.

Between 18 and 25 November, U-331 carried out the second half of its mission, patrolling off the North African coast in the neighbourhood of Sollum and Mersa Matruh. The U-boat remained submerged during the day and surfaced during the night. At the time Tobruk was being held by the Allies although surrounded by enemy forces and the U-boat was ordered to prevent any supplies reaching the garrison by sea. The supplies had been arriving from Alexandria in small, heavily protected convoys but all U-331 saw every time it gingerly surfaced during the day was aircraft, which forced it down again.

At 0800 on 25 November the faint sound of propellers in a northerly direction was picked up by the operator on the hydrophone aboard the U-boat. The commander ordered the boat to periscope depth and cautiously swept round the horizon, making sure first of all that there were no aircraft around that could pick up the U-boat on radar or see the feather wake caused by the periscope. The surface of the sea was empty, the commander could see nothing. He surfaced, saw an aircraft nearby and crash dived right away. There were no bombs but in that short moment he had also searched the horizon in the direction where the propellers had last been heard. Nothing could be seen. The U-boat was ordered down again to 50 -metres, which was considered to be the best depth for HE listening, so as to check up on the sounds. The U-boat carried on the hunt under water and its commander carries on with the story:

> *After the first unsuccessful surfacing, the boat stayed submerged until shortly after noon. Then there were two aircraft; the first one at a safe distance but later a second approached too close for the U-boat to stay on the surface.*
>
> *The wide band of faint propeller noises was now in a north-easterly direction. We didn't stay down too long and after surfacing again we proceeded in the direction of the last bearing with high speed, but still nothing could be seen for some time. Suddenly a yellowish thickening over the horizon was made out and some needlelike masts could be distinguished. This group of ships moved in a southerly direction and then seemed to disappear to the east altogether, only to grow again after turning west. It became quite clear that this was a fleet of warships. We approached each other on a reciprocal course and from now on things happened in a rather quick succession; by some inexplicably intuitive order the boat turned around full circle and dived. This delay later turned out to be crucial.*
>
> *There were three battleships steaming west in a line ahead formation with a protective screen of eight destroyers. The three were Queen Elizabeth class ships but it was not possible to establish names.*

In the U-boat the crew had closed up to full action stations. The time was just after 1600. The late afternoon sun was shining in a south-westerly direction behind the U-boat, perfect weather for an attack.

Tension inside the U-boat rose tangibly in the next few moments as unknowingly the British formation approached fast on a collision course. In his periscope the U-boat commander could now see three battleships steaming in line astern, flanked by four destroyers on each side. Two destroyers, *Jervis* and *Griffin*, leading the formation, moved forward.

A lieutenant aboard *Jervis* said that the destroyer was steering a mean course of 290 degrees at 1615. Two minutes later the anti-submarine cabinet reported an echo bearing 220-degrees, range 900-yards. Because the extensive target was between 40 and 60-degrees he considered it to be 'non-sub' and told the A/S cabinet to disregard and carry on the sweep by which time the range was 400-500-yards on the port beam. It was thought that the echo must have been some form of water layer or difference in temperature of water found on warm days.

The U-boat slipped through between *Jervis* and *Griffin* at periscope depth and was now on the port side of the first battleship. Unsuspectingly

Queen Elizabeth had led her two sister-ships directly toward the submerged U-boat and von Tiesenhausen could hardly have found himself in a better position to attack. He saw flags at the yard-arm of the battleships, which obviously heralded a change in formation. The U-boat found itself on the port side of the battleships. The first was already too close as it took up more space than the periscope's field of vision could accommodate. Then the second battleship in line, *Barham*, appeared. A quick glance showed the prospective target growing bigger and bigger in the cross-wires.

The torpedo men were ready but the angle of over 90-degrees was still too great. The forward torpedo room reported '*Hartlage*', through the speaking tube but the button could not be pressed as the U-boat was lying almost broadside on to the target which was so close that the periscope could only accommodate part of the battleship.

Strong action had to be taken to overcome the 90-degrees: one engine stopped, the other full speed ahead and the rudder hard to port was a delicate situation in itself. In addition four torpedoes now left their tubes in proper sequence. The distance to the target was 375-metres. Unknown to von Tiesenhausen all the battleships had turned to port, that is, toward him. After the torpedoes had been fired U-331 came very close to the third battleship, *Valiant*. In fact, in a quick sweep with the periscope von Tiesenhausen had seen a huge mass of grey steel approaching and was sure that his boat would be rammed any moment. Especially so, as a report came from the engineering officer in the control room that the conning-tower had broken surface. In addition to these difficulties, the U-boat was probably forced out of the water by the movement of *Valiant* so close by. The commander was the only one to realize the dangerous situation. There had been no time to inform the crew of the happenings. He ordered the room in the conning-tower to be abandoned quickly; *Obersteuermann* Walther closed the watertight hatch. After having been visible on the surface for 45-seconds and disappearing only 30-yards off the starboard side of *Valiant*, too close even to be hit by pom-pom fire, U-331 submerged down deep into the dark safety of the sea. The expected ramming never happened. Up top the captain of *Valiant* recorded:

At 1625 the officer of the watch was taking the distance of Barham *when he observed a large explosion on the port side of the battleship abreast the mainmast. He realised immediately that* Barham *had been struck by a torpedo fired from somewhere on the port side and quite correctly ordered 'Hard-a-port'. I was not on the compass platform at the moment of the explosion, but on reaching the front of it ten seconds later, I observed a very large column of water and smoke alongside* Barham, *only the after end of the quarterdeck being then visible. I immediately ordered 'Full speed ahead together'; at the same time the officer of the watch informed me that the wheel was hard-a-port, and I observed that the ship was just beginning to swing to port under the influence of full port rudder.*

About fifteen seconds later a U-boat broke surface between five and ten degrees on the port bow at a distance of approximately 150-yards and moving from left to right. By then Valiant had swung about eight degrees to port... I ordered 'Amidships', and then 'hard-a-starboard' in an endeavour to ram the U-boat, but before the rudder was hard over it was obvious that it would not be possible to check the swing to port before it was across the bow. Actually the swing was just about checked when the U-boat passed down the starboard side, and submerged again when abreast Valiant's bridge at a distance of about fifty yards. As it appeared on the starboard side a pom-pom fired 19 rounds at it with the maximum depression, but all rounds appeared to pass over. The wheel was then again reversed so as to keep clear of Barham. The only portion of the U-boat which appeared was the periscope and about two to three feet of the conning-tower which was flat-topped. A certain amount of disturbed water before and abaft the conning-tower indicated the fore and after ends of the hull, and enabled an accurate estimate of its course to be made.

A petty officer also in *Valiant* recorded:

The battleships had just come into line abreast, as part of their zig-zag and this put Barham immediately abreast of us, about two cable lengths distant. I then saw a huge column of water rise abreast Barham's forward turrets; and I thought it was a bomb dropped without any air-raid warning. I changed my mind when I saw a couple more huge water spouts along her side and realised that they were torpedo hits. I immediately closed the port, but before I had pulled the dead light down Barham was completely on her port side with her funnel touching the water. I went quickly up on to the upper deck, and as I looked at Barham there was a terrific explosion and I thought that obviously a magazine had gone up. I actually saw a twin 4-inch AA gun hundreds of feet up in the air and then bits and pieces began falling all around us. Probably as the result of having fired a salvo of torpedoes the conning-tower of the U-boat shot up quite close to our bows and one of the forward pom-poms opened up on it but couldn't depress enough to obtain any hits. I don't know what action was taken to try and catch the U-boat, but fortunately no depth charges were dropped otherwise the casualty list would have been worse.

Meanwhile, down below, the U-boat began sinking like a brick, three detonations were heard, and shortly afterwards a fourth; these were incidental at this time to the U-boatmen, but at least they knew a target had been hit. The elation turned to tension at the speed of the rapid descent of the Emden-built boat, loose articles crashed about and the needle of the depth gauge registered increasing depths. At 70-metres there was a slow down and an evening out at 80-metres. However, since the boat was bow heavy and the screws were still turning, U-331 continued to go deeper. Going deeper gave the U-boat a better chance of escaping the explosions of depth charges, the crew were mystified why none had so far rained down on them.

The U-boat continued plummeting toward the bottom; it was indeed fortunate for the crew that they were in deep water, otherwise they would have been in deep trouble. The forward depth gauge showed 265-metres and the commander knew this was the deepest any U-boat in action had ever recorded and survived to make the claim. The U-boat was designed for a depth of 150-metres, but with a safety factor of 2.5, The commander continues:

> *Finally compressed air blew water out of the tanks and the involuntary descent was halted. The boat was brought up higher, but still was 150-metres below the surface.*
>
> *This experience gave the crew great confidence in the structure of the boat. No damage was found, although the temporary deformation of the hull at such tremendous pressure – 26-kilograms on every square centimetre – caused sparks at the propeller shafts.*

Slowly the boat rose as it crept away northward. As soon as he felt certain that he was clear von Tiesenhausen signalled his success and his intention of returning to Salamis. He arrived on 3 December.

His report of the attack was not over-optimistic and on the following day the German radio reported that a U-boat commanded by von Tiesenhausen had attacked a British battleship off Sollum, scoring a direct hit with one torpedo. After putting ashore at the Greek port the commander went to Berlin but found that the secret had been kept so well that the authorities there were as much in the dark as he was. On 16 December he broadcast a description of the attack but, denied the full enjoyment of his achievement, could only say that he had certainly hit the battleship.

Hans-Dietrich von Tiesenhausen was one of two U-boat commanders being interviewed about the war in the Mediterranean. He was the first to speak and was later given a copy of the recording which, in translation, is reproduced here:

> Interviewer: *It is only a few weeks since the first report on the presence of U-boats in the Mediterranean has reached us. Since then, they scored a number of successes. In the middle of November, Ark Royal was sunk and the battleship Malaya damaged in the western Mediterranean. At the end of November, the German communique announced that a U-boat commanded by* Oberleutnant Freiherr *von Tiesenhausen scored a heavy torpedo hit on a British battleship off Sollum.*

Commander: *It was about noon on 25 November when we saw a column of smoke in the north. Fifteen minutes later, the mast of a destroyer became visible, I took course in this direction, and before long we sighted three battleships, recognisable by their high masts, and the superstructure on the front mast. I remained on the surface and made full speed ahead towards the enemy ships. The opportunity of having a crack at a formation of battleships is a unique chance for a U-boat commander; so we did all we could to get close, and fire. Immediately after submerging I turned towards the formation which headed for us. I moved ahead, under water, just at periscope depth, and thus was able to have a good look at them. There were three battleships sailing not in line-ahead-formation but in port-line-formation, flanked on each side by four destroyers. I ordered the crew to action stations, and made preparations for the coming torpedo attack. It was a sunny day, but there were many clouds, strength of sea-swell two to three, conditions quite favourable for a U-boat attack. When I approached, two of the destroyers escorting the battleships on the port side moved forward until one of them was sailing just in front of the leading battleship, and the other to the left of the first destroyer. It was our task to get through between these two destroyers.*

Interviewer: *How far apart were these destroyers?*

Commander: *About 500 to 600-metres. I had a good look at them, and if I had made less sparing use of the periscope I could have observed every movement on board – say, whether they served coffee on the bridge to while away time. A signal was flying from the battleships, perhaps the order for the change of formation that had just been carried out. Slipping through between the two destroyers was, of course, a ticklish business and great care was required in handling the periscope. 'Up, down.' Thus my commands alternated but in the end we got past the greatest obstacle in our way. Then I had reached the first battleship. Three detonations ensued, and subsequently the customary noises accompanying a successful torpedo hit, such as water rushing into the ship and so forth. After the attack, I took another look round. I did not know at first whether the third battleship had already passed us or not – we had been too preoccupied with our attacking manoeuvres to notice that – but suddenly I saw her rushing directly towards us. We dived at full speed – it was a delicate situation and I had already visions of the bows of a battleship making an appearance in the control room – but all went well. For some time, we heard the noise of the ship's screw. After some time light depth charges and later on, heavy ones began to come down, but apparently there was no great pursuit at first.*

Interviewer: *Anyway, your boat was not hit, was it?*

Commander: *No, we were unscathed. In the evening when we surfaced again we saw a large fire in the direction of the scene of attack. Probably the fuel of the ship we had torpedoed caught fire.*

Many of the crew of U-331 heard their commander's broadcast as leave had been given in watches when they arrived back at Salamis and they all spent Christmas and the New Year ashore as the U-boat was not due to put to sea until mid-January.

However, before this the Admiralty thought that U-331 had been sunk. On 12 January the British submarine *Unbeaten* sank U-374 in the Mediterranean. The one survivor rescued told his captors that the U-boat sunk was U-331! This news was passed on and it was officially thought that the U-boat that had sunk the 33,000-ton battleship *Barham*, with a heavy loss of life, had itself perished.

The U-boat sailed on its fourth patrol on 14 January 1942 from Salamis. Its area of operation was off Tobruk and was most unprofitable. On arrival it lay in the mud and could not be moved until all torpedoes had been fired, without pistols, and a quantity of oil pumped overboard. Shortly afterwards, while off the North African coast it rescued five Italian airmen who had fallen into the sea.

On 27 January 1942, there was great rejoicing aboard the U-boat because the British Admiralty issued the following communique to the Press:

> *The Board of Admiralty regrets to announce that HMS* Barham *(Captain G C Cooke RN), flying the flag of Vice Admiral H D Pridham-Wippell KCB, CVO, second-in-command of the Mediterranean Fleet, has been sunk. Vice Admiral Pridham-Wippell is safe, but Captain Cooke lost his life. HMS* Barham *was sunk on the 25th November, 1941. The next of kin of casualties were informed, but the loss of the ship was not announced since it was clear at the time that the enemy did not know she had been sunk, and it was important to make certain dispositions before the loss of the ship was made public. The German radio has from time to time made statements with the obvious intention of endeavouring to discover whether a battleship of the* Queen Elizabeth *class, which they claimed to have hit with torpedoes had, in fact, sunk. This information has been denied to the enemy for the reason given above, but, as it is clear that they are now aware the* Barham *was sunk, her loss can be announced.*

Later the same day the German radio announced that the Knight's Cross had been awarded to von Tiesenhausen for this exploit and various members of the ship's company received other decorations.

The U-boat then set course for La Spezia which it reached on 21 February. The crew went on leave in watches. For the fifth patrol, from the North Italian port, U-331 had the luxury of a supernumerary as its former midshipman had returned on board as *Oberfähnrich zur See* Hartwig after undergoing a course at the Pillau U-boat training school.

The U-boat departed on 4 April, destination the Beirut area of the eastern Mediterranean. After passing through the Straits of Messina and while on passage, in daylight, off Crete U-331 was attacked by an aircraft. The commander quickly took his boat down and three explosions were heard, but all were too distant to effect any damage. An hour later the boat surfaced after a careful look around but the aircraft had gone.

Arriving off Beirut on the afternoon of 8 April U-331 lay on the bottom so as to not attract attention. The commander was amazed at the lack of defences; through the periscope he could clearly recognise the traffic on the shore. The echo-sounder often showed very shallow depths below the boat's keel. During this time a large sailing ship was sighted but no attack was made for fear of exposing the U-boat's position.

The U-boat remained off Beirut for some days; then being dissatisfied with the lack of targets the commander extended his patrol further out to sea. The U-boat returned to Beirut on the 15th and in the evening a ship inside the harbour was attacked while barges were alongside. A large fire and a smoke column was seen but the target, a 4,000 ton Norwegian steamer *Lyder Sagen*, was not damaged. Nine hours later there was a further failure; a freighter of about 4,000-tons was attacked leaving the harbour, A torpedo was fired and this was seen running on the surface, but it did not explode.

Later that night two small boats were sunk by gunfire. The commander thought they could be carrying oil but they were probably fishing vessels. Early the next morning, the 17th, a sailing ship was intercepted between Beirut and Cyprus and her crew were given time to abandon ship before that too was despatched by gunfire. During this engagement one man injured his hand, resulting in the loss of his little finger, so the commander decided to put back to Salamis to land him. A signal was intercepted from Guggenberger in U-81 reporting the sinking of a tanker and a column of fire was seen to the westward. Between Cyprus and Crete U-331 sighted an aircraft and dived, but no attack developed. The U-boat surfaced an hour later.

On 19 April U-331 arrived at Salamis and lay at the pier off Paloukia, near the dockyards of the Salamis Strait. The wounded rating was taken to hospital and the 1WO left the boat at this time with the 2WO moving up to 1WO and the ex-midshipman was installed as the 2WO. While at Salamis advantage was taken to install the new SBT gear. This submarine bubble target was a device that ejected chemical pills which activated on contact with sea water and created an echo to asdic transmission and so created a disturbance which effected a false target of approximately the same extent as a U-boat. The pill, or Pillenwerfer as the Germans called it, started to operate two minutes after ejection and lasted for the six minutes considered necessary for the U-boat to escape.

The U-boat was also given a fresh coat of paint while at the Greek port. Naturally Hitler's 53rd birthday was celebrated by all on 20 April.

With orders to operate in the area off Mersa Matruh, U-331 sailed alone on its sixth patrol from Salamis on 9 May, passing Gendos Island to port.

For some days the U-boat sighted nothing, then at 1000 on 19 May U-331 received a signal reporting an eastbound convoy and four hours later sighted it. Air escort proved too strong for a daylight attack, and during the afternoon touch was lost, but a further signal gave the position and course. In the dark hours of the next morning the commander attacked from the north firing three angled torpedoes from the surface at the second merchantman in the column nearest to him. Two explosions were heard and the Bristol registered *Eocene* of 4,216-tons sank. The U-boat immediately submerged and altered course 35-degrees to port. Subsequently four depth charge explosions, fairly close, were heard; the gear for blowing Tank No 5 was broken. The commander then ordered one SBT charge to be released, but the sound of asdics was heard shortly afterwards, closely followed by the explosion of further depth charges. One more pill was released and no further depth charge explosions were heard.

On surfacing at 0800, the commander decided, as the boat was no longer able to crash dive efficiently, to cut short the patrol and made for Messina where he could effect the necessary repairs. On 23 May, U-331 entered the Sicilian port and made fast at the pier, opposite the Via Zuncle. As the stay was only going to be of short duration the U-boat refuelled from a tanker which came alongside. Some of the crew stayed on board and others were accommodated in barracks. In Messina there were facilities for U-boats to carry out just minor repairs, there being no dry docks. All the labour was Italian.

The U-boat was ready to put to sea again at 1700 on 25 May and as the repairs entailed spending more than 24 hours in port, U-331 was allowed to count this next sortie, its seventh, as a separate patrol. The crew had met some of their colleagues from U-568 while at Messina – the U-boat was sunk at sea three days later.

U-331 was escorted by an Italian destroyer until well to the south of the Straits of Messina. The patrol which lasted until 16 June, was spent between Mersa Matruh and Tobruk, and during that time only one attack was made. Three tank landing craft were attacked with three torpedoes in the evening of 4 June; there were no hits and two end of run detonations were heard after running for over seven minutes. The commander considered it too dangerous to wait any longer owing to the shallows in the area. The only other thing of note during the patrol was the number of aircraft alarms; as many as fourteen or fifteen were counted on one day. Diesel trouble forced the U-boat to return and La Spezia was nominated as the port for repairs to be effected. The boat was to have a complete overhaul.

All the crew were given leave and many went to Düsseldorf, the boat's town of adoption, where they were feted. However, the problems of life ashore were quickly brought home to some of them as the sirens wailed out on 29 July, but this was only a minor raid. A major Bomber Command attack by 630 aircraft took place on the last night of the month and 900-tons of bombs were dropped. The crew had all been given 18 days' leave on three overlapping watches and those that had been unfortunate enough to draw the last leave could not wait to get back to sea again. When they did arrive back at the North Italian port they found that new batteries had been fitted and the diesels repaired; it was thought that trouble had developed in one engine owing to having proceeded too long at full speed. New fittings were installed in the bow compartment and the twin 12.7-mm machine-guns and their housings were fitted. Two additional ratings to man these guns were embarked and the remainder of the seamen were given instruction in these weapons. Another lick of paint was applied to complete the refit and the boat was once more ready for sea.

The boat's badge, a serpent, had been renewed on the conning-tower but it was not as deadly as the boat's armament, which beside the new 12.7-mm guns included the 88-mm gun forward, one 20-mm, two Type C.30 and two Type C.34 machine guns also on the bridge. The new guns were forward of the 20-mm gun on either side of the bridge. They were on retractable mountings and pivoted on a conical-shaped pedestal, which in turn was fixed to a retractable circular plate. To lower the gun it had to be elevated to an almost vertical position, by means of a catch under the stock. The latter could be folded backwards so that it lay between the gun barrels. The gun was then ready for lowering into the casing.

The ammunition for the four forward machine guns was stowed inside the conning-tower in ammunition boxes containing ten clips for the 20-mm and fifteen clips for the 12.7-mm machine guns. Each clip held 20-30 rounds in the following order: two tracer bullets, one explosive and one ordinary bullet.

The U-boat carried twelve electric torpedoes for its five tubes, four of which were forward and one aft. Before going on patrol its crash diving time was rechecked and showed: to 98-feet, 27-seconds; to 197-feet, 60-seconds. The speed was 17-knots and the fuel capacity was 128-tons and at slow speed it burned 1.7-tons per day.

Tried and tested, and looking spanking new, U-331 sailed from `La Spezia escorted by an Italian destroyer for its eighth patrol on Wednesday, 5 August. The U-boat parted company with the destroyer a few hours out to sea where it saw U-73. The refitted U-boat set course to the north of Corsica and tried out its new diesel at full speed on the surface. On 8 August the Balearic Islands were sighted on the starboard beam. Suddenly the U-boat was attacked by an aircraft which appeared off its starboard bow and released three bombs, but these did not drop close enough to do any damage. The blame for this unexpected attack fell to a new seamen who was on watch and failed to spot the aircraft in time. The U-boat immediately submerged on the orders of the 1WO, but the commander countermanded these and ordered it to surface and man the guns.

The bombing attack had been carried out by Hudson A-Able of No 233 Squadron, and when U-331 resurfaced an inconclusive gun duel took place in which two of the crew, the 1WO and a seaman petty officer were wounded. The commander was disappointed at not having brought the aircraft down with the new guns. He decided to put back to La Spezia to land the wounded men. He then had further cause for disappointment because he thus missed taking part against Operation *Pedestal* in which U-73 had sunk HMS *Eagle* on 12 August. His U-boat arrived at La Spezia on the morning of this day. The wounded men were landed and the boat refuelled from an oiler and sailed again just before midnight for the Balearics. The patrol was relatively uneventful and U-331 was again back in La Spezia on 15 September.

On 18 October, while U-331 was in port, *Kapitan zur See* Kreisch issued a statement from his Rome headquarters; he was operational commander of the Mediterranean U-boats, known as FdU, and was housed in the same building as the *Deutsches Marine Kommando*. His statement read: 'The ban on attacking warships smaller than cruisers, in force until now, has been raised.'

The boats were granted freedom of action against enemy destroyers and escort vessels. The order restricting attacks was made at a time when it was considered desirable that the operation of the U-boats in the western Mediterranean should be concealed from the enemy until a worthwhile target was encountered; but nolonger could the U-boats be expected to surprise the Allied ships.

It was about this time, when U-331 was having an overhaul, that a German Search Receiver was fitted. The commander had reported that he had often spent the entire night searching for targets which he knew to be in the vicinity without once finding one. This was a defect which could obviously be remedied by fitting some kind of surface search gear. He had accordingly proceeded to Berlin and Kiel in the latter half of the year to put forward such a request. However, subsequently, the commander had no high opinion of the GSR. The commander thought that the receiver, as fitted to his boat, was of little practical value. Firstly, it rarely functioned properly. Secondly, the long cable that had to be connected to the aerial seriously hindered crash-diving, as it and the aerial had first to be stowed below. He regarded the whole apparatus as provisional.

When U-331 sailed from its berth on the port side of Bassin No 1 at La Spezia in the late forenoon of 7 November it carried a complement of forty-nine for its ninth patrol. This consisted of five officers, three chief petty officers, twelve petty officers and twenty-nine other ratings. The only new officer was the midshipman *Oberfahnrich zur See* Franz Stanzel. He had joined the *Kriegsmarine* at Stralsund in September 1940, undergoing a three month course of recruit training. He then underwent courses at the Naval College at Flensburg-Mürwik and served some time thereafter in patrol boats in the English Channel. Further courses at Flensburg were followed by training at the U-boat school at Pillau. After promotion in June of that year he was due to be commissioned shortly. This was his first operational U-boat. On being commissioned he was to have remained on board as 2WO, with Hartwig promoted to 1WO and Nehls appointed elsewhere.

Kapitänleutnant Mehl, the officer commanding the drafting depot at La Spezia, also embarked fourteen new ratings; twelve to replace old hands required elsewhere and two as supernumeraries for experience.

As the ropes were cast off from their bollards the commander glanced across the basin to the administrative office of the 29th Flotilla in the former barracks opposite. There were always friends waiting to see the U-boats off through the boom between the breakwater and Santa Maria point.

The U-boat had put to sea about a week earlier than had been originally intended. Although it has always been, correctly, stated that the Axis was unaware of Operation *Torch* – the North African landings - the monitoring of W/T signals had shown unusual activity to the west of Gibraltar, and thus that obviously something was afoot. By 3 November the Eighth Army had Rommel in full retreat and two days later the British were advancing along the whole front from El Alamein. The following day General Montgomery announced that the battle had ended in complete and absolute victory. As we now know, the African second front troops were already in the Atlantic, ready to land at Algiers and Oran.

Before sailing the commander of U-331 told his men that Hitler had sent the FdU a signal of the 'do or die' variety to be issued to all boats.

The U-boat sailed north of Corsica and then south at full speed on the surface: the operational area was to be in the neighbourhood of Algiers.

While U-331 was making for Algiers the Allies were also making for the same spot. By the evening of 7 November the advance forces and convoys were well inside the Mediterranean. Among the ships was USS *Leedstown*, a transport of 9,135-tons. The American ship carried twenty-four landing craft, the 1st Commando and the 3rd Battalion of the US Army 39th Combat Team. These were to be held in reserve ready to land at two hours' notice on the beaches although, in fact, many of the craft were used in the initial attack in the early hours of 8 November.

The whole invasion went well and the airfields at Maison Blanche and Blida were in Allied hands by 0830 and in use by the RAF ninety minutes later. However, Axis aircraft made determined attacks on the ships later in the day and in the early evening *Leedstown* became a target for their attention. The transport, loaded with troops, was anchored off the lee shore in 21-fathoms of water twelve miles from Algiers and just over three miles from Cape Matifon light. The enemy torpedo bombers hit the starboard side and with a single torpedo badly damaged the ship. In the early afternoon of the following day two enemy aircraft were seen directly overhead and three bombs straddled the ship, one being a very near miss. There was a Force 6 wind blowing at the time.

The look-outs in *Leedstown*, no doubt distracted by the aircraft and the damage, completely failed to see the periscope of U-331 as it approached, and just fifteen minutes after the last aircraft attack was struck on the starboard side amidships by two torpedoes fired from the U-boat. Two terrific explosions followed, causing a violent heaving and shaking motion through the ship. Simultaneously, water, smoke and debris was blown out of the forward stack. The ship fell away instantly to starboard and then partly righted herself. Immediately the transport settled by the head with an increased starboard list. The main deck amidships was submerged three feet. Ten minutes after the attack 'Abandon ship positions' was ordered and seventy minutes later, when those still alive had been taken off, the captain went over the side. He was rescued by the corvette HMS *Samphire* some eighty minutes later. The corvette landed 104 survivors at Algiers the next morning.

It was not until the evening that U-boat headquarters received from U-331: 'At 1404 sank a two-funnel troopship at anchor'. The position was given as off Algiers.

Three days later, at 2240 on 12 November, U-331 sent another signal:

> *Observed this morning while attacking Algiers convoy, heavily depth-charged. The forward hydroplane, damaged by touching the sea bed during a shallow water attack, can now only be moved with difficulty by hand, request short period in dock.*

The situation in the western Mediterranean was such that the withdrawal of a U-boat from the area was extremely awkward and so U-331 was ordered to remain in the operational area unless it was absolutely necessary for it to dock. In view of the damage to the boat a proposed operation off Algiers was abandoned.

As the U-boat surfaced to send signals the next day, it was spotted by destroyers and depth-charged but escaped. For the Mediterranean boats there were regularly daily VLF broadcasts from Berlin at 1100, 1500 and 2100 as well as local bulletins from Rome and Salamis. To receive the W/T routines U-boats had to surface, at least to aerial depth. It was to receive this first broadcast that U-331 surfaced to periscope depth on Friday, 13 November. The 1WO was at the periscope and reported enemy destroyers on either beam. The commander satisfied himself that this was the case and promptly dived deeper. He intended to submerge to 30-metres. At 20-metres, however, a depth charge attack developed and U-331 promptly altered course. Shortly afterwards, another twenty-five depth charges were counted.

Von Tiesenhausen then ordered one SBT charge to be ejected, and shortly afterwards the sound of asdics ceased. Half an hour later the sound of asdics was once more evident, and thirty more depth charge explosions were counted. Another SBT was ejected. This was followed by the detonation of another ten depth charges, all of which sounded much fainter than previously. The only damage caused in this attack was to the forward hydroplane motor. The crew were unable to see how deep their boat submerged during this attack as all the depth-gauges, except the one the commander read, had been disconnected.

This attack lasted for six to seven hours, and when U-331 finally surfaced it was already growing dark.

During the night of the 15/16th U-331 sighted one destroyer, but took no action. On 17 November the U-boat was proceeding westward at periscope depth north-west of Algiers. There was no sign of enemy activity and the commander gave the order to surface; the boat continued at slow speed westward. The GSR was not in position as during the day-time the crew relied more on visual than other methods for spotting aircraft. It was usually the officer of the watch's duty to mount the equipment in position.

After the U-boat surfaced, an aircraft was spotted flying eastwards on the port bow. The bridge watch consisted of four men: the officer of the watch covering port 90-degrees to right astern; one seaman port 90-degrees to right ahead; one petty officer of the watch right ahead to starboard 90-

degrees; and one seaman starboard 90-degrees to right astern. All were issued with binoculars and anti-dazzle glasses. Watch-keeping on the bridge was a fatiguing and exacting task, yet at all times the men had to be alert. Visual sighting was the key. With the noise of the diesels, the look-outs could not hear the sound of approaching aircraft; this was known and made use of by Coastal Command aircraft. If an enemy aircraft was sighted an electric bell gave the alarm, the petty officer of the watch went below to his action station in the conning-tower with the commander. The starboard quarter look-out went to the after hydroplanes and the officer of the watch was the last below. It was his duty to remove the aerial and to close the hatch. He then went to his action station in the control-room. The responsibility for choosing between diving and fighting lay with the officer of the watch. It was recommended that the U-boat should dive if it sighted the aircraft in good time to avoid a surprise attack, that is one in which the aircraft approached to within 2,000 to 3,000-metres without being sighted, in which case the U-boat was encouraged to fight it out on the surface.

As the aircraft sighted was some distance away, it was thought that it would not see the U-boat, but, when it turned towards it, the U-boat immediately dived. No attack was heard, so two hours later U-331 surfaced to periscope depth and, as there was no sign of the enemy, the order was given to surface fully.

This was exactly the move that the New Zealand pilot Ian Patterson, flying Hudson Z-Zebra from Tafouri airfield, near Oran, had been waiting for; everything was working to plan.

After the first sighting, he decided his only hope was to 'bait' his quarry. This entailed flying eastwards and up-sun for nearly 100-miles and climbing to a height where white camouflage could be most effective – 10,000-feet on such a day. Returning to the U-boat's last seen position two hours later, he was rewarded by the sight, through binoculars, of a wake, which could only mean one thing.

Warning the crew that the target was in sight, he began a long dive, overcoming the difficulty of reducing the speed as much as possible by flattening the pitch of the airscrews. One mistake was made, not opening the bomb door until half-way down, at maximum speed, which seriously upset the trim of the aircraft, but when completed, helped to keep the needle below the red line.

In the U-boat the starboard quarter lookout did not see the aircraft. The port quarter look-out, on his first operational patrol, saw it too late and it was the commander himself who sounded the alarm which started the U-boat diving.

For the pilot of the attacking Hudson everything was working well; within a thousand yards of the U-boat, he reduced height to 20-feet and, just before the Hudson lifted over the conning-tower, four Mark XI Torpex depth charges set to shallow depth and spaced 35-feet apart were released. Three straddled the target and the fourth hung up.

Von Tiesenhausen suffered from shock after the explosions, and in the confusion that followed was under the impression that one of his crew was wounded by machine-gun fire. This was not so because the attacking aircraft did not fire on the run-up.

The 88-mm gun was put out of action and the forward hatch burst open and jammed. This led to water entering the forward compartment, which the commander then ordered to be cleared and the forward watertight bulkhead closed. The diesels were also damaged and one battery put out of action. Von Tiesenhausen then switched over to the other battery and continued ahead as fast as possible on the surface. The pressure hull was still undamaged.

Patterson claimed that the stick straddled, exploding on each side of the U-boat, which lifted it up in the water. Von Tiesenhausen was under the impression that three depth charges were dropped and that they exploded fifteen yards distant to port. He at once ordered the crew to put on life-jackets in case a larger scale attack developed, necessitating abandoning ship.

The Hudson pulled round steeply to port, and passing over the U-boat again, machine-gunned the decks in an effort to saturate any attempt to man the guns. It then climbed to 1,000-feet and sent off a signal reporting the attack. Two further Hudsons then appeared. These were L-Lucy and C-Charlie both of No 500 Squadron. Attacking from the U-boat's starboard quarter at 60-degrees to track, from a height of 50-feet, L-Lucy released four Mark XI Torpex depth-charges set to shallow depth and spaced 36-feet apart. The pilot stated that No 1 depth-charge exploded on the starboard side, No 2 against the port side and Nos 3 and 4 over on the port side. When spray subsided, the U-boat remained stationary on the surface. This attack wrecked all the depth-gauges and compasses and put the steering out of order, so that U-331 inclined to circle.

The U-boat commander then ordered men not on duty below on to the upper deck, in case it should be necessary to abandon ship.

The remaining aircraft now dropped a further three Mark XI Torpex depth-charges released from a height of 50-feet in an attack made from the U-boat's port quarter at 60-degrees to track. The depth-charges were set at shallow depth and spaced about 36-feet apart. At this point the U-boat was fully surfaced and several of the crew were seen on the bridge. The No 4 depth-charge failed to release. This stick straddled the U-boat and explosions were seen on either side of the conning-tower. After the spray had settled some of the crew, presumably those who had been on the bridge, were seen in the water. The U-boat was still on the surface and stopped. The depth-charges dropped in this attack blasted a number of those on deck overboard and killed a crew member. These two attacking aircraft then set course for base.

At this point a serious attempt was made to man the guns but those who tried were either cut down by machine-gun fire from the Hudson, or jumped overboard to avoid it. Each time the aircraft approached and swept the conning-tower more men fell to the guns of the attacker, and the deck became red with blood. A number of the crew came up from below, and waiting until Z-Zebra had finished a run, donned life-jackets and began swimming away from their crippled boat. The pilot, thinking that an attempt was being made to scuttle U-331, dropped a 100-Ib A/S bomb, instantaneously fused, among them, and those that survived returned to the U-boat. By this time Ian Patterson was having difficulty with a smoke-blackened windscreen, and most of the ammunition in the Hudson had been expended. As a last effort the Hudson pilot started a climb to carry out a dive-bombing attack with the one remaining 100-Ib bomb.

Below, with his U-boat totally unable to dive with the forward hatch open and no chance of being able to cover it, the commander ordered a white flag to be hoisted on humanitarian grounds to save the loss of further lives to his crew.

The Hudson acknowledged this sign and the crew took stock of the situation. Fuel was running low and calculated insufficient to take the aircraft right back to base. Signals had been sent requesting assistance with the U-boat but no shipping could be seen in the vicinity. The nearest airfield was Maison Blanche, Algiers, so the navigator set course for there. On arrival Ian Patterson spoke by telephone to the Navy giving the exact position of U-331. He was informed that a destroyer, HMS *Wilton*, was being despatched and he stated that as soon as his aircraft had been refuelled and re-armed he would return to the U-boat and guide the ship to the spot.

Concurrently, those remaining on board U-331 had been making efforts to rescue their shipmates swimming in the water. By this time, as a result of the flooding of the forward compartment, the U-boat was down by the bows to the extent that its screws were practically out of the water. The commander gave the order to go astern on the motors, realising that this would be their only chance of escape.

Meanwhile, the engine-room personnel had managed to repair the diesels so that they could be made to function at slow speed. The U-boat therefore proceeded very slowly towards the North African coast, estimated by the commander to be about twelve miles distant, partly on diesels and partly on motors. The aim in proceeding astern towards the coast was not so much to save their lives as to make land and escape. Von Tiesenhausen said that it was hopeless to proceed to sea as he was already so close to the coast and could not submerge. The U-boat commander then ordered U-331 to be prepared for sinking and destroyed all secret documents and made an open signal describing his position.

The U-boat then abandoned all attempts to make land, as the propellers were practically exposed. The ship's company tended their wounded and U-331 remained stopped. Some of the men tried to make rafts out of sections of the deck covering, their rubber dinghies having been destroyed by blast from the depth-charges.

Elsewhere in the Mediterranean the signal from Z-Zebra about the U-boat surrendering was having effect. It was picked up by the aircraft carrier HMS *Formidable* and she at once despatched a striking force consisting of three Albacore biplanes and an escort of Grumman Martlet fighters to the scene. When they arrived the Hudson was back guarding her prize and *Wilton* was about eight miles away. The presence of these aircraft gave cause for alarm to Ian Patterson as, everything being under perfect control, he was afraid that they might attack. To ward off this possibility he endeavoured to keep his aircraft between the U-boat and the new arrivals, and by every means possible warn them that their help was not needed. Nevertheless, a Martlet dived on the men waving white flags and machine-gunned the decks from bow to stern. The gunfire penetrated U-331's conning-tower killing some and wounding others. Von Tiesenhausen and his 2WO were both wounded. One of the Albacores then penetrated the Hudson's 'screen' and from 700-yards dropped one 18-inch torpedo. Mark XII, duplex pistol, set to 12-feet, speed 40-knots. The torpedo track was clearly evident and von Tiesenhausen ordered hard-a-starboard on the hand operated rudder, but it was too late. The ensuing explosion nearly hit the Hudson which was almost immediately overhead, some of the pieces and crew of U-331 being above it, in the air.

The torpedo struck U-331 on the starboard side, killing men who were still below; the remainder were thrown into the water. A second explosion was observed under water and wreckage was seen.

The attacks by the Martlet and the Albacore were observed from *Wilton* but she was too far away to prevent them. A Walrus flying-boat then appeared on the scene, picked up the survivors, about nine in number, endeavoured to take off but found that her cargo was too heavy. She accordingly put some of the men back in the water and took off with the remainder. Those left swimming were then picked up by *Wilton* which continued searching for a long period for further survivors, but found none.

Ian Patterson and his crew in Z-Zebra were disgusted at what had happened and left the scene while the destroyer was searching for further survivors.

Squadron Leader Ian Patterson was awarded the Distinguished Service Order early in 1943, in the meantime the Albacore pilot was court-martialled for having torpedoed U-331 while it was flying the white flag.

A total of seventeen survivors from U-331 were landed at Gibraltar; five were badly wounded, including the commander. The 1WO, 2WO, midshipman, four chief and petty officers and nine ratings made up the total. One of these was shot and killed as he tried to escape from the Rock.

This was the end of the wartime career of Hans-Dietrich von Tiesenhausen whose attack on *Barham* Admiral Cunningham, Commander-in-Chief Mediterranean, had described as 'a most daring and brilliant attack'. There can be no higher praise from an enemy.

CHAPTER FIVE

EAGLE-EYED

When HMS *Eagle* was commissioned early in 1924 it was the first aircraft carrier worthy of its name. The hull, originally built as the battleship *Almirante Cochrane* for the Chilean Navy on Tyneside, was completed in 1920 after work on the vessel had been suspended at the outbreak of the Kaiser's war in 1914.

Trials carried out in 1920 showed that the 667-foot carrier with its island on the starboard side could launch and land aircraft and it was completed by the autumn of 1923. No 444 (RAF) Fleet Reconnaissance Flight were embarked for trials.

In 1925 *Eagle* was with the Mediterranean Fleet at Malta standing by so that its aircraft could fly to Constantinople if a threatened confrontation between Turkey and Iraq materialised. The trouble blew over and the Navy reverted to peacetime status.

Eight years later, while serving with the Royal Navy on the China station, at Tsingtao, HMS *Eagle* was visited by a party of sailors from the cruiser *Köln* which was carrying out a worldwide cruise. Among the German visitors was a cadet, Helmut Rosenbaum, who would see the carrier again in a different part of the world nine years later and whose name would always be associated with *Eagle*.

In 1933 the displacement of the carrier was 22,600-tons – and this is the figure usually referred to, but by the time it was sunk this had risen by almost five thousand tons with its increased wartime loadings.

At the beginning of the war *Eagle* carried eighteen Fairey Swordfish aircraft as its strike force. It was switched from the China station to the Indian Ocean and stationed at Trincomalee in Ceylon, together with two cruisers. In the spring of 1940 the carrier sailed through the Suez Canal and linked up with Admiral Cunningham's Mediterranean Fleet at Alexandria.

The carrier's torpedo bombers were in action on 9 June attempting to slow down an Italian force so that British ships could catch them. At the beginning of September aircraft from the carriers *Eagle* and *Illustrious* bombed the airfields on Rhodes but lost four Swordfish aircraft. In mid-October aircraft from the same carriers dropped more than one hundred bombs on Leros in the Dodecanese.

Eagle missed the successful attack at Taranto on Armistice Day as defects were found in her fuel system, probably caused as a result of several near misses sustained during bombing attacks on her.

In February 1941 the First Sea Lord decided to take *Eagle* from the Mediterranean. The carrier, with its unarmoured flight deck, was vulnerable against the German Stuka dive bombers, now increasingly being brought into the action from Italian bases.

It was intended to use *Eagle*'s aircraft to search for surface raiders in the Indian Ocean and South Atlantic, including enemy supply ships.

Towards the end of April Winston Churchill wrote to President Roosevelt:

> There are certain areas in the North and South Atlantic, off the trade routes, in which the enemy maintain their supply ships and where they go to refuel. Up to the present time we have been unable to search out these areas, as we have not had the ships to do it with.

On 17 May *Eagle*, accompanied by the battleship HMS *Nelson*, was sighted by *Atlantis*, one of the successful raiders, in the South Atlantic. The German ship was not seen by the British force.

The big round-up of the supply ships began early in June following the *Hood* and *Bismarck* action. Documents had been captured from a sinking German weather ship and U-110 and this enabled the Admiralty to decode the German naval wireless transmissions with the result that they knew the overall position of the supply ships at sea.

Eagle's contribution was the bombing and sinking of a small German supply ship *Elbe* on 9 June, but much more important was the capture of *Lothringen*, with HMS *Dunedin*, six days later. Aircraft from *Eagle* located the large supply tanker and held it, under threat of being bombed, until the cruiser arrived.

Lothringen had left La Pallice on 11 May and was sailing out to the mid-Atlantic supply area. Its loss was particularly serious as there were U-boats waiting to be refuelled; its non-arrival forced operations to be abandoned and the U-boats had to return to port. When they were interrogated the crew stated that the manning of the ship by both merchant marine and naval personnel was experimental, being the first time this had been done in the case of a supply ship. The naval ratings pronounced the experiment a failure!

After the Allies had discovered all the secrets of German refuelling the ship was turned over to the Royal Fleet Auxiliary and served as the *Empire Salvage*.

Four months later, on 21 October, *Eagle* slipped from the mole at Gibraltar with a destroyer escort bound for Britain. Five days later, in the forenoon, nine aircraft from No 813 Squadron and two Sea Hurricanes disembarked from *Eagle* and flew to Machrihanish and Belfast respectively. Later a further nine aircraft, of No 825 Squadron, also flew off to the Scottish base. *Eagle* herself anchored at Greenock just before midday.

Throughout 1941 Malta, sandwiched as it was between the Italian mainland, Sicily and the Axis-held North Africa, suffered many heavy air raids from German and Italian aircraft. It was essential that aircraft were ferried in to the beleaguered island to help keep the enemy at bay. In the first two months of 1942 there was a total of almost 500 air raids on the island, and only thirteen nights were raid-free. Convoys from both ends of the Mediterranean attempted to bring supplies to the island and submarines transferred fuel. It was essential that a target of four merchant ships a month reached the island.

Modern fighters were urgently required to replace the Gladiators and Hurricanes that had fought valiantly, and in late February the first Spitfires to arrive were flown in from the carriers *Argus* and *Eagle*. In the next six months *Eagle* completed a total of nine aircraft ferrying trips, despatching a total of 183 Spitfires to Malta.

In June, out of a double-pronged convoy from Port Said and Gibraltar, only two merchantmen from Gibraltar arrived and the Port Said convoy was forced to turn back. The island, which had been awarded the George Cross by King George VI earlier in the year, was getting desperate; food supplies were extremely short and fuel oil for the defending ships and aircraft was running dangerously low.

In August 1942 a vital attempt to relieve the island fortress was launched:

Operation *Pedestal*, a force of fourteen merchant ships with the heaviest escort that could be supplied, set out to relieve the island. Four aircraft carriers were included in the force, *Furious* was carrying thirty-eight Spitfires for Malta while *Victorious*, *Eagle* and *Indomitable* carried seventy-two fighters for the protection of the convoy.

Before commencing with Operation *Pedestal* from the Allied perspective, we will go back two years to the launch of U-73, a Type VIIB boat, in Germany, which features prominently in the operation. In July 1940 U-73 slipped from its blocks at the Bremer Vulkan yard in Vegesack. Helmut Rosenbaum was appointed commander and a young officer, Horst Deckert, who had been born in Egypt of German-American parents, was chosen to be his 2WO.

At this stage of the war England was on her own, Germany was in command of all the European mainland; most of France was occupied, so after leaving Heligoland for its first operation on 8 February 1941, U-73 was detailed to put in to Lorient. On this initial patrol U-73 bagged its first victim when the 4,260-ton British ship *Waynegate* was torpedoed while sailing in a convoy outward bound from Liverpool to North American. The steamer was one of nine ships in convoy OB288 sunk by U-boats that night. In its first wolf pack attack U-73 had notched up a success. Four days later U-73 was safely escorted into Lorient. These were the days of celebrations, with flowers and bands, when a U-boat reached port. The U-boat remained at the 10th Flotilla base for four weeks before commencing its next patrol, to the North Atlantic.

A pack of U-boats were awaiting convoy SC26 of fully laden ships sailing from Nova Scotia to Britain. Six ships of the, then unescorted, convoy were sunk and U-73 was in part responsible for three of them. First the 5,724-ton British steamer *Westpool* was sunk at 0410 on 3 April and 25-minutes later the 6,895-ton ship *British Viscount* was also torpedoed and sunk. After remaining submerged throughout the day, U-73 surfaced in the evening when the 5,351-ton British ship *Athenic* was seen through the periscope. The ship had been torpedoed earlier in the day by Endrass in U-46 but did not sink, so U-73 delivered the coup de grâce.

The next success did not come until Hitler's birthday, seventeen days later, and this was a three-in-one sinking. In darkness, during the early hours, U-73 torpedoed the British 8,570-ton steamer *Empire Endurance* which was carrying two motor launches, ML 1003 and ML 1037, as deck cargo. Three days later U-73 returned to Lorient claiming over 26,000-tons of shipping sunk on the patrol.

After leave U-73 left Lorient, on 20 May, for the last time, bound for the North Atlantic again. Bad luck dogged the patrol. In broad daylight on 4 June the commander attacked a 7,000-ton ship; watching through the periscope he saw a torpedo hit the ship, but it did not explode.

After a month at sea U-73 returned to France, this time to the base at St Nazaire, where it came under the control of the 6th Flotilla. While serving with the new flotilla the partnership was not at all productive. After leaving for patrol on 29 June U-73 had to return five days later with an engine defect. The next two patrols produced no successes.

When wished 'A Happy New Year' Helmut Rosenbaum could not have visualised what 1942 held in store for him. He was under orders to sail for the Mediterranean, and warmer climes, on 3 January and passed through the Straits of Gibraltar on the night of the 13/14th of the month.

The first Mediterranean patrol, under the command of the 29th Flotilla, was off the North African coast, here, just before midnight on 3 February, an attack was carried out on a destroyer. Two detonations were heard but no ship was reported sunk.

Although, like all the other Mediterranean boats, U-73 was kept very busy, it was not until August that it had its greatest succcess.

Returning to Operation *Pedestal*: besides the convoy of fourteen merchant ships and the four aircraft carriers already mentioned, there were two battleships, *Nelson* and *Rodney*, three light cruisers and fifteen destroyers with the main force: four light cruisers and eleven more destroyers with Force X, the fleet oilers, corvettes and tugs.

The Germans and Italians, intent on maintaining their stranglehold over Malta, were alerted and ready to meet this last-ditch attempt at relief; they let fly with their shore-based aircraft on an unprecedented scale, operating at short range from Sardinia and Sicily. They set up a U-boat trap deploying their boats in a triple line of attack. Five Italian submarines and two German U-boats were ordered to first locate, and then to attack the convoy, special targets were specified as the aircraft-carriers. The German boats were U-73 and U-205. It will be remembered that the latter had also taken second place in the sinking of the carrier *Ark Royal* nine months earlier.

For protection against air attacks *Eagle* carried four 4-inch AA guns, two 40-mm AA pom-poms and twelve 20-mm oerlikons. Nine 6-inch low-angle guns were also carried. For protection against U-boat attack *Eagle* had a broad anti-torpedo bulge underwater and a 4.5-inch armoured waterline belt as protection to the machinery and magazines.

In the early afternoon on 11 August the ships' crews were tensed and ready for the first sight of Axis aircraft; *Eagle* had a patrol of four Sea

Hurricanes aloft sharing the duty with four others from *Victorious*. However, it was from beneath the waves that the first serious attack materialised. The veteran carrier *Eagle* was stationed well over on the starboard quarter of the convoy, steaming at thirteen knots, on the starboard leg of a zig-zag.

Owing to a shortage of escorts, due to the refuelling programme, the ships on the wings had been opened out to 2,000-yards. At 1300 *Laforey* turned over the escort to *Westcott*, the latter taking up her position, *Westcott* had come from the starboard wing position and *Laforey* proceeded ahead at 28-knots on completing the turn-over aproximately four miles ahead of *Eagle*.

At 1315 observers saw four explosions along the port side of *Eagle* and she immediately began to list to port. In fact the first torpedo had struck the carrier's port quarter and was followed in ten seconds by three more. After the first hit *Eagle* heeled five degrees to port and this increased to fifteen degrees after the final hit. All the explosions occurred in the vicinity of the port-side engine room; no immediate damage was caused in the centre or starboard engine-rooms. A, C and D boiler rooms in the centre flooded and in each case the port wing bulkhead collapsed. One of the escorting destroyers reported later:

> We watched, hypnotised by the speed of events, for her list was rapidly increasing. By the time she had swung ninety degrees to starboard she was right over on her beam ends, with the port side of her flight deck in the water. Then she disappeared into the cloud of smoke and steam which hung around her.

Reuters had a special correspondent aboard *Eagle*, who said:

> Terrific explosions shook the ship from stem to stern. I asked the commander, before jumping over the side, 'Is this the end?': the officer could not reply with words, he could only nod.

Eagle finally settled bodily at thirty degrees and sank within eight minutes. It was the experienced *Kapitänleutnant* Helmut Rosenbaum, operating out of Spezia in U-73, who had carried out the attack. He had detected the approach of the convoy by the sound of advancing propeller noises and had at once come up to periscope depth and made his approach. A quarter of an hour later the masts of a destroyer approaching were sighted and at the same time the commander caught sight of a carrier. He estimated the speed of the carrier at twelve knots, she was zig-zagging with six escorts around her as she passed the U-boat some four miles away. Cursing his misfortune, Rosenbaum continued his course.

An hour passed, then another destroyer came up at high speed, passing close by U-73's position and continued in the direction taken by the carrier group. When almost out of sight she started signalling and then returned the way she had come, again passing almost over the U-boat without detecting it. That is what the commander thought although it was probably two different destroyers, *Laforey* and *Westcott*.

Helmut Rosenbaum waited until the destroyer passed and then took another look through the periscope and at once sighted the convoy approaching him from the west. He counted eight freighters, a battleship, two cruisers and eight destroyers. Now was the time that all the things learned in training and from experience were brought to bear. This was the culmination of a U-boat commander's dreams: an enemy fleet approaching and he was himself undetected. Working up to full speed Rosenbaum closed the target and identified a carrier as the last ship in the starboard line.

Rosenbaum counted seven destroyers between him and his target, which he correctly identified as *Eagle*, the carrier he had visited as a cadet in Tsingtao nine years earlier!

Undisturbed by the fact that his boat was operating at less than full efficiency – defects included an unserviceable direction-finding aerial, a leaking exhaust cut-out, leaks in the bilge pump and periscope – he at once went into the attack making a text-book approach on the carrier – the target he had been ordered to give top priority. He closed undetected by the destroyer screen, to within five hundred metres of the carrier before firing a full salvo of four torpedoes from the bow tubes.

In making its approach the U-boat had passed between two destroyers with under four hundred yards to spare on either side.

After the attack U-73 dived deeply, flooding the bow tanks with all spare hands crowded for'ard as four explosions were heard and twelve minutes later the roar of the carrier's boilers blowing under water shook the submerged boat.

Only then did the first depth charges arrive. *Lookout* and *Charybdis* attacked at random, unable to obtain a contact. Other ships went to the rescue of the crew. Captain L G Mackintosh and some 900 of the crew were picked up.

For about an hour-and-a-half after the sinking, numerous sightings of U-boats and torpedoes and asdic contacts were reported but none was of U-73 which had crept away at 500-feet, its hull creaking frighteningly at such unaccustomed pressures. All the auxiliary machinery was stopped and the bilge-pump stationary, with water leaking in through the defective cut-out and periscope. For three hours the commander stayed at this depth but no further depth-charges arrived so the U-boat was brought carefully to the surface. Oil leaking from the hull was mingled with that from the sunken carrier, successfully hiding its whereabouts. Rosenbaum signalled to Admiral Kreisch, Commander-in-Chief in the Mediterranean, the composition, speed and bearing of the convoy, adding that he had sunk *Eagle*. At 2200 the Deutscher Rundfunk broadcast a special news bulletin; Rosenbaum was awarded the Knight's Cross of the Iron Cross for this brilliant attack.

Only five of the fourteen merchant ships, including the tanker *Ohio*, reached Malta and two of these were badly damaged. The cruisers *Nigeria* and *Kenya* with the aircraft carrier *Indomitable* had all been damaged while, as well as *Eagle*, HM ships *Manchester*, *Cairo* and *Foresight* had all been sunk.

So Malta's defenders and people survived but at a heavy cost. Admiral Cunningham said of *Eagle*: 'A fine old ship which had done an outstanding job during the war and had paid an ample dividend.'

A month after the attack, on 12 September, an article appeared in the *Völkischer Beobachter* entitled '*The end of* HMS *Eagle*', a conversation with U-boat commander Rosenbaum and war reporter Edgar Schroder.

Although obviously showing the hand of Doctor Goebbels' propaganda ministry, the piece is certainly worthy of translation and reproduction:

> We won't waste any time over the fact that the English reported, 'The German U-boat, which sank the aircraft carrier Eagle *in the Western Mediterranean on 11 August 1942, was later itself destroyed; it was cut in two by ramming, none of the crew surviving.'*
>
> We saw this brave and successful boat put into harbour, we took part in the plain but ceremonial welcome at the base, heard the words spoken by the C-in-C German U-boats in the Mediterranean when he addressed the crew and their young commander, Kapitänleutnant Rosenbaum, *were witnesses when the commander received from the Senior Officer U-boats the Knight's Insignia of the Iron Cross awarded to him by the Führer, and we looked into the eyes of this man, the only one of the crew to see the* Eagle – through the periscope – before she sank.
>
> In those grey-blue eyes, as in the happy faces of his men, life, which had triumphed over death in the stern [sic] attack on the great British ship, was shining.
>
> For closely had death approached this U-boat while it was executing its unprecedentedly daring attack; death – and all men knew it – stood behind the commander as he gave his orders.
>
> 'Put on life-jackets and escape apparatus! We are attacking. Our target is the Eagle.'
>
> 'We are attacking.' These words, spoken that noon, when the U-boat was alone, at the moment of contact with a superior force, were more than a promise; it was a pronouncement, whose weight must have been felt even by the youngest seaman. To attack in a U-boat demands more of a seaman than the order to go forward requires of a soldier on the field of battle; for in a U-boat each man has the same chance of escape; either all return or a great silence covers boat and crew.

'Target - Eagle' These two words have a double meaning. The sinking of this aircraft-carrier, as the Senior Officer U-boats said in his address to the crew was no 'chance success'; it was the last link in a chain of deliberations and decisions. We cannot, of course, discuss them here. It is enough to say that they aimed at the most effective use of the U-boat in the most promising position.

The decisive final link in the chain was, as the Senior Officer, U-boats, particularly emphasised in terms of the highest praise, forged by Rosenbaum's U-boat. He described the attack as 'a classic' carried out by men sustained by a pitiless will to destroy the enemy, an attack which has written a new and particularly beautiful page in the history now being made by the German U-boats in the Mediterranean.

It is so easy to read all this and, without forgetting the deadly seriousness of the situation in which the U-boat found herself, the reader may perhaps smile at being told that the commander, who for 2.25-hours was passing orders, as he concentrated all his will and ability at the periscope, asked for one brandy when he sighted Eagle *and another two later on. There was not much sea and great was the danger that the periscope would be sighted and give away the presence of the U-boat.*

Not content with one target, the U-boat made ceaseless efforts to get into a position for an attack on one or other of the warships which crossed its sights; for there was the dread lest the attack on the aircraft-carrier might miscarry and leave the U-boat mourning missed opportunities to attack other ships. But the young commander kept his head and, waiting for his opening, obtained the best target of his career.

'I never saw so many British flags before,' he said with a smile, as he described to us his impressions at the periscope. A German U-boat commander is not easily upset, even by such a huge number of ships – he did not say this himself, of course, but his action proves that we are right in this.

'I only once saw the commander excited,' one of the crew told me, 'and that was when the great aircraft carrier came in sight, but he had himself in hand again in an instant and from then on every movement was the controlled action of a man completely concentrated on his target. This wonderful outward calm – our own hearts told us how his must have been beating – had its effect upon us all. It was an experience to see how exactly and how surely the orders of the commander and of the Engineer Officer – the latter responsible for keeping the boat at periscope depth – came swiftly following one after the other, especially at the time when the destroyer dashed past us only eighty metres away and we had to go deeper as quickly as we could. But it wasn't long before our boat stuck its nose out again I can tell you.'

On this occasion there was that most desirable thing – good luck wedded to good management. Mere words cannot really describe Rosenbaum's achievement, that of bringing his U-boat through a double screen of warships to Eagle, *in broad daylight, at periscope depth and in circumstances generally unfavourable to him.*

The achievement met its reward. When the ring of ships was pierced, Rosenbaum had placed his boat only 500-metres distant from Eagle *– and he was ready to fire.*

Eagle was zig-zagging, as the whole formation was, but at the critical moment her zig-zag brought her beam on to the U-boat even as it fired its torpedoes. The time was 1315.

The death throes lasted for two minutes and then Eagle went down. Her sinking was heard in the U-boat; a nerve-racking noise, which those who heard it will never forget, the cracking rustling sounds of bursting bulkheads, the noise of boilers exploding under water – and then the quiet after the hull had sunk down past the U-boat and had reached the bottom.

The hunting craft were so startled that they dropped their depth charges more or less at random. It would have been a bad day for us if the torpedoes had missed and there had been no men swimming about in the water to be rescued distracting the attention of the destroyers.

The U-boat is extricated from the danger area by every artifice that our skilful U-boat men are capable of. Soon the depth charges are being dropped fairly far away and then stillness returns to the sea. In the U-boat all has been still since that first muffled outburst of joy.

The sinking of HMS *Eagle* was a glorious way for *Kapitänleutnant* Helmut Rosenbaum to finish his eighteen-month reign as commander of U-73. On arrival back at La Spezia he and his crew were feted and later he was appointed to a shore posting. So ended a fruitful partnership between officers and crewmen that began at the end of July 1940 when the Type VIIB boat was launched at Vegesack.

The new commander was Horst Deckert, who at the beginning of the commission had been 2WO of the boat. A product of the first 1937 class for *Kriegsmarine* officers, he had progressed from 2WO to 1WO, had then taken his commander's course, on the recommendation of Helmut Rosenbaum. Now he was to follow his illustrious former commander, in command. The crew were pleased at the continuity: 'better the devil you know'.

This Egyptian-born, German-educated U-boat commander must surely have been the only one serving whose parents were living in America, in Chicago to be exact!

The new commander was unfortunate with his first attack. His target was the 20,000-ton ship *Otranto* which had carried ten assault landing craft and the 1st Battalion of the US 168th Combat Team to Algiers for Operation *Torch* on 8 November. Just after midday on 11 November U-boat headquarters Italy received a message from U-73, which said: 'At 1136 fan of three torpedoes on large single transport, two pistol failures, course 250-degrees, speed 11-knots, am in pursuit.'

The position given indicated that U-73 was off the south-east coast of Spain. The Axis intelligence service picked up a radio report from *Otranto* saying that a U-boat had attacked her and that torpedoes missed below the stern. A comparison of positions showed that it was the transport attacked by U-73. The U-boat was informed that there had been no pistol failures.

Obviously *Otranto* was riding high in the water having disembarked its heavy load and the new commander had set his torpedoes to run too deep.

Two days later, in the evening, Deckert signalled that at 1600 he had identified the carriers HMS *Argus* and HMS *Furious* but he had been forced to submerge but was in pursuit. No attack was forthcoming so the new commander had been unable to emulate the success of his predecessor with an attack on an aircraft carrier. However, in the early morning of the following day, the 14th, the 7,453 ton British steamer *Lalande* was torpedoed and damaged, twenty survivors were seen in the water.

The U-boat was thankful to return to La Spezia as during the time that it had been on patrol U-660, U-605, U-595, U-259, U-331 and four Italian boats had been sunk by Allied air and sea forces in the Mediterranean.

The U-boat put to sea again just three days before Christmas, much to the chagrin of the crew. The outer harbour boom was opened outward by a tug to let through U-73 which had cast off at 2200 for the western Mediterranean.

Four days later, at 1857 on Boxing Day, U-73 reported fourteen freighters, one tanker, one submarine, escort vessels and destroyers, barrage balloons and anti-torpedo nets putting into Algiers as it became light. Two torpedoes fired at a tanker missed because of anti-torpedo nets.

On New Year's Day there was an attack taken straight from the text book of U-boat commander's instructions:

The classical attack from the stern tubes is only carried out when the U-boat is ahead of the enemy, or else when, owing to an unexpected alteration of course on the part of the enemy, it turns out to be more advantageous to fire from stern tubes than from bow tubes. If the U-boat is ahead of the enemy it must steer towards him for a stern shot; steering towards him is more advantageous than allowing itself to be overtaken by the enemy, because when it has to turn on to the attacking course it makes a turn smaller by two director angles than in the opposite case. Do not turn too soon, or the range of firing will be too great. Keep a good hold on your nerves.

In mid-afternoon, off the North African coast near Oran, the American 7,176-ton ship *Arthur Middleton* was at a range of only 250-metres when the stern tube was fired. Just seventeen seconds later the ship exploded as the torpedo struck home. Two days later, in the same area, another attack was made, two detonations were heard, but the Allies lost no ships on this day.

At some time during this period U-73 landed French-speaking spies off Oran. The crew were not told anything about their passengers and the commander was acting under sealed orders.

Towards the end of March U-77 was sunk by aircraft from Nos 233 and 48 Squadrons in the western Mediterranean. At the time U-73 was quite close and one of the crew reported:

> Our boat got a hell of a battering too. The boat was badly damaged; a bomb went through the torpedo hatch at a depth of 42-metres. The pressure hull and everything was smashed. The torpedo hatch was stove in. We surfaced and managed to reach base, where the pressure hull was repaired.

By now the Allies had cleared the Axis forces from North Africa and their next objective was Sicily, before attacking the mainland of Italy. The build up of shipping for the forthcoming invasion meant plenty of targets for the hard-pressed U-boats.

On 21 June the small British boat *Brinkburn* was torpedoed and sunk by U-73 and six days later a most desirable target, the 8,300-ton Royal Fleet Auxiliary *Abbeydale* was seen through the periscope. This tanker had been replenishing the Mediterranean fleet at sea. The RFA was torpedoed, but did not sink; nevertheless, this was a blow for the Allies.

The next target for U-73 was the American cruiser USS *Philadelphia*. Three months earlier the cruiser had collided with a destroyer, putting both ships out of action temporarily. Now, on 11 August, while assisting in the invasion of Sicily it was sighted by U-73. In the evening the U-boat fired at the cruiser, heard two hits and assumed it had sunk; it hadn't. This was the thirteenth war patrol of the U-boat, the superstitious crew members were apprehensive when told the American cruiser was their target. They need not have worried, for they escaped without a depth charge being dropped or even an aircraft search. This was in direct contrast to another occasion when they remained submerged for forty hours. The chief engineer and some of his ratings were poisoned and the remainder of the crew had pains in their chests and ached all over.

On 18 October U-73 attacked a 6,000-ton freighter fifty miles west of Algiers; it was claimed sunk, but in fact it wasn't even hit. The next proper success came just after midnight on 3 November when the French 4,581-ton steamer *Mont Viso* was torpedoed and sunk.

The successful U-boat, that had far exceeded the eighty day expectation for survival, commenced its fifteenth, and last patrol on 3 December. For *Kapitänleutnant* Horst Deckert it was his sixth patrol in command, and his charge was one of only thirteen U-boats still on operations in the Mediterranean. As has been seen earlier the Allies were stepping up pressure with sustained anti-U-boat saturation hunting techniques,

An eight-and-a-half knot convoy, of twenty-four ships with escorts, left

Alexandria, dropped some ships off at Bône and picked up others from the Algerian port. Among the US-bound ships was the American 7,176-ton tanker *John S Copley*. On 16 December this tanker was the target singled out for attention by Horst Deckert. The ship was hit by a triple fan salvo from U-73; she listed to port but did not sink. Two lifeboats were seen to leave the tanker, but it later made harbour.

Hunting U-73 were HMS *Brilliant* and US destroyers *Edison*, *Trippe* and *Woolsey*. The Americans sailed out of Mers-el-Kebir to track down U-73. *Edison* was detailed to assist in the screening and to pick up survivors from the tanker. The force reached the area in the late afternoon and started an anti-U-boat search. Within 45-minutes *Woolsey* picked up a contact. As the others in the force closed the contact evaporated so the hunters held their depth charges, waiting for a sharper materialisation of the target. This came just after 1830, *Woolsey* regained a sound contact and the attack commenced. What happened is best described by one of the U-boat's crew:

> *About midday we attacked an 8,000-ton ship, a corvette and a transport. I don't know whether they were sunk. One hunter after another came after us all afternoon. We were at 20-metres the whole time, we didn't go any deeper, but none of them dropped depth charges.*
>
> *At about 1830 another one joined, and crash'. They dropped depth charges on us. They landed right under the boat and immediately there was an inrush of water for'ard, by the torpedo compartment; water from the diesel got into the electric motors and the air was almost all used up – we had to keep blowing the tanks. We had plunged to 160-metres, then up again and down again and up again. We had to surface. It was dark, there was nothing to be seen.*
>
> *'Three-quarter speed ahead,' ordered the commander – the diesels were still working. Suddenly there was a shout from all sides, they had got us amidships. Then the firing really began, Everybody got out of the boat, but some drowned as there was quite a heavy sea.*

Woolsey's radar picked up the now surfaced and damaged U-73 at a range of over a mile. *Woolsey* and *Trippe* shot the ray of a powerful searchlight across the sea. As the beams fastened on to the U-boat, the German gunners opened fire. *Woolsey* was the target and hot steel whistled across the deck and two ratings were wounded. The destroyers returned the fire and U-73 was lashed into sinking wreckage. USS *Trippe* and *Woolsey* were credited with sinking U-73 25-miles north-west of Oran, seventeen months after *Eagle* had been sunk in the same sea. The aircraft carrier had been avenged. *Kapitänleutnant* Horst Deckert and thirty-three members of his successful U-boat's crew were plucked from the water and taken prisoner.

CHAPTER SIX

NINETEENTH CENTURY
WW2 U-BOAT COMMANDER

In October 1942, for the first time in the war, the British lost some of the large and valuable liners that had served so well after being converted to troop transports. Such fine ships could never be replaced. On the 9th the Italian submarine *Archimede* sank *Oronsay* just north of the Equator. The following day *Orcades* was sunk off the Cape by U-172, and the *Duchess of Atholl* was sunk by U-178 north of Ascension Island.

The Type IXD2 boat U-178 was built by A G Weser at Bremen. It had six torpedo tubes, four forward and two aft and a bunker capacity of 442-tons which allowed it a range of about 30,000 miles.

The U-cruiser, as the type was often referred to was launched on 25 October 1941 and four months later *Kapitänleutnant* Hans Ibbeken was appointed as its first commander. This was remarkable on two counts: First, he was then forty-two years old, having been born at the end of the last century. He graduated in the officers' class of 1918. Secondly, at the outbreak of war Hans Ibbeken was leader of the 2nd U-Boat Flotilla at Wilhelmshaven, with Fritz Lemp, Otto Schuhart and Hans Jenisch under his command.

The U-cruiser commenced its first war patrol from Kiel on 8 September 1942. It was among a group of Type IX boats that had been sent to probe the 'soft spots' off Capetown and the Indian Ocean. However, on 21

September the Admiralty tracking room had learned that a southward movement of U-boats appeared imminent. At that time the Allies did not have sufficient anti-U-boat trawlers on station in that area to deal with a concentrated U-boat attack, although on the evening of 8 October U-179, which had just sunk the *City of Athens* with its first attack, was depth-charged and sunk by HM destroyer *Active* on the same day.

It was 36-hours later that Hans Ibbeken was to have his greatest success, in his first attack, and one that was to prove the wisdom of appointing senior officers to the U-cruisers.

The 20,119-ton liner *Duchess of Atholl* was proceeding from Capetown to England at a speed of 17-knots. Sunrise was at 0620 and fifteen minutes later the ship, which was zig-zagging, was struck by a torpedo on the port side in the centre of the engine room. Immediately the ship began to lose speed. In the W/T cabin the receiving set was put out of action and no confirmation could be received acknowledging that the distress call had been received.

All lights in the liner were extinguished and she soon became immobile. At 0650 the chief engineer reported the engine room flooded and that he could do nothing. The passengers and crew were then standing by at 'Abandon Ship' stations, as they had previously rehearsed.

Just as the engineer was making his report a second torpedo struck the ship at about the same place on the port side. Orders were then given to put women and children in the boats and send them away. This was done without any untoward incident.

At 0725 a third torpedo found its mark on the starboard side and the ship began to settle and it was decided to abandon her. All this time the ship had remained perfectly upright and there was no difficulty with the launching of the boats.

The captain was the last to leave, at 0745, after all the confidential books and mail had been weighted down and put over the side. Three boats were smashed by the explosion and one motor boat was damaged to such an extent that it had to be abandoned about twenty minutes after being launched and then the engine of another motor boat broke down shortly after getting away from the ship due to water getting into the clutch and magneto. Although the boat contained many engineers the clutch could not be freed.

Just before the *Duchess of Atholl* sank at 0925 U-178 surfaced near the boats and the U-boat crew were seen to be dressed in khaki shirts and shorts, without any caps, and an officer, who spoke good English asked questions of the crew. The weather at this time was a moderate south-east trade wind, with a moderate swell and slight sea. The sky was cloudy with occasional light rain showers and this weather continued until the arrival of the rescue vessel the next day.

Rather strangely U-178 was seen again by the survivors about four hours before the rescue vessel arrived at 0830 on the 11th to pick up the remaining survivors, four of the engine room staff were unaccounted for.

The *Duchess of Atholl* was irreplaceable and its loss gave U-178 its first and, what turned out to be, its greatest success.

For the next twenty days U-178 continued on to its patrol area, round the Cape of Good Hope and in to the Indian Ocean. On 1 November it was off southern Mozambique and in the afternoon the British 8,233-ton steamer *Mendoza* crossed its sights and was torpedoed. One of the senior officers recorded:

> At about 1530 I was standing on the starboard promenade deck when I heard a loud explosion at the after end of the ship, accompanied by a blinding flash of light. The torpedo struck the stern near the rudder and on the starboard side, I immediately went to the engine room and found both engines stopped, orders to this effect having been rung down from the bridge. I also found that the main injection pipe on the starboard side was fractured and a smaller pipe on the port side broken at the flange. These pipes were pouring a large amount of water into the ship and I concentrated on trying to stop this inrush. The necessary valves were shut, pumps started on the bilges and so on. In addition a number of lubricating oil pipes were broken.
>
> The master had been aft to examine the damage and on his return shouted down to the engine room that both propellers and the rudder had gone and he intended to abandon the ship, which was settling down aft. The Chinese greasers and firemen left the engine room and stokehold at the first alarm and were not seen again. Before the engineers finally left, the fires were extinguished and the fuel pump stopped.
>
> After assuring myself that the engine room and stokehold were clear of men I joined the captain who suggested I should go down to a boat on the port side, and he would follow shortly. Standing on the port side of the promenade deck I saw the track of a second torpedo coming towards the ship. I started to run round to the other side but before I reached it the torpedo struck and the ship was enveloped in flame and smoke, and took a heavy list to port. I estimate she was struck just forward of 'midships. There seemed to be a double explosion and I think the torpedo struck the fuel oil tanks which are situated in this part of the ship causing an almost simultaneous explosion in the oil. As there were now no boats alongside we threw a small raft over the side and eventually the captain, second engineer, medical officer and myself succeeded in reaching a boat where the captain took charge.
>
> Aircraft had now made their appearance and signalled that help was coming. The captain kept the boats together until dark and then ordered them to make sail for Durban,

keeping in touch if possible.

At dawn the US motorship Cape Alava *was sighted and the captain of this vessel stopped for a considerable time to pick us up although the ship was loaded with explosives. It was while trying to board this ship that the captain of the* Mendoza *lost his life. He was so exhausted that he could not retain his hold on the ladder and fell into the sea. He managed to grasp a rope net a little further aft and here the struggle for his life went on for some time but he finally died.*

The U-boat commander signalled that he had sunk a ship called *Laurentic* but U-boat headquarters knew this was wrong as Otto Kretschmer had sunk it two years earlier! Hans Ibbeken also signalled that there were light air and sea patrols operating in the area.

The next attack was quite daring as it was close to the coast and took place in daylight. It was just before midday on 4 November, as the Greek vessel *Fane Romoni* was proceeding out of Lourenco Marques harbour, that she saw the 2,561-ton Norwegian steamer *Hai Hing* torpedoed. The U-boat then surfaced and the gunners on the Greek ship fired off four rounds at U-l 78, which was about three miles away. All the shots fell short. The Greek ship then prudently returned to harbour. The Norwegian ship had left Bombay for Durban on 18 October, but was diverted to Lourenco Marques. It was steaming at 12-knots when the torpedo struck No 3 hold on the starboard side and it sank in two minutes taking the master and twenty-four of the crew with it. The remainder were picked up by a tug and taken into port. The U-boat commander described the ship as a passenger freighter.

It was only three hours later that U-178 struck again. The British steamer *Trekieve* was en route to the United Kingdom, via Durban, having left the Seychelles on 27 October, when she too was diverted to Lourenco Marques. There was a light sea running when the torpedo struck the port side of the 5,244-ton ship. The ship settled very quickly and the master left when water was practically at deck level. Three men were lost. Once again U-178 surfaced, this time 25-minutes after the attack.

The U-boat then proceeded out to sea in a south-easterly direction and here the collier *Louise Moller* was to be unlucky on Friday, 13th November. The 3,764-ton ship had loaded a full cargo of coal at Durban two days earlier, for Mombasa, and when 300-miles south-east of Durban, at 0620, a torpedo struck the ship under the bridge on the starboard side. The collier stopped immediately and remained at a standstill. It settled very gently, and appeared to crack under the bridge, and sank within five minutes, on an even keel. At the time of the torpedoing the captain had just left the bridge and entered his cabin. After regaining the bridge, from which he gave orders to abandon ship, he dived overboard with the second officer. The captain received injuries on the forehead, probably due to wreckage, and was in the water over an hour before he was picked up.

The ship was fitted with two lifeboats 'midships. With the force of the explosion the front falls on the starboard lifeboat were carried away, leaving the lifeboat stern in the air, and the bow in the water. Happily, the ship was at a standstill so the lifeboat remained hanging in one davit. All the Indian crew ran to the port lifeboat, climbed in and seated themselves, and refused to move – even when ordered to do so by the chief officer. They even refused to give a hand at lowering the lifeboat in which they were seated, and it had to be lowered by the officers and engineers. The strops around the lifeboat were not untied, and broke as the lifeboat was lowered. The remaining fall of the starboard lifeboat was cut, causing it to be launched. There was practically no damage to the boat and those still left of the crew entered it and rowed over towards the other lifeboat.

Once again U-178 surfaced, between the two lifeboats, and remained on the surface for about an hour, and after asking the name of the ship, cargo, from where to where, the commander, using a powerful pair of binoculars, assisted in pointing out the various members of the crew who were picked up one by one by the lifeboats. The commander was wearing a fair-coloured beard and was said to speak perfect English.

On the day of the torpedoing, the captain's lifeboat parted company with the other boat. This second lifeboat was picked up by HMS *Douglas* after four days and the survivors were landed at Durban. The captain and his boat's crew had to wait a week for rescue and they were landed at East London.

It was two days later, on the Sunday, that U-178 failed for the only time in its career, to sink a ship that it had torpedoed.

The British 6,348-ton ship *Adviser* had left Durban the previous day loaded with 2,000-tons of graphite, bound for New York. No warning had been given of the presence of a U-boat in the area and the ship was proceeding in the dark; there was a moderate sea and swell with a north-east wind, force 4, it was an hour after midnight. No one saw the track of the torpedo, which struck in No 1 hold, on the port side. There was a very heavy explosion, and a high column of water was thrown up. The beams, hatches and derricks from the hold were destroyed, there were bulges down both the port and starboard sides of the ship amidships, the port side bulge being badly split, the hole extending well below the waterline. Orders were given for the engines to be stopped, and in view of the extent of the damage 'Abandon ship' was ordered. All four lifeboats, which were swung outboard, were safely lowered, and everyone was clear of the vessel by 0120. The boats remained in the vicinity during the night, and at daybreak the ship was circled to make a further examination. By this time the ship was well down by the head with her propellers more than half out of the water. She was still working badly with the shell plates throwing out a number of rivets, one of which hit a lifeboat.

At daybreak the master, the carpenter and radio officer reboarded the ship; the carpenter took soundings and found the fore peak and No 1 hold completely flooded, five feet of water in No 2 hold and four feet in No 3 hold. A distress message was transmitted with the ship's main wireless, giving her position, to which an acknowledgement was received from a shore station. It was then decided to return to the lifeboats to await the arrival of assistance which was promised. At 1105 the master again reboarded the ship, with all hands, and raised steam. The guns' crew were ordered to their gun stations, the two starboard lifeboats were hoisted back on board, but the port ones were left alongside in case of an emergency.

At midday a further message was sent in code stating that with the assistance of a tug the ship could reach port. A code message was received from the shore stating, 'Corvette and tug coming to your assistance'. In the early evening a further code message was sent, giving the damaged ship's corrected position. Bad weather was experienced throughout that day, with a fresh northerly wind, a rough sea and swell, which caused the ship to strain and work badly.

During the night of the 15/16th a gale warning was received from the shore station. Just after midnight a corvette was sighted and various signals about the situation on board passed between the ships. At daybreak the port boats were hoisted inboard and later a tug arrived and commenced preparations for towing the ship by the stern. After many trials and tribulations with bad weather, *Adviser* arrived in harbour at Durban on the afternoon of 19 November and permanent repairs were effected which allowed the ship to sail once more nine months later.

Hans Ibbeken says that *Adviser* was hit twice amidships but says he did not observe the sinking because of air patrols. The U-boat also heard depth charges being dropped at some distance during the day.

For the crew aboard the U-boat it was time to think about going home. Conditions on board were now much better, torpedoes had been fired, provisions had been used up and so there was more room for the crew members to move about in.

A week after the attack on *Adviser*, U-178 fired a two shot spread which missed a freighter. On 26 November U-178 sent a signal to headquarters saying that nothing had been seen for five days, but the next day, south of the Cape, a British steamer was seen in the afternoon, sailing independently and without escort. It was *Jeremiah Wadsworth* of 7,176-tons, bound from New Orleans to Bombay.

The first intimation of an attack was when two torpedoes hit the ship within a space of 30-seconds. She was zig-zagging and had lookouts posted, visibility was about seven miles. The first torpedo struck the starboard side forward of the bridge to No 3 hatch; the second hit No 5 hatch on the starboard side. Ten minutes later a third hit under the bridge and a fourth missed. The ship was abandoned at 1603. The ship had had no opportunity to take offensive action although guns were fired in the direction from which the torpedo came, engines were not stopped and boats were therefore swamped.

Once again U-178 surfaced, and for the last time the commander asked the men in the boats where the ship was from and its destination and what tonnage; the name of the ship had been taken from the bow. The U-boat commander told those in the motor boat where the other boats were and all were picked up.

A United States Navy officer was aboard the torpedoed ship; he recalls:

> An SOS with our position was sent at 1547 giving noon position and signal letters. In my opinion the U-boat was German and the commander was German. We were adrift in boats for eight days. We recovered rations and water from one of the damaged boats and we had sufficient rations for 42-days and water for 30-days. All boats were towed during the day and night for four days. The weather was bad with high seas and rain. We were picked up 45 miles from Georgetown.

The last torpedo remaining on board was fired from U-178 on 8 December at a 5,000-ton freighter, but the torpedo was faulty and a circle runner. On the 16th, perhaps Hans Ibbeken regretted the excessive use of four torpedoes in the sinking of *Jeremiah Wadsworth* when he saw two steamers in mid-Atlantic, but now had no torpedoes left.

A week later the U-boat sent an uncoded message which was picked up at Freetown signal station. Translated it read: 'Christmas greetings to all at home. So far 58,000 GRT sunk now being celebrated in a tropical heat with ship's company and myself.'

The receiving station added their own comment: 'This message would appear to have been inspired by a stronger spirit than wistful sinking!'

The old commander, who had successfully negotiated the Indian Ocean, the South and North Atlantic and now the Bay of Biscay brought his boat and crew safely home to France, to Bordeaux, the base of many of the U-cruisers. The date was 9 January 1943, the U-boat had been at sea for 123 days. For Hans Ibbeken it was his last sea appointment. In February, after he and his crew had enjoyed some well deserved leave he was appointed to be commander of the torpedo school at Mürwik.

Korvettenkapitän Dommes was appointed as the new commander of U-178. The former commander of U-431, he had experienced mixed fortunes. He had his fair share of torpedo malfunctions, yet had sunk the famous Dutch destroyer *Isaac Sweers* in the Mediterranean and merchant ships. However he had also had the ill-fortune to miss the aircraft carrier HMS *Furious* with a four-torpedo salvo. A Knight's Cross holder and a member of the 1931 class, Wilhelm Dommes was an East Prussian farm owner and hunter. Although not as old as his predecessor, he was older than most U-boat commanders.

For its second patrol, off South Africa and in the Indian Ocean, the fully refitted U-178 left Bordeaux on 28 March, 1943, made its way down the river to the Bay of Biscay. The U-cruiser proceeded south, round the Cape and on 1 June caught a ship in a Capetown-Durban convoy that had been attacked four days earlier by U-177 in which Robert Gysae had sunk two ships. The first victory for Wilhelm Dommes in his new command was the Dutch steamer *Salabangka* of 6,586-tons. It was mid-morning when the ship was torpedoed and damaged. He decided the ship was salvageable; it was taken in tow, but sank that same evening.

It was nearly five weeks before his next success, but then it was a double victory. First, in the early afternoon of 4 July, a convoy straggler from Durban was torpedoed and sunk. This was the 2,659-ton Norwegian steamer *Breiviken*. Just over four hours later, at 1830, the Greek ship *Michael Livanos*, of 4,774 tons, was torpedoed and sunk. A week later its sister ship *Mary Livanos* was also sunk, in mid-mirning on 11 July off Mozambique.

In a night attack, three days later, the 7,191-ton American ship *Robert Bacon* was torpedoed and sunk in much the same area. Two days later, in a late evening attack, Wilhelm Dommes was to sink his last ship. The 6,692-ton British ship *City of Canton* was torpedoed off the coast of Mozambique. This last victory was on 16 July and U-178 headed north and east and on 29 August entered the Japanese-held Malaysian port of Penang.

The U-cruiser spent almost three months at the port, and when it left, it did so without Wilhelm Dommes, who was appointed in charge of the 33rd U-boat Flotilla at the port.

Logistic problems beset the Far Eastern base, since it was so far from Germany. There was a shortage of torpedoes and fuel and maintenance and repairs were difficult to carry out. In October the RAF dropped mines round the base and all seaworthy boats at Penang were ordered to return to Europe.

Wilhelm Dommes moved on to become U-boat liaison officer in Tokyo. The third commander, for the third patrol was the watch officer *Kapitänleutnant* Wilhelm Spahr. His U-boat war is worthy of a book of its own for he had been with Günther Prien, in U-47, from December 1938 through until February 1940 and was with the 'Bull of Scapa Flow' when he sank *Royal Oak*.

The six-month voyage from Asia to Europe began on 27 November when the U-boat was escorted out from Penang. At Christmas, four weeks later, U-178 had reached a position to the south of India, and two days later it sank the 7,244-ton American steamer *Jose Navarro* to the south-west of India. It was the first and only success for Wilhelm Spahr. Nevertheless, the sinking was welcomed at U-boat headquarters as there were only three other sinkings in that area in the last four months of 1943 and this was the first for over two months.

After refuelling from the tanker *Charlotte Schliemann*, 100 miles south-east of Mauritius on 28 January, the U-cruiser returned to the 12th Flotilla base at Bordeaux, after its 180-day sea voyage, just two weeks before D-Day. When it secured to a dockyard bollard, the fighting days of U-178 were over.

By mid-August the Allied troops were fast approaching the port. On the 18th a force of sixty-four Lancasters bombed the oil storage depot at Bordeaux and the following night mines were laid off the Biscay bases. The 12th U-boat Flotilla was disbanded and the withdrawal began. Two U-boats, U-178 and U-188, were unable to sail and were scuttled. So, ignominiously, U-178 which had sunk thirteen ships and damaged another, in total 100,000-tons met its end 22-months after the success that made Hans Ibbeken a U-boat ace.

CHAPTER SEVEN

ON A RAFT FOR 130 DAYS

Carl Emmermann sank twenty-seven ships, totalling 152,656-tons during his two-year career as commander of U-172 and ranked thirteenth in the list of successful U-boat commanders of the Second World War.

Born in Hamburg in 1915, Carl Emmermann attended the officers' class of 1934 and from November 1940 until August 1941 was a watch officer in UA, the ex-Turkish U-boat. His first command, U-172, was a Type IXC boat launched from the AC Weser yard at Bremen on 5 August 1941. He joined the boat a month after its launch and *Oberleutnant* Hermann Hoffmann was shortly afterwards appointed as watch officer.

The first war cruise from Kiel, on 22 April 1942, was an eleven day shakedown patrol which took the boat to Lorient to join the 10th U-boat Flotilla at its base on the River Scorfe.

The boat did not remain long at the French base, for eight days later, on 11 May, its commander conned it through the narrows and into the Bay of Biscay, en route for the Caribbean. Once it arrived on station success came thick and fast for U-172. After sighting two independently routed ships the first victim, torpedoed and gunned, was the British motor tanker *Athel Knight* on the night of 27 May. The U-boat then made for the Mona passage and five nights later an American 5,447-ton steamer, *Illinois*, was torpedoed and sunk. Two nights later another American steamer, *Delfina*, of 3,480-tons was also torpedoed and sunk. Three nights later on 8 June a small American motor ship, *Sicilien*, was torpedoed. In the morning of 14 June another American steamer, the 8,289-ton *Lebore*, was torpedoed. The following evening a small Norwegian steamer, *Bennestvet*, was sunk. Three days later, in the early hours the guns' crew were given more practice and they sank the *Motorex*, a small American motor tanker. On the 23rd a small Colombian sailing ship was sunk. The last victim of the patrol was the 8,379-ton steamer *Santa Rita* which was sunk to the east of the West Indies on the afternoon of 9 July, but it took gunfire as well as torpedoes to sink the American ship.

Commander Carl Emmermann had a mixed bag of successes to report when he arrived back at Lorient on 21 July flying nine victory pennants after completing his Caribbean patrol; the total of nine ships sunk varied in size from the 35-ton sailing ship to a steamer of nearly 9,000-tons.

The crew only spent a month ashore before embarking on their third war patrol, and a long one it was to be. Setting out in mid-summer on 19 August they would not return until mid-winter, just after Christmas. During the-period 16-19 August other U-boats leaving their French bases were U-68, U-504 and U-156. All were to operate in company with the replenishment milch-cow U-459, off Capetown and all received permission to attack merchant shipping. Mines had been laid off Lorient by RAF aircraft earlier in the month but U-172 was escorted through a swept channel and by 5 October, after having refuelled, arrived in the Capetown Roads which were found to be empty and Carl Emmermann requested freedom of action.

At 0600 on 7 October the 6,200-ton American steamer *Chickasaw City* was torpedoed and sunk with two torpedoes. The U-boat then came right alongside the master's boat after the sinking. The commander enquired the ship's name, port sailed from and destination, and cargo carried. One of the seamen aboard told him the name of the ship saying it was sailing from the Cape to the United States and the master was extremely upset that this information had been given. Carl Emmermann then consulted a brown backed book and appeared to obtain from it full information of the ship's tonnage, and cargo carried and did not appear happy when the master insisted that his ship had been in ballast. The U-boat commander and crew were described as remarkably young and neatly dressed, Emmermann in blue uniform with lieutenant's stripes, the remainder in khaki. The 1WO had a goatee beard. The U-boat was reported to be in excellent condition with few signs of wear and tear, and no rust. This fact made a strong impression on all the survivors, who stated that the U-boat's exhaust threw up water exactly like a whale spout. Seven members of the crew of

Chickasaw City lost their lives in the sinking, but the remaining forty-two were all picked up the next day by the Flower Class corvette HMS *Rockrose*.

In the same area, just over four hours later, the Panamanian ship *Firethorn* of 4,700 tons became the next victim, again hit by two torpedoes, on the port side. The U-boat closed the survivors and an officer spoke to the chief officer of the sunken ship. However the U-boat commander appeared to have been in a hurry as he did not press his questions when the chief officer gave evasive answers. A United States Naval Reserve lieutenant was carried on the ship for gunnery duties and he made a careful observation of the U-boat, the nearest it approached was 75-yards, and he noticed an emblem on the conning-tower, white paint on blue background. In his opinion the hull was in good condition, showing little, if any rust: it was a dark aluminium colour. Of the fifty-nine aboard *Firethorn*, twenty-one were picked up by the South African naval trawler *Springs*, and twenty-seven by HMS *Rockrose*.

Amazingly on the very next morning, in the early hours a Greek steamer *Pantelis*, of just under 4,000-tons was sunk nearby. The ship had left Capetown the previous day bound for Buenos Aires and two torpedoes sank it in two minutes. The ubiquitous HMS *Rockrose* rescued the survivors two days later, but twenty-eight had been lost. The U-boat was then detected and Carl Emmermann reported that he was hunted by air and sea patrols for 28-hours and although depth charges were dropped his U-boat was undamaged.

Despite the three sinkings by U-l 72, and others in much the same area by Merten in U-68 and Witte in U-159, the troopship *Orcades* was allowed to sail from Capetown for the United Kingdom. This 23,456-ton former Orient line, Vickers-built ship carried over 1,000 passengers and crew, 2,000 bags of parcel post and 3,000-tons of general cargo. The master recalls:

Prior to sailing from Capetown I visited the control office to find out about my routing instructions. I read a number of signals stating that ships had been torpedoed about 300-miles off the coast and saw, to my horror, that my track was plotted right through the middle of this dangerous area. I asked the Royal Navy captain if this was intended and he said it would be quite all right for me to sail on the track mapped out for me. Accordingly at 1530 on 9 October I sailed from Capetown and proceeded as instructed. We passed HMS Hecia and, as I knew her captain, we exchanged signals and she signalled saying that three ships had been torpedoed on my track during the previous afternoon and wanted to know why I was using that route, and who had given permission to sail. I told him I had been instructed to proceed and therefore could not do otherwise.

Orcades continued without incident until the late morning on the 10th when the weather was poor with heavy rain squalls, and visibility about two miles. There was a rough sea with a very heavy swell and a south-westerly wind force 7. At 1123 when steaming at 15-knots on a westerly course *Orcades* was struck by two torpedoes.

The master continues:

> *The cracks of the torpedoes were not seen although there were a large number of look-outs on duty. The first torpedo struck on the port side between No's 1 and 2 holds. The explosion was rather muffled and no water was thrown up nor was any flash or flame seen. A minute after the first explosion a second torpedo struck the ship aft in No 6 hold. Again the explosion was muffled, but the port engine and the steering gear were put out of action. Emergency stations was sounded and all the passengers were mustered ready for abandoning ship. The ship was still proceeding with the starboard engine and making 5-knots when at 1130 a third torpedo hit the ship in No 3 hold amidships – No 6 hold was flooded by now and the hatches were blown off, also the hatches of No 3 were blown off. Boxes of oranges were slipping out into the sea. The water was up to the 'tween decks in No 1 and the ship settled bodily several feet.*

Immediately after the third explosion it was decided to disembark all the passengers and as many of the crew as possible leaving on board enough of the crew to get the ship to port. A total of twenty-two lifeboats were successfully lowered and the passengers abandoned ship. *Orcades* still had plenty of buoyancy and although down by the bow she was rising welt to the sea and swell. When the boats were clear the ship went ahead with the Starboard engine. Later the port engine was restarted at slow speed and *Orcades* proceeded at about 5-knots. The steering gear was still out of action but the wind and uneven speed of the two engines held the ship fairly steady and she yawed to and fro.

As time went on hope was entertained that perhaps it might be possible to save the ship. Repairs to the steering gear were in hand. At 1420, however, the ship was struck by a fourth torpedo, followed a few moments later by two more. It was clear that the end had come and the ship immediately took a list to starboard and commenced to sink rapidly. The order to abandon ship was given and those remaining on board proceeded to man the four remaining lifeboats which had been turned out and prepared since the first boats had left.

The ship sank very quickly after receiving her death blow and she disappeared at 1430, some 300-miles from Capetown.

The four lifeboats pulled around amongst the wreckage and collected all those who had not been fortunate enough to reach a boat and who were clinging to wreckage. As many oranges as possible were recovered from the sea.

An aircraft passed within about two miles at about 1530 but gave no indication of having seen the four boats although yellow flags were displayed. Shortly before midnight a darkened ship was sighted and red flares were burned. These were observed and the ship turned towards the boats. The ship proved to be the Polish merchant vessel *Narvik*, and it was learned that she had rescued the majority of those who had left *Orcades* earlier. The four boats were cleared by 0045 after the occupants had been in them for about ten and a half hours.

At noon two destroyers arrived to escort *Narvik* back, to lead her into harbour clear of the minefields. She arrived at Capetown on the morning of 12 October and landed the survivors from *Orcades*. Of the crew, twenty-three out of 326 had been lost, and from the 741 carried twenty-three passengers were also missing.

The loss of *Orcades* was a body blow to the British Ministry of War Transport, for in two days three troopships had been torpedoed and sunk in the southern hemisphere, the others being the *Duchess of Atholl* and *Oronsay*.

After the sinking U-172 moved away from the coast westwards and on the 18th Emmermann fired two torpedoes at a freighter, which missed. There were air patrols and the U-boat commander presumed that traffic had been halted. He signalled U-boat headquarters a week later, on the 25th, saying that he had sighted nothing.

However, on the last day of October the British motor steamer *Aldington Court*, of just under 5,000-tons, was struck by two torpedoes and sank. The senior surviving officer when landed at Montevideo stated that he was on watch on the forebridge and heard the torpedoes approaching and saw their tracks just a few seconds before they struck. The noise was like that of an approaching aircraft and the torpedoes appeared to be running very close to the surface,

When U-172 came to the surface, fifteen minutes after the vessel was sunk, an officer speaking in good English but with a German accent, ordered the boats to come alongside. The officer asked for the master, but on being told that the master had not been saved, the chief mate was ordered on board the U-boat, and after being blindfolded, was taken below for questioning.

The second radio officer stated that at 0900 on the day the vessel was sunk W/T had been used to acknowledge diversion signals which had been received from the Admiralty with instructions to acknowledge receipt. On other days, two or three days before the vessel was sunk, W/T had been used for several hours in order to acknowledge receipt of diversion instructions.

Another survivor who was in his quarters, under the topgallant fo'c'sle, said he heard a noise which he thought was an approaching aircraft. He heard this noise a minute or two before the torpedoes struck and had time to get his lifebelt and get to the door before the explosion of the torpedoes. He thought they were torpedoes running on a circular track.

The U-boats operating in the Capetown-Durban area sank twenty-four ships totalling over 161,000-tons during the month. The Admiralty were compelled to reinforce the escorts in the area and sent out twenty ships, of which a dozen were trawlers from the Western Approaches.

The faulty black-out on the London registered ship *Llandilo* of nearly 5,000 tons, probably caused it to be torpedoed on the very dark night of 2 November as it was sailing from Trinidad to South Africa. There was a smooth sea with a slight swell and no moon when the ship was torpedoed on the starboard side under the bridge. An SOS was acknowledged by Capetown wireless station.

After the sinking U-172 surfaced about half-a-mile away and then came alongside the lifeboat. The lifeboat crew were allowed on the U-boat for fifteen minutes while their boat was being baled out. The U-boat sailed off on the surface and the twenty survivors were picked up by a Norwegian vessel five days later and returned to Trinidad.

The crew of U-172 must have misheard the name of the sunken ship, *Llandilo* for it claimed that the ship *Clandille*, on course from Trinidad to Capetown, had been sunk.

On 7 November U-172 and U-68 were given freedom of movement but the following day they were ordered to stay in the area in which they were operating in for the next four days. When this time had expired, on 12 November, Carl Emmermann requested permission to operate in a position to the north-east of Brazil, just below the Equator. However, it was just north of the Equator, on its way home, that U-172 intercepted the British 6,630-ton steamer *Benlomond* sailing from Capetown to Paramaribo on 23 November. It was just before midday when a torpedo hit the engine room as the steamer was making 12-knots.

The following is the story of the sole survivor, Poom Lim, a second steward who was rescued on 5 April, 1943, 130 days after the sinking: He was in his cabin at the time of the explosion, grabbed his lifebelt and put it on while running down the alley along the saloon and towards his boat station. When he got there he found two of the officers and one seaman trying to lower the lifeboat. He joined them and they had just raised her off the chocks when he was washed away by a green sea. He was carried deep under and when his lifebelt brought him to the surface he could no longer see the *Benlomond* nor any trace of her except some planks floating around him. He got hold of one of these to hold himself up and paddled about for a long time, 'two hours, maybe' he said, but it is probable that his estimate of time just then was not very exact. He says that all the crew, except the watch, were below, either in the engine room or in the holds which they were scraping and cleaning out, with the hatches off. He thinks that the torpedo blew off a large part of the ship's bottom as she was very light and high, carrying no cargo and that the water finding no resistance from air pressure very rapidly filled the ship which he says must have sunk in about three minutes.

After paddling around he came across a life-raft, swam towards it and climbed on to it. He was then able to look around and saw another raft so far away he could not recognize the four men on it. He thinks they were the gun crew, who had been on deck by their gun. These men waved to him to join them but he could not get his raft to move, being alone on it. He states that he saw no other members of the crew but did hear several calling out and crying for help. Later the two rafts were drawn apart and he lost sight of the other one.

About this time he suddenly saw a U-boat, at some distance. It was on the surface when he saw it first and remained so, moving away and disappearing. He described it as very big, but he had never before seen a U-boat close up. The bow was higher than the stern over which the water was washing and he recalls there was one heavy wire strung from the bow to the top of the bridge. He did not know what a periscope was, but insists that there were no masts standing up from the bridge/conning-tower. There was, however, a gun with some men around it forward of the bridge and, quite definitely, on the deck itself, which ran level, upwards from stern to bow. He also saw a flag, or insignia, painted on the side of the conning-tower. It had three colours but he only remembers white and green. He recalls a rectangular, up and down, marking on the white in the centre of the flag. He was absolutely sure it was not a swastika. The crew he saw, on the bridge were not fair but dark and had brown or black hair. He did not know the difference in appearance between an Italian or a German. He called to the U-boat for help, but was merely waved away with laughter.

On the raft he found water and food stored which sufficed for him for fifty days. He drifted about without being able to direct or move the raft. He saw several ships, one of which was quite close to him. For this one he fired a flare he found on the raft, but the ship did not respond and steamed on. Before the fifty days were up he dug a nail out of a plank of the raft with his teeth, and with the same tools formed it into a fish hook. He unravelled the life line round the raft and made a fishing line. He baited his hook with some biscuit, made into a paste, and soon caught a fish which resembled a whiting. This he used as bait for bigger fish, and caught some eventually as heavy as 'fifty pounds'. It may be deduced that by this time the currents had brought him in nearer to South America off the mouth of the Amazon. He also caught seagulls which settled on the raft while he was lying down between the benches over which he spread the material of his lifebelt as a protection from the sun and to catch rain water. He was washed by sea water all the time and was stark naked. He was burned on shoulders, back and arms a deep black-brown colour, but did not blister and showed no salt water sores, though when found he was scratched and showing signs of old scars. When his water ran out he was able to gather enough rain water to fill the tins. It rained very often, which also seems to show he was not far off the Brazilian coast at the time. For five days only did he have to go without water. These occurred after he had been one hundred days on the raft and he seems to have suffered then the worst mental anxiety of all his 130 days on the raft. He also saw several aircraft, again showing that he must have been drifting for some time along the Brazilian coast. One came right down to inspect him and in fact did report him to the US Naval authorities at Belem. An aircraft went out to search for him, but did not find him.

At last a Brazilian fisherman sighted him some ten miles out to sea off the coast of the state of Para east of Salmas. He sailed out to him and picked him up. He had to be lifted off the raft as he was too weak to get up. He was overjoyed and sang and laughed and ate voraciously. The fisherman particularly observed that he ate a red pepper of very powerful pepperiness by the handful and seemed to enjoy the bite or not notice it. Three days later, 5 April, he landed at Belem, able to walk and amazingly agile, though very weak.

He was taken charge of by the British Consulate and put to bed in hospital under the doctor's care. The doctor reported that he was in need of rest and building up with tonics and that the only thing really wrong with him otherwise was a stomach derangement probably due to the raw food he had eaten for so long and exposure. A fortnight later he was up and about and fit enough to be returned to the United Kingdom. Almost at once after his arrival he expressed the desire to return to duty. He had lost all his belongings and particularly missed his wrist watch. The British colony subscribed to donate him a new one, with inscriptions all complete.

There was no sign of wreckage or other survivors from *Benlomond*. When U-172 reported the sinking of *Benlomond* it said it was in ballast to Capetown when in fact it was sailing in the opposite direction. The U-boat also reported seeing a flight of six bombers, presumably being ferried from Ascension Island to Africa. A similar group had been observed on the outward passage.

On 27 November U-172 stalked a 14-knot steamer on a south- easterly course without attacking, but the following day the last victim of the patrol was caught in mid-ocean between South America and Africa and in a dawn attack the guns' crew were given some practice after a torpedo had failed to sink the American steamer *Alaskan* of 5,364-tons. Again the ship was wrongly named as *Laskan* in a signal to U-boat headquarters and it was added that it was on route from Capetown to New York via Trinidad.

The following day U-172 stalked a ship for eight hours before giving up, realising that the steamer was probably Spanish. News was received in the U-boat that Carl Emmermann had been awarded the Knight's Cross on 27 November, and it was an occasion of much rejoicing for all the crew.

Now running short of fuel, U-172 was directed to a mid-Atlantic supply rendezvous. The crew could hardly believe their eyes; here in the middle of the ocean were seven U-boats and the milch-cow Type XIV supply boat. Among those present were Ernst Bauer with U-126, Albrecht Achilles with U-161, Ulrich Thilo with U-174, Helmut Witte with U-159, and U-128. Witte and Emmermann were friends, having been together in the 1934 class; and they both visited Ulrich Heyse in U-128; Heyse had graduated a year earlier.

Fully replenished, U-172 reported a westerly-bound convoy on 11 December, sailing at 10-knots in mid-Atlantic. It was ordered to exploit the chances of attack until the 13th and then to continue the return journey. In a dusk attack, with the last two torpedoes, an attack was made on an 8,000 and a 4,000-ton steamer. After 3-minutes and 5-seconds and 3-minutes and 16-seconds, detonations were heard. No ships were sunk and the detonations were probably depth charges from a destroyer. U-boats in the area, U-105 and U-124, were told of the convoy and U-105 sank one of the ships on the 14th.

Owing to stormy weather in the Bay of Biscay Carl Emmermann just failed to return in time for Christmas, arriving on 27 December with eight victory pennants flying above the conning-tower, on which the insignia was, in fact, a picture of Neptune holding a trumpet and a trident. The crew made up for lost time in welcoming in the New Year and in fact they were not called on again for another two months.

During mid-January Allied bombers laid waste large parts of Lorient, with night raids, but U-172 was safe in the bunkers, and many of the crew were on home leave in Germany.

The fourth war patrol commenced on 21 February and the crew were relieved to hear it was to be to the eastern seaboard of the United States. In a dawn attack, in mid-Atlantic, on 4 March the British steamer *City of Pretoria* was sunk by U-172 and later in the day, and in the same area, U-515 sank another ship of a similar size, 8,000-tons. A night victim of U-172 two days later was the 3,000-ton Norwegian motorship *Thorstrand*. March was the month that cost the Allies 108 ships with 627,000 lost tonnage. A week after its last attack U-172 joined with a pack that attacked UGS6, a slow convoy from the United States to Gibraltar. In a night attack Emmermann sank *Keystone* and three days later, the 16th, in an evening attack U-172 fired a four-torpedo spread which resulted in the sinking of *Benjamin Harrison*. Both victims had been American steamers, of 5,500 and 7,000-tons respectively. *Freiherr* Walter von Steinaecker in U-524 was another to record a success against the convoy. Nearly a fortnight later U-172, with U-167 and U-159, fell upon convoy RS3 from Gibraltar to Sierra Leone and sank *Silverbeach*, a British 5,000-tonner, just after midnight on 29 March. It was time to return to base.

The U-boat spent six weeks in Lorient before commencing its fifth war cruise, the last with Carl Emmermann in command. On 29 May he conned U-172 out of the river Scorfe into the Bay of Biscay for a new patrol area, off the South American coast. The departure was unusual in that just days earlier Admiral Dönitz had ordered all his Atlantic boats back to their bases following the loss of 41 U-boats during this May month.

South of the Equator, midway across the South Atlantic, between South America and Africa, the British 4,748-ton steamer *Vernon City* was sunk in a dawn attack on 28 June. The U-boat continued with its patrol and with another dawn attack off the Brazilian coast on 12 July torpedoed and sank the American steamer *Africa Star* of 6,500-tons. Three days later and further out to sea Emmermann sank the British 4,000-ton ship *Harmonic* at dusk. Nine days later, on 24 July, in another dusk attack U-172 sank its last victim, a 7,000-ton British steamer *Fort Chilcotin*.

A message was sent to U-172 and U-185 to proceed to a position off Pernambuco to rescue the crew of U-604. The Type VIIC boat on its sixth war patrol had been depth-charged by US aircraft and the destroyer *Moffet* on 3 August. Although badly damaged, U-604 attempted to return to base.

When this was found to be impossible the crew were taken off by U-172 and U-185 and U-604 was scuttled on 11 August.

That same day U-172 reported it had been damaged by an aircraft attack but the survivors aboard were more fortunate than their colleagues rescued by U-185 for this U-boat was sunk the next day, 12 August.

Now U-172 was on its way back to Lorient; there is no doubt that the cramped crew were anxious to shake off their sea-legs after spending all the summer at sea, and so on 7 September Carl Emmermann took his boat into Lorient for the last time. In a space of fourteen months he had sent 27 Allied ships to the bottom. It was time for him to have a shore posting and he was appointed in command of the 6th U-boat Flotilla at St Nazaire.

Strangely, U-172, having been a Lorient-based boat all its operational life, was also transferred to St Nazaire and *Oberleumant* Hermann Hoffmann was promoted from watch officer to command the boat.

When the boat set off on Monday, 22 November, for its sixth war patrol, there was a new operational area, the Indian Ocean, although the boat had skirted the area on its South African patrol. The boat was one of three of the larger ones sent to the distant operational area. Their instructions were to remain unseen and not to attack targets until the patrol area was reached. On 30 November U-172 signalled in, confirming its safe passage through the Bay of Biscay and into the Atlantic. It was the last message received from the boat by U-boat headquarters. Almost a fortnight later, when 180 miles south-west of the Canary Islands and 600-miles north-north-west of Cape Verde, U-172 inadvertently came too close to convoy GUS23 crossing from Casablanca back to the United States. Worse still the carrier *Bogue* was in the vicinity of the convoy with, in turn, its escort of USS *George E Badger*, *Dupont*, *Clemson* and *George W Ingram*.

On 11 December U-219 had already replenished three boats but the lines were still attached to U-172 when aircraft from *Bogue* were sighted. The auxiliary tanker quickly submerged but U-172 was still on the surface and the hunt was on. The U-boat submerged immediately and *Clemson* was ordered to the spot. On arrival asdic contact was established and a depth charge pattern dropped. While this was being done, a carrier-borne aircraft patrol overhead looked for telltale signs of destruction.

The other escorts steamed to join *Clemson* hunting U-172. Down below, the U-boat crew were observing silent routine; the motors were cut, the crew lay down wherever there was a space. It was a cat and mouse game with the hunters knowing that their quarry would have to surface eventually for air and to charge the batteries. The escorts waited throughout the day and into the night. How long could the U-boat remain submerged? Although lying deep, U-172 was located time and again by the destroyers and each time another pattern of depth charges was dropped. The U-boat was unable to escape the unwelcome attention of its attackers and sheer desperation caused its new commander to surface in the early hours of 12 December. The crew needed air and the batteries needed charging. As soon as the U-boat's silhouette was seen all hell was let loose; the destroyers opened fire with their guns and as U-172 scrambled below, depth charges were released. It was the beginning of the end. The U-boat's pressure hull was damaged and U-172 was fatally leaking oil.

As dawn broke the Wildcats from *Bogue* were back again. Just after 0800 the telltale oil slick was spotted and the information radioed to the ships below. It was now nearly all over. The asdic was superfluous; the oil leaking to the surface gave away U-172's position. The depth charges rained down from *Clemson* and *Ingram* but still the U-boat couldn't or wouldn't surface. The depth charges were running short and by mid-morning there was no sign of the Germans giving up the struggle.

Then it happened, a quick rise to the surface and a run for it. It was really no contest. As soon as U-172 broke through, it was seen by an excited pilot who communicated his delight in clear. Two more flights were scrambled from the flight deck of the carrier and together the three aircraft strafed the U-boat, machine-gunning the conning-tower. Some of the U-boat crew were knocked, or jumped, into the sea. The aircraft veered off, thinking the crew were abandoning U-172, but it was not so.

Other crewmen manned the guns and the U-boat opened fire. One shell struck *Ingram*'s quarterdeck, killing one and injuring eight members of the crew. The one sided fight could have only one end, but the crew of U-172 kept firing. The gunnery from the American destroyers was soon on target and U-172 was drifting helplessly round in circles. In six minutes its deck was awash and the crew poured out of the conning-tower as it plunged for the last time.

Oberleutnant Hermann Hofrmann, his 1WO and thirty-three of the crew were rescued. So ended the life of the U-boat, the crew of which had helped to make its former commander a U-boat ace.

CHAPTER EIGHT

LAST MEDITERRANEAN U-BOAT SUNK

In 1940 the *Danziger Werft* secured an order to build thirty Type VIIC U-boats. Between the end of 1940 and the end of 1942, twenty-five had been launched and every one of them was sunk – not one survived the war. The boat U-407, which features in this chapter, and U-413, in the next, were among the victims and it is little wonder that these Danzig-built boats were unpopular with the U-boat men. The U-boat U-407 had been launched on 16 August 1941 and when it was completed, four months later, the 24-year-old *Kapitänleutnant* Ernst-Ulrich Brüller of the 1935 class was appointed as the first commander. All his war service had been as a watch officer or commander in low-numbered U-boats.

It was not until mid-August that U-407 was deemed suitable to be a 'front-boat' and it left the 5th Flotilla U-boat base at Kiel, just one day short of the anniversary of its launching and after an unsuccessful patrol in the North Atlantic joined the 9th Flotilla at Brest on 9 October. Four weeks later U-407 left the French base to join the 29th Flotilla in the Mediterranean, passing through the Straits of Gibraltar on the night of 7/8 November. The U-boat was just one of a group sent to work off Algiers and Oran, and other reinforcements arrived off Gibraltar. A group of seven penetrated the Straits and, at the very time that U-407 was passing through the Straits, the first ship it was to sink, *Viceroy of India*, was taking up its position for the forthcoming invasion of North Africa. Probably the sheer

volume of Allied traffic that was entering the Mediterranean allowed the
U-boats to enter unseen.

The *Viceroy of India* had been launched thirteen years earlier. The
Peninsular and Oriental luxury liner had been ordered, with its owners,
undeterred by the spectre of the depression, for the Bombay run.

Unlike her predecessors. *Viceroy of India* the most luxurious ship to date,
was powered by turbo-electric drive, which could push her through the
water at 19-knots, more smoothly and more quietly than ever before. She
was also the first P&O liner to have an indoor swimming pool; but what
made her special, set her apart from all her rivals before or since, was her
dreamlike opulence. This was not a floating hotel but a lavish stately home,
with an eighteenth-century music room, an Adam-style reading room;
and, most spectacular of all, the first-class smoking room, designed like a
Scots baronial hall with panelled walls and a large fireplace. Pre-war this
was the ship the posh people sailed in to India: port outward, starboard
home. Like many other P&O ships, *Viceroy of India* was requisitioned by the
Ministry of War Transport and was classified for Operation *Torch* as an LSI
– landing ship infantry.

Now, armed with a 6-inch gun, a Bofors, two 12-pounders, sixteen
machine-guns and three depth charges, the wartime displacement must
have been more than the original 19,627-tons.

Along with many similar designated LSI's *Viceroy of India* was assigned to
the landings off Algiers. By the eve of 7 November the convoys with the
advanced forces were well inside the Mediterranean. Algiers stands on the
western shore of Algiers Bay, which lies between Pescade Point and Cape
Matifu and is bordered, for the most part, by a sandy beach. Three beaches
were selected for the Allied landing at Algiers. The *Viceroy of India* was to
operate off 'Apples' which had a release position five or six miles to seaward.
A portion of the fast convoy, of which the ex-liner was part, was due at the
position at 2245 on the 7th, being 'homed' there by HMs/m *Shakespeare*.
Viceroy of India was in this portion, herself carrying the 2nd Battalion
Lancashire Fusiliers and the assault party of the East Surreys. The ships for
the 'Apples' section sighted the submarine ahead at 2214. A few minutes
later they stopped and went to landing stations while the escort carried out
an endless chain of anti-U-boat patrols around them. The troops from the
ex-liner landed at 0110. Although the beach proved very bad and dangerous,
the landings were carried out safely and according to plan.

The next day HMS *Bulolo*, the headquarters ship carrying the Admiral's
flag, entered the harbour and berthed alongside, receiving an enthusastic
welcome from a large crowd of onlookers. Thus the city of Algiers passed

safely into Allied hands.

The difficult part of the operation, ferrying and landing the troops, now successfully completed the seemingly easier part of returning the transports, began the next day and *Viceroy of India* sailed independently from Algiers at 1800 on 10 November. The master of the ship continues with the story:

> We were bound for Gibraltar in ballast. The crew, including twenty-nine gunners, numbered 432, also on board we had twenty-two passengers. After dark we heard aircraft overhead, but saw nothing of them, so continued without firing at them as I did not want to give our position away, the identity of the planes being unknown.
>
> We proceeded without incident until the early morning of the 11th, the weather was fine with good visibility, smooth sea, and easterly wind force 2. We were steering a westerly course, zig-zagging at 18$\frac{1}{2}$ knots when at 0428 we were struck by a torpedo on the port side in the engine room. I understand from those on watch that it was a noisy explosion, there was no flash, but a huge column of water was thrown up to a considerable height. The ship shook violently, all the lights went out and she heeled over 3$\frac{1}{2}$ degrees to port. The upper deck was badly torn and rolled back, but no split in the ship's side was visible above the water line.
>
> The emergency dynamo was brought into action, an SSS message was sent out with the crew standing by. The engines were shattered, but I had great hopes of saving the ship if we could arrange to be towed. At daylight a small drifter came along and signalled, 'How long will you take to sink?' which appeared to me to be rather premature; shortly afterwards a destroyer appeared, and she too signalled to know if we were sinking. This was HMS Boadicea, and I replied that although the ship was sinking slowly, I thought there would be a chance to save her if they would take us in tow, first taking off most of the crew. This was agreed upon, and while the destroyer carried out a U-boat sweep the men got into the boats and all six were successfully lowered. These boats accommodated eighty people, and the six were just sufficient for the personnel on board. They boarded Boadicea, whilst forty of us remained in the *Viceroy of India* as a working party. We made tow lines fast, but the vessel was already 18-feet lower in the water, going down all the time by the stern and listing more heavily, until at 0700 I decided to abandon ship. We held on a little longer, but she continued to sink, and at 0740 we left the ship and boarded Boadicea. She stood by and we watched the vessel slowly sinking until she finally disappeared at 0807, going down by the stern.
>
> We arrived in Gibraltar, landing at 1800 from HMS Boadicea.

Four of the crew had been killed in the explosion. The SSS U-boat attack call had been picked up by German monitoring stations, and the news that U-407 had opened its account within three days of reaching the Mediterranean was most welcome.

It is strange then that, with a potential ace in command, the U-boat did

HMS Eagle – *the carrier with two funnels.*

U-73 which sank Eagle.

HMS Eagle *sinking, taken from HMS* Kenya *with* Glenorchy *in the picture.*

Kapitänleutnant *Helmut Rosenbaum* in *U-73* at *25-metres after the hit on HMS* Eagle.

The 1942 commissioning photograph of U-179. A few months later the whole crew were lost after just one sinking. Outboard is U-178 which enjoyed a much longer and more successful career.

Duchess of Atholl.

Kapitänleutnant *Hans Ibbeken* and *U-178*.

U-172.

Orcades.

Viceroy of India *pre-war.*

U-407.

The crew of Viceroy of India *abandon ship before she finally sinks.*

HMS Birmingham *(pre-war) – the cruiser was escorted to Alexandria by…*

HMS Pathfinder *which was also an escort in Operation* Pedestal.

Royal Mail Steamer Warwick Castle *in peacetime…*

Warwick Castle *at war.*

Kapitänleutnant *Gustav Poel and U-413.*

HMS Warwick – *before conversion to a long-range escort.*

HMS Vidette – *before conversion to a long range escort.*

Kapitänleutnant *Adolf Piening*.

U-155.

Hedgehog – forward firing missiles which exploded on contact with a U-Boat.

HMS Avenger.

Within the image:
O. R.M.S. STRATHALLAN, 23,500 TONS.
arrying First-class and Tourist-class Passengers
India and Australia Mail Service.

Royal Mail Steamer Strathallan *pre-war.*

U-562.

not strike again until the next invasion, the invasion of Sicily nine months later. It was on Saturday, 10 July, that Operation *Husky* commenced. Sicilian coastal defences and communications were bombarded and 3,680 Allied aircraft participated in a prolonged series of raids on the island's airfields.

As has been seen earlier, U-81 harassed Allied transports in harbour and Axis U-boats attacked men-of-war at sea. On 18 July an Italian U-boat attacked HMS *Cleopatra* and on the 23rd U-407 torpedoed HMS *Newfoundland*. Both the cruisers, although damaged, reached Malta safely - in time to hear the news of Mussolini's downfall.

Four months later U-407 attacked another British cruiser, HMS *Birmingham*. The U-boat had been patrolling an area about 70-miles east-south-east of Malta, but on 19 November it moved south and patrolled fifty miles off the coast of Cyrenaica. There was plenty of heavy traffic inshore of the U-boat, but the depth of water there was not great.

An eastbound convoy had been sighted from the air and U-407 was moving towards it, when fortuitously it came across the unescorted cruiser on 28 November. HMS *Birmingham,* with a newly commissioned ship's company, was on passage to the Levant, steaming at 25-knots and zig-zagging. In part, the captain's report reads:

> At 1118, while still making good speed, and six minutes after altering 50-degrees to starboard to the starboard leg of the zig-zag there was a violent explosion under the fo'c'sle. Water was thrown high over the bridge and when the splash had subsided speed was reduced to 10-knots. Then, perhaps half-a-minute after the explosion, I observed very distinctly in the calm sea a swirl or discharge bubble about five cables on the port beam. I was surprised at its nearness. I think the U-boat must have fired from fine on the port bow. Had he fired a salvo at such short range at a broad track angle more than one torpedo must have hit.
>
> The ship swung to port, listed 8-degrees to port and settled by the head. The wheel was put to starboard to put us stern on to the U-boat and the ship answered her helm. The engine room reported main machinery compartments all correct. It was apparent that the torpedo had hit well forward.
>
> The damage control organisation worked smoothly and well, in spite of the fact that most of the forward section damage control parties were knocked out and overcome by gas fumes, and had to be rescued by later arrivals.
>
> The ship was taken closer inshore and then headed east to make Alexandria. Speed was increased to revolutions for 12 and then 14-knots and this latter gave her about 12-knots through the water. At 1225 the Greek destroyer Themistocles and ORP Krakowiak were sighted closing. They were formed on Birmingham as an anti-U-boat screen. I thought it probable that a patrol line of more than one U-boat might be spread along the

known convoy route. It was decided to join the convoy known to be close ahead. At 2155 Faulknor was sighted approaching and was stationed one mile ahead for the night. It became apparent that the convoy had been spurred on to greater speed and that Birmingham could not expect to join up until after daylight. The convoy was overhauled at 0750 the next morning.

Fury and Pathfinder joined the escort later and Birmingham arrived off Alexandria at 0630 on the 30th without further incident, drawing 33-feet forward and 16-feet aft. Fortunately the sea was calm for the whole passage, the flooding boundaries held, and free water on the two lower messdecks was cleared by the pumps.

The casualties were twenty-seven dead, twenty-six wounded hospital cases, and seventy-two others had to receive attention.

It seems probable that the U-boat commander over-estimated *Birmingham's*, speed and that the rest of the salvo passed ahead, the last one hitting the cruiser forward. From the German point of view it was a pity that the cruiser was not sunk, it would have lifted the spirits of old U-boat men, because the previous HMS *Birmingham* was the first British warship ever to sink a U-boat, five days after the outbreak of the Kaiser's war.

So far, U-407 had made three attacks, all against major targets. After the attack U-407, which had been the only U-boat in the area, returned to base and early in 1944 *Kapitänleutnant* Brüller was succeeded by *Oberleutnant* Herbertus Korndorfer.

As a 19-year-old, the new commander attended the first wartime officer's class in 1939 and from its commissioning in October 1941 until July 1943 had the good fortune to serve with Gerd Kelbling in U-593, a most successful boat. After his commander's course and a short stint in U-139, Herbertus Korndörfer took charge of U-407 in January 1944.

Unlike his predecessor the new commander patrolled close inshore, and was prepared to attack any target. On 27 February off the Palestinian coast the small sailing ship *Rod El Farag* was shelled and sank; two days later, a little further north, the British tanker *Ensis* of 6,207-tons was torpedoed and damaged.

The next patrol was off the coast of Cyrenaica and on 16 April a good torpedo attack was made on two 7,000-ton American ships. The steamers were off Derna when hit. *Thomas G Masaryk* was torpedoed and damaged and subsequently towed to Alexandria, but it was declared a total loss but *Meyer London* was sunk on the spot. These were the last successes for the U-boat.

In the middle of the year the ex-commander of the Mediterranean U-boats U-421 and U-596, *Oberleutnant* Hans Kolbus, was appointed to command U-407, which had been fitted with a schnorkel.

In July the abortive attempt on Hitler's life took place and although it hardly affected the *Kriegsmarine* Admiral Dönitz issued a general order, part of which said:

> The Kriegsmarine *stands true to its oath, in proven loyalty to the Führer, unconditional in readiness for battle. Take orders only from me and your own commanders so that errors through false instructions will be impossible.*

When U-407 ventured to sea for the last time, there was a groan from the crew, for they were carrying a passenger, a war correspondent. So not only were they in a Danzig-built boat, but they now had the added burden of a guest. To the superstitious among them it could only bring bad luck, and of course, they were proved right.

The U-boat had been to sea for over a week when a powerful squadron of escort carriers, cruisers and destroyers on its way to carry out offensive sweeps in the Aegean, prior to a landing, chanced upon it.

In the evening of 18 September the Polish destroyer ORP *Garland* was detached from the force and ordered to proceed to the eastward on patrol. While on course at twenty knots smoke was sighted about eight miles off. Course was altered towards and a visual signal flashed to Captain D, but as *Garland* was down wind nothing was sighted behind the smoke and no echo was obtained on radar at a range of three miles. When the range had closed to 700-yards, speed was reduced to ten knots and at 400-yards an object, resembling a stick or galley-funnel, was sighted as the source of the smoke. This, however, was not identified as a schnorkel until the range had closed to 200-yards, when a periscope was seen some three feet abaft the funnel. The Polish destroyer now sent an 'Immediate' signal confirming a U-boat sighting, but its text was not immediately decoded owing to the movements of the other ships in dispersing to night stations and changing from visual signalling to R/T and W/T.

Until *Garland* was 200-yards off, U-407 was quite unaware of the fact that it had been detected, but then it dived on a northerly course. It had no time to acquaint U-boat headquarters of the situation.

Garland immediately altered course for the diving position. Initial asdic contact was then obtained on the port side at a range of 700-yards. A hedgehog attack was now delivered, although contact was lost at 520-yards. No results accrued from this attack, by the forward throwing projectiles, and no explosions were heard.

The rear admiral of the escort carriers now ordered the destroyers HMS *Troubridge* and HMS *Terpsichore* to proceed in support of *Garland*, which they did, while the other British destroyers *Zetland* and *Brecon* were diverted and ordered to close the position from the south. On sighting *Garland* at 1800, *Troubridge* closed *Garland*'s markers, endeavouring to obtain contact, while *Terpsichore* commenced a square search at a distance of three miles from the position. As *Garland* had reported losing contact after her first attack, a line abreast search at 7-knots, passing close to the original markers, on a northerly course, was ordered.

In the course of this sweep *Troubridge* gained asdic contact at 1,200-yards. This was classified as a U-boat which appeared to be moving at 4-knots. The ship was now manoeuvred into position for an attack, with depth charges being set at 100 and 225-feet. Nothing was observed from this attack, but at 1850 contact was regained and the U-boat plotted still on a northerly course but at reduced speed. Despite the lack of visible results it was evident that this attack must have shaken the U-boat crew badly.

While *Troubridge* held the echo *Terpsichore* came up on the starboard quarter of U-407, eventually gaining contact at a range of 1,200-yards. Meanwhile *Zetland* and *Brecon* were ordered to commence a box search round the hunting vessels at a distance of three miles. Later *Brecon* was ordered to join the hunt, approaching from the southward in order to obtain contact from astern. This was done and the U-boat appeared to be zig-zagging wildly at speeds of up to 3-knots. Unfortunately *Brecon* crossed *Troubridge*'s bow as she closed, thereby causing the latter to lose contact. This was soon regained as a few minutes later *Brecon* picked up an echo thought to be the U-boat. The echo faded, however, and it was not until 2145 that firm contact was again established by *Troubridge* and *Brecon*. The U-boat now appeared to be moving at 2-knots.

At 2235 another attack was carried out by *Troubridge*, using a ten charge pattern set to 500 and 850-feet. It had been expected, before the attack, that the U-boat would not be deep, hence the depth settings employed. On the run in, however, the target was held to 250-yards, indicating that the U-boat had only gone to a moderate depth. On this assumption, the settings were too deep, and, although probably little material damage to the U-boat resulted from this attack, the moral effect on the crew was probably considerable, as hydrophone effect and tank blowing noises were reported frequently during the next quarter of an hour.

Contact was lost only for a short period after *Troubridge*'s second attack, being regained then by *Terpsichore* and *Brecon*. No attack was made, however, until all three ships were in contact, but as soon as *Troubridge* had regained the target, *Terpsichore* was sent in. This latter ship on regaining contact had heard whistle effects from the U-boat. The depth settings used for the attack were 250 and 385-feet. However, contact was lost at 400 –

yards and no results were observed.

The U-boat commander now made an alteration of course in an attempt to evade his pursuers. This was held until 0100 when an alteration to port was noticed, followed by a final alteration to the northward, U-407 weaving at slow speed. From these movements it was appreciated that it would endeavour to make the islands some twenty miles to the northward.

Weather conditions at this time were such that difficulty was experienced in holding the target by all three ships. In view of this, Captain D decided to withhold further attacks until dawn unless at least two ships were in firm contact. However, one last attack before the night period ended was decided upon, and *Terpsichore* who had been in firm contact for a short time, was ordered to carry this out. The U-boat at this time was noticed to have made a large alteration of course to starboard, thereby causing much manoeuvring on the part of *Terpsichore* to gain a good attacking position. As a result, some delay was caused in making the attack, but at 0430 the run-in was commenced.

The range had been opened to about 1,000 yards and the depth charges were ready for firing, when suddenly U-407 surfaced on the port bow, passing rapidly aft down the port side on a north-westerly course. Fire was opened immediately with close-range weapons, several hits being observed on the conning-tower and hull.

As the target drew clear of *Terpsichore*'s stern, *Troubridge* opened fire, being joined by *Garland* with some long-range shots, while other ships joined in the general action as opportunity afforded. Several of the crew were then seen to abandon the U-boat but it was not fully appreciated at this time, due to the poor light, that the U-boat had been completely abandoned. *Garland* was therefore sent in to destroy it with a shallow pattern. Although a straddle was obtained the U-boat was still afloat when the water subsided. *Troubridge* now fired a torpedo but missed as the target still had a slight headway and was turning. Gunfire was again opened but at 0500 U-407 sank in 220-fathoms.

To complete the destruction *Zetland*, whilst in brief asdic contact, dropped a final depth charge pattern on the position. Thereafter, ships proceeded to rescue forty-eight survivors, including the commander.

The destruction of U-407 was essentially the result of *Garland* sighting smoke at eight miles. Her initial attack by hedgehog, while failing to damage the U-boat, contributed largely to a lowering of morale of the U-boat's crew; when they heard the projectiles swishing through the water, they recognized them as the 'secret weapon' and were alarmed.

The first depth charge attack by *Troubridge* was considered to have been accurate and caused considerable damage. A big shock was felt, lights were extinguished, water pumps ceased to function and water, which caused the U-boat to trim by the stern, had to be pumped by hand. All gauges became defective and the air began to deteriorate, while the speed of the boat was reduced to 3-knots.

Troubridge's second attack was described as being near, but did no further damage, as the U-boat had dived deep. The final attack by *Terpsichore* also did not cause further damage, but contributed to the surfacing of the U-boat.

When the order was given to abandon the U-boat, several members of the crew escaped through an escape hatch while the boat was still submerged. The war correspondent, the 1WO and four or five ratings were killed. The survivors expressed surprise at seeing so many destroyers as it had been thought that they were being attacked by only one ship.

The last message from U-407 had been picked up ashore on 12 September 1944 – it was the last message any 29th Flotilla wireless operator would ever receive, for U-407 was the last U-boat to be sunk at sea in the Mediterranean. Two others, in port, Hans Kolbus's former boat, U-596 and U-565 were sunk in a USAAF bombing raid on Salamis five days later. It was the final elimination of U-boats in the Mediterranean. Gradually wartime restrictions were lifted: ships no longer had to sail in convoy; and at the end of October the Commander-in-Chief of the Mediterranean noted in his war diary: 'For the first time in five years merchantmen are now permitted to burn navigation lights in certain areas.'

CHAPTER NINE

A REMARKABLE COINCIDENCE

The sinkings in this chapter throw up a coincidence that has not been highlighted previously.

The main casualty, *Warwick Castle*, had a brush with a U-boat, or boats, in the first week of the war. The Union Castle liner was returning from South Africa and on Friday, 8 September, 1939, a look-out reported:

> *We sighted two U-boats. The first we saw ahead of us, and we immediately began to manoeuvre, zig-zagging about, and slipped it. Shortly afterwards another U-boat, it may have been the same one, although I scarcely think so, was sighted about three miles ahead. A call went out to British naval vessels from the liner and.nothing more was seen of the U-boats.*

At this time the liner was sailing under its peacetime colours and was not armed. The next time it was sighted by a U-boat, three years later, it was a different story. By now, daubed all over in an anonymous battleship grey, it carried a 6-inch gun, three 12-pounders, fourteen Oerlikons, nine twin Hotchkisses, various small weapons and four depth charges. To operate this armament the crew included fifteen naval gunners, fifteen army gunners and a naval gunnery officer.

On 15 February, 1942, Singapore surrendered and *Warwick Castle* had been in the last convoy carrying troops and stores from Bombay to bolster up the beleaguered garrison. The liner was attacked by Japanese aircraft while passing through the Bangka Strait but escaped undamaged.

Nine months later *Warwick Castle* again carried troops, this time for Operation *Torch*, described elsewhere in this book, and it was torpedoed while returning to the United Kingdom from this operation, off Lisbon. The U-boat that sank the liner was U-413, under the command of *Kapitänleutnant* Gustav Poel. This Type VIIC boat, launched at the Danziger Werft on 15 January 1942 was on its very first war patrol, having left the 8th Flotilla base at Kiel on 22 October.

The 20,107-ton *Warwick Castle*, flying the red ensign, left Gibraltar in convoy for the Clyde on 12 November, sailing light. The convoy comprised fourteen ships, formed into six columns and included two escort carriers, HM ships *Biter* and *Dasher*, all returning from Operation *Torch*, and they were escorted by eight destroyers. A convoy conference was held at 1445 on the day of sailing, and owing to this and the necessity for destroyers to proceed at 1545, very little time was available for the commodore, senior officer ocean escort in HMS *Biter* and destroyer commanding officers to discuss detailed arrangements for the conduct of the escort. In view of the known heavy concentration of U-boats in the western approaches to the Straits, the importance of the ships in the convoy, and the odd assortment of destroyers forming the anti-U-boat escort, this was felt to be unfortunate, but was inevitable in the circumstances. The best that could be done in the few minutes available was to agree that the provisions of Western Approaches Command Instructions would be adhered to as closely as possible.

The weather was calm during the first night at sea, but during the forenoon of 13 November the wind freshened considerably from the northward, becoming Force 6 to 7 by noon and increasing to gale force by nightfall. A heavy swell and rough sea made progress extremely wet for the destroyers, who were only able to maintain the convoy speed of 12 to 13-knots with difficulty. These conditions resulted in severe reduction of the destroyers' anti-U-boat efficiency, also involving some damage; *Achates* lost her topmast, *Eskdale* reported losing her asdic dome and had her motor boat smashed by seas, and *Albrighton* reported a defective asdic dome due to heavy pounding. In addition, severe 'quenching' of the asdic was experienced due to the motion, and the almost continuous heavy spray over the ships seriously impaired the efficiency of look-outs. As far as the Hunt Class destroyers were concerned, the manning of the forward guns was out of the question, and the ability to fight the after mounting with any degree of efficiency was very much in doubt.

It was in such weather conditions, a rough sea, heavy rain squalls in which visibility was from moderate to nil that, at 0847, a visual signal was sent by the commodore: '*Winchester Castle* has just reported a U-boat diving bearing 270-degrees distance 8-miles.'

While action was being taken by the destroyer escort to deal with the report, two rockets were seen to be fired from a ship on the port side of the convoy. The ship was *Warwick Castle* which had been zig-zagging for the past hour at a speed of 11-knots. Her first officer recalls;

> *At 0850 we were struck by a torpedo on the port side in the way of Nos 2 and 3 holds. Nothing was seen of the track of the torpedo, nor of the U-boat, although all gunners were closed up at action stations. It was not a very loud explosion, and I do not think much water was thrown up, but hatch covers from the two holds were blown right over the crow's nest; these appeared to be scorched, but no flame was seen with the explosion. When I came up from below, I found that No 3 hold was already full of water, but I could not see any hole in the ship's side, nor was the deck split.*
>
> *I stopped the engines, all the crew went to their emergency stations and boats were lowered as far as the embarkation rail. At 0900 a second torpedo struck the ship in almost the same place on the port side. This was a much louder explosion, there was no flame, but a huge column of water was thrown up. I think this torpedo went into the hole made by the first one and exploded inside the ship. Again nothing was seen of the track. This explosion brought down the foremast and everything in the vicinity was wrecked. The ship at once settled by the head and listed very heavily to port. No 2 hold was now rapidly filling, and at 0905 the captain ordered, 'Abandon ship', which order I passed verbally to those on deck and informed the engine-room staff by telephone.*
>
> *Fortunately no boats had been damaged and these were all lowered into the water without mishap, although it was rather difficult on the starboard side owing to the heavy list to port; this side was the weather side, but the boats were fitted with Schatt skates and slid down into the water without being damaged.*
>
> *The list to port was increasing, and at 0920 I climbed down a scrambling net and swam to a Carley float; I believe I was one of the last to leave the ship. The last I saw of the master and chief officer was when they were both standing on the bridge. I did not see the ship sink, but I understand she went down at 1015, the fore part having already broken off abreast of where she was struck by the torpedoes, and sunk. I was hanging on to the Carley float for over two hours, until rescued by HMS Achates. I think I was one of the last to be picked up by this ship, but HMS Vansittart and a converted Cross-Channel steamer Valentina, were also rescuing survivors from the many rafts, boats and ALC's, which were spread over the sea for a considerable area. It was terribly rough with big seas breaking over rafts and boats, so I think many of those who are missing were probably drowned whilst waiting to be picked up, especially those on rafts, as although there were plenty of ropes to hang on to, it was very difficult to remain on a raft owing to the huge waves breaking over them all the time.*

After the torpedo attack *Eskdale* and *Vansittart* were detached to hunt the U-boat and do everything possible to keep it down until the convoy was out of sight. After which *Eskdale* was ordered to rejoin and *Vansittart* to stand by *Warwick Castle*. *Leinster*, who had been detailed as rescue ship, also stayed behind to pick up survivors, ultimately following the convoy in company with *Vansittart*. These two ships between them rescued 150 survivors and a further 140 were picked up by *Achates*. Sixty of the 295 crew and fifty-four of the 133 service personnel passengers were lost. Gustav Poel knew exactly which ship he had sunk and notified U-boat headquarters. The U-boat was attacked from the air before it arrived at Brest, to join the 1st U-boat Flotilla, at the end of its first patrol on 25 November. Hamburg-born 25-year-old Gustav Poel and his watch officer, *Oberleutnant* Dietrich Sachse, just twenty days younger than his commander, and their young crew – were acclaimed on reaching their French base. Any success on a first patrol was an achievement, but a large enemy troopship sunk on a first patrol by a new U-boat was probably unique.

The crew were to spend Christmas ashore, but not the New Year, for on 27 December, U-413 left Brest on its second patrol, to the North Atlantic. The U-boat was one of many seeking out homeward-bound convoys from North America to Britain. The convoy it fell upon was SC117, obviously an ill-disciplined one as its commodore reported: 'I have been on twenty-nine convoys and have never seen such bad stationkeeping as during the first two days out of New York.' Some ships detached to Halifax and others joined. Included in the latter was the 3,556-ton Greek ship *Mount Mycale*.

The convoy commodore continued to complain; one Flower Class escort was out of position, one merchant vessel made too much smoke, another 'sparks badly from the funnel'. On the night of 20 January, the convoy ran into a heavy south-south-westerly gale and blizzard and some ships hove to without orders and some became not under control. The order was therefore given to heave to. One of the serious features of this blizzard was that for some time afterwards merchant ships and escorts were dangerously conspicuous at night due to the coating of ice still present on the hull and upperworks.

Course was resumed by the convoy on the following afternoon and it was probably first sighted by U-boats 24-hours later for that evening a signal was made by the Commander-in-Chief US Fleet indicating that a wolf-pack was forming up on the convoy.

During the night H/F D/F bearings indicated U-boats in contact on both sides of the convoy. At 2253 an SSS signal was heard which faded before a call sign or position was made. *Mount Mycale* was the victim, U-

413 had struck again. The success was signalled to headquarters with the information that the victim was a straggler from the convoy.

On the 24th the convoy's course was altered from 330 degrees to 050 degrees, in the hope of passing under the stern of the U-boat which appeared to be moving ahead of the convoy. This ploy worked as only another straggler was sunk, by U-624, the next day. Just two ships from the convoy were torpedoed but the Report of Proceedings penned by the commodore probably kept the Admiralty busy for many days.

Convoy SC118 originally consisted of sixty-three ships. On 5 February U-262 made the first attack and later in the day U-413 sank the 5,376-ton American steamer *West Portal*. Eight ships were sunk by U-402, including the gallant rescue ship *Toward*, mentioned in the next chapter. A total of thirteen ships was lost to the pack of twenty U-boats. The U-boats U-265 and U-624 were sunk and two others were badly damaged.

Two victory pennants were flying when U-413 returned to Brest on 17 February. The crew were ashore for most of March while their colleagues were playing havoc with the Atlantic convoys; U-413 sailed on 30 March, but by then the seas were nearly clear.

Only one attack was carried out on the patrol, that in the afternoon of 25 April when south of Iceland. An attack was carried out against a large ship but only end of run detonations were heard. Really the big bonus of the patrol was that U-413 managed to keep out of the way during May when forty-one U-boats were sunk by the Allies and Admiral Dönitz was forced to recall the Atlantic boats. It was 13 June before U-413 arrived back at Brest.

The Allied sea and air escorts were searching the Bay of Biscay with mixed fortunes during the summer of 1943 and it was not until 8 September that U-413 put to sea again, though it had to return to base ten days later with a defect. Two weeks later all was well and U-413 left Brest for a North Atlantic patrol on 2 October. This patrol was a barren one and no successes were reported when the U-boat returned on 21 November. Those Berliners aboard fortunate enough to get home leave must have wished they were back at sea as this was the time the RAF was blitzing the captial with continual night raids. For those crew members who remained at Brest there was more rest, the bombers were concentrating on Germany.

It was not until 3 February that U-413 was ordered to sea again to the Atlantic and then patrol round the Scilly Isles area, looking particularly to attack convoys sailing between Portsmouth and the Bristol Channel area and to make a reconnaissance of the inshore shipping routes.

On this patrol Gnats were carried, torpedoes that were guided on to their target acoustically, to strike the noisiest part of a target. Unfortunately, the first two fired, in a night attack on 11 February, were heard to detonate at the end of their runs after eleven and twelve minutes without hitting their intended convoy victims. In the next few days the U-boat moved closer inshore, to the North Cornish coast. The first victim was not to be a ship in convoy but an escort destroyer that had been sent to hunt for the U-boat as the Admiralty had got wind of the plans for U-413. The victim was to be HMS *Warwick* the veteran 'V and W' Class destroyer. This is the remarkable coincidence – a U-boat that had sunk the former liner *Warwick Castle* should now sink HMS *Warwick*!

The old 1,100-ton destroyer had been built by Hawthorne Leslie and launched at the end of 1917 and completed in March 1918 just in time to be Admiral Roger Keyes' flagship for the Zeebrugge raid at the end of April. The destroyer was damaged by a mine in the blockade of Ostend but succeeded in reaching Dover and like many of her class, and indeed her former admiral, was pressed into service, and did good work, in Hitler's war.

From January to May 1943 *Warwick* was in Dundee being converted to a long-range escort. The forward boiler was removed and the space fitted as a fuel tank to provide additional endurance for North Atlantic convoy work. The destroyer had left Ardrossan after a refit on 15 February and four days later was with other destroyers hunting U-413.

That evening, between 2100 and 2200 hours, the skipper of a fishing vessel had seen U-413 skulking among vessels working in the area off Trevose Head Cornwall. He did not report it at the time. On that night *Warwick*, with another Kaiser's War destroyer, HMS *Scimitar*, was carrying out an anti-U-boat patrol in an area, which the Germans were exploring for the first time since 1940, between Pendeen Head and Trevose Head. A very great number of fishing vessels were operating within four miles westward of the searched channel. They were bottom fishing with either beam or Otter trawls. Owing to the encumbrance these vessels caused to the patrol and the great difficulty of detecting an enemy by radar, a signal was made advising that trawlers were greatly hindering the patrol and air co-operation was requested.

At 0815 on the 20th an echo was obtained by asdic and attacked. This proved to be a shoal of fish and thereafter a large number of non-sub echoes of a fish nature were obtained. Buckets on ropes were streamed over the side and the stunned fish were quickly taken to the galley.

At 1135 the asdic operator in *Warwick* commenced to tune his set. In view of the number of trawlers in the vicinity permission had been given for this to be carried out. At 'tot-time' ten minutes later, while *Warwick* was on the southward leg of the patrol and in a position fifteen miles from Trevose Head a violent explosion occurred in way of the after magazine which cut the ship in half abaft the bulkhead of the captain's cabin. The after part of the ship floated away and the bulkhead abaft the engine room held for about four minutes, the forward part of the ship thus remaining buoyant. At the end of this four minute period she suddenly turned over, the watertight integrity being destroyed, probably by the collapse of the after bulkhead of the engine room; this collapse may have been aggravated by the fact that one or both propeller shafts were continuing to revolve, for although the steam throttles had been closed, no astern steam had been applied before the engine room had to be abandoned on account of fire.

While the stern of *Warwick* was still visible HM destroyers *Scimitar* and *Wensleydale* attacked an asdic contact, classified as a U-boat by both ships, about a mile away to the south-westward.

Despite the searching destroyers locating U-413, there was still a question mark about the cause of the loss of the *Warwick*. Possible causes, such as a mine, British or German, or an internal explosion from the warhead magazine or the inflammable store – the spirit room was open at the time for getting up spirits at tot-time, were all explored. It was not until the fishing boat skipper told of 'a strange vessel, darkened except for the display of a lantern of unusual appearance which was proceeding faster and more steadily in the water than the fishing vessels' that the loss of Admiral Keyes's ex-flagship was credited to a U-boat. There were ninety-three survivors, including the destroyer's captain.

The U-boat commander had shown great enterprise and put his boat at some risk by mingling with the fishing vessels but the result justified his action. Having seen the I 25 pendant painted on the destroyer's side Gustav Poel was able to signal U-boat headquarters of his success. The following day, having moved westward out to sea, there was disappointment for U-413. In an attack just before midnight, on a destroyer and a steamer, U-413 heard one end of run Gnat detonation after 2 minutes 35 seconds and after firing a FAT spread of circling torpedoes another end of run detonation was heard after 13 minutes. A possible 'damaged' was reported on the steamer, but this proved not to be so. By having moved out from the scene of the *Warwick* sinking U-413 avoided the ships and aircraft sent to search for it.

On 21 March the award of the Knight's Cross to Gustav Poel was promulgated much to the delight of the crew of U-413. At the time they did not know he would only be their commander for another six days at sea and they returned to Brest on 27 March.

In April Gustav Poel was replaced as commander by Dietrich Sachse, who, it will be remembered, commissioned the U-boat with him as the watch officer. Dietrich Sachse served with U-413 for a year before taking his commander's course and was then commander of U-1162 for three months. He was in charge of the training boat U-28, out of Neustadt, when it sank accidentally in the Baltic, in March.

The crew of U-413 therefore had mixed feelings about their new commander. He was known to the crew veterans, but he had been unfortunate enough to lose a U-boat! His bad luck was to continue, for the day U-413 next sailed from Brest was D-Day, 6 June, when there was maximum Allied air activity. It was therefore no surprise when it was attacked two days later by Halifax F-Freddie of No 502 Squadron operating out of St David's. The U-boat returned to Brest the following day.

During those first vital four days from D-Day Coastal Command sighted thirty-seven U-boats, of which twenty-four were attacked. In every case the U-boat fought back desperately with flak, but six were sunk during these four days, so U-413 can be said to have been fortunate.

The U-boat slipped past the anti-torpedo net into the bunker and remained in the Brittany port until its eighth patrol on 2 August, this time to the English Channel. Just three days later the dam-busting No 617 Squadron Lancasters made Brest their target, carrying Barnes Wallis's 12,000-lb Tallboy bombs. There were five direct hits on the bunkers and more in future raids but U-413 was reaching its position and was soon to run into problems of its own.

Operation *Neptune*, the naval side of Operation *Overlord*, the invasion, was still very much in operation and the Royal Navy was keeping a close watch for U-boats in the Channel. In the middle of August eight U-boats were active in the area. On the 6th U-736 and on the 15th U-741 were sunk by surface escorts.

The U-boacs U-480, U-764, U-989, as well as U-413, were stalking Channel traffic supporting the invasion.

Oberleutnant Dietrich Sachse was the first commander to attack convoy ETC72. He torpedoed what he described as an 8,000-ton ship, but his claim was not accurate, for it was the British steamer *Saint Enogat*, of 2,360-tons, that he sank.

It was the sinking of this vessel at 1055 on 19 August that was to cause the loss of the U-boat 24 hours later. After sinking the steamer the U-boat had been located and attacked by the surface escort, but had escaped. However, HMS *Forester*, which had been launched not very far away in Cowes, Isle of Wight, ten years previously, persisted on the track of U-413.

Her captain decided to remain on the longitude and downtide from the scene of the attack and his patience was rewarded the following morning when a contact was made and held on the U-boat. Other destroyers, the Hunt Class *Wensleydale* and *Melbreak* and the 'V and W' Class *Vidette*, were called to assist and the end was near for U-413. It was appropriate that after the U-boat had sunk the old 'V and W' class *Warwick* that another of that class, *Vidette*, should be responsible for the U-boat's demise. In fact *Vidette* had already sunk U-125 and had a hand in the sinking of U-274 and U-292 in the past fifteen months. Now, with her hedgehog forward throwing projectiles, fitted at Sheerness dockyard, she was again to play a vital role.

Forester gained the initial contact at a range of 2,100 yards when her speed was 20-knots, a most creditable performance. The location was 25-miles off Beachy Head on the Sussex coast. At 0824 on 20 August *Forester* reported that she was in firm contact. Just before 0900 the other destroyers arrived and *Forester*'s echo sounder indicated an object at a depth of 15-fathoms, in 32-fathoms of water. *Wensleydale* confirmed the contact was a U-boat and *Forester* attacked with depth charges. The U-boat then proceeded on a northerly course at 4-knots. *Vidette* was warned to stand by with hedgehog. Then a heavy rain squall reduced visibility to nil for several minutes. At 0934 *Vidette* attacked. The projectiles were observed to fall on the course bearing of the target, from *Wensleydale*, and two distinct explosions were heard some seconds before the remainder of the pattern exploded on the bottom. Thirteen minutes later light oil was beginning to appear near the disturbance caused by the hedgehog explosions. This attack had been extremely accurate and caused U-413 to leak badly forward and it became heavy and went to the bottom.

Wensleydale next carried out an attack with depth charges; a five-charge diamond pattern was fired with throwers set to 100-feet and rails to 150-feet. A diesel oil slick resulted and some air bubbles surfaced.

Suddenly, one of the U-boat's crew appeared on the surface. He was quickly rescued by *Wensleydale* and he told his interrogator that the U-boat was badly smashed. His insistence on this story, to save his comrades, and a lack of wreckage of any sort, and movement of the U-boat indicated on the plot decided the captain of *Wensleydale* that further attacks were necessary. When the sound of tanks being blown were clearly audible from the loud speaker on the bridge it was decided to discourage further resistance. At 1045 *Forester* attacked with depth charges. The attack was accurate and oil slick increased in volume.

Wensleydale then attacked as another destroyer, HMS *Watchman*, joined – but by then it was all over.

That final attack by *Wensleydale* undoubtedly split the hull of U-413 abreast the commander's cabin and wardroom since all identifiable clothes and personal effects obtained were those of officers; and the fact that confidential books were blown to the surface confirmed this.

The one survivor, the engineering officer, had gone forward to the torpedo room to investigate the damage caused by the hedgehog hits. He found the water rising fast and there was only one way to get out, upwards! The forward escape hatch afforded him the opportunity to float the 90 feet to the surface and safety. He could count himself fortunate that no depth charges were being fired at this time.

With the loss of U-413, once again a U-boat had been lost on the patrol after a long-serving commander had left the boat.

Kapitänleutnant Gustav Poel had pulled off two remarkable coincidences, putting two torpedoes, at an interval, into the same spot on *Warwick Castle* and then sinking the other, destroyer, representative from the county town of *Warwick*.

CHAPTER TEN

THE AVENGER

Adolf Piening'was commander of U-155 for two-and-a-half years – both he and his boat survived the war. This in itself was a rare achievement as the U-boat arm had an 80-percent loss of personnel. Without doubt, using any yardstick, Adolf Piening was a U-boat ace.

Born on 16 September 1910 in Süderende, Adolf Piening attended the 1930 officers' training class. When opting for U-boats he was fortunate to serve under Heinrich Bleichrodt in U-48, the most successful U-boat of the war, for ten months before getting his own command. His boat, U-155, was the larger Type IXC boat, and the third of the type launched from the yard of AG Weser at Bremen. The boat carried twenty-two torpedoes for its six torpedo tubes, four forward and two aft.

While the boat was being constructed during the second quarter of 1941 Winston Churchill ordered Bomber Command to divert from their main objective to concentrate on the destruction of U-boats. He said:

> We must take the offensive against the U-boat and the Focke-Wulf wherever we can and whenever we can. The U-boat at sea must be hunted, the U-boat in the building yard or in dock must be bombed.

The list of targets selected by the Air Ministry included the three U-boat shipbuilding yards at Kiel, the two at Hamburg and those at Vegesack and Bremen. Thus, on the night of 8/9 May Hamburg and Bremen were the targets for Bomber Command. The shipbuilding yards and city targets were the main objective for the bomber force of 133 aircraft that raided Bremen, but not one bomb struck the AG Weser yard. It was just as well for U-155 which was vulnerable, waiting to be launched.

Three nights later Bomber Command mounted another attack against both ports and eighty-one aircraft set out for Bremen. This raid was more successful, the bombs dropping in the harbour area and a floating dock at AG Weser was sunk. Later in the day, on that Monday, 12 May, the blocks were knocked away and U-155 was launched; it had survived the first two of many aircraft attacks it was to experience in its four year career.

Kapitänleutnant Adolf Piening, who had completed the commanding officer's course, was appointed to command U-155 in August. The crew were drafted and the officers appointed. After acceptance and sea trials in the Baltic the boat was ready to commence its first war cruise, from Kiel, on 7 February, 1942. The boat sailed from the 1st Flotilla base and it would be over three years before it would return.

The area for the large bunkered-boat's first patrol was off the American seaboard. The Americans had been in the war for only two months and Admiral Dönitz correctly estimated there would be some initial easy pickings.

He had recorded in his war diary:

> *There is an area in which the assembly of ships at the few points of departure of Atlantic convoys is in single-ship traffic. Here, therefore, is an opportunity of getting at enemy merchant ships in conditions which elsewhere have ceased almost completely for a long time. Further, in the American coastal area, there can hardly be any question of an efficient patrol, at least a patrol used to U-boats. Attempts must be made as quickly as possible to utilize these advantages, which will disappear shortly, and to 'beat the drum' along the American coast.*

The new U-boat, on its first patrol was in the third wave of U-boats assigned to Operation *Drumbeat* and at the end of the month U-155 sighted the outward-bound convoy ONS67 some 600-miles north-east of Cape Race, Newfoundland, on a south-westerly course. For more than three days the U-boat was used as a shadower while five more U-boats that were within a 2-300-mile radius were called in to make a pack attack. As well as U-155, U-558, U-162, U-158 and U-587 all made successful attacks in which eight ships were sunk, of which six were large tankers and no U-boats were lost. Adolf Piening was the first to attack. His very first salvo was aimed at two tankers and a freighter.

The first live torpedoes fired from the boat left the tubes just after 0700 on 22 February. The Norwegian 1,800-ton freighter *Sama* was the first victim and the British tanker *Adellen* of 7,984-tons was the second. When torpedoed, the tanker tried to fire white rockets but they would not work so snow flakes were fired instead. There was no time to send out a W/T message.

The tanker was armed and carried four Navy and six Army gunners amongst its crew of fifty. It had left Belfast a week earlier and was bound for Trinidad in ballast. The master said:

> We proceeded, in convoy, without incident until the Sama was struck by a torpedo, and at the same time we experienced a slight shivering in the ship and she immediately commenced to sink.
>
> There was no noise at all, no smoke, but a small burst of flame came through the engine room skylight. From mv experience the slight vibration was Just tike putting the helm over and pushing up against a sea with the bow, and if the ship had not commenced to settle, we should never have known that we had been torpedoed. I think the torpedo must have struck on the port side, but I am not really sure. There was no visible damage at all on deck, but the bulkhead between the engine room and the bunkers must have been opened by the explosion as the water poured through into the engine room. The lights remained on for a few seconds and then went out. The ship immediately settled aft with the water breaking round the poop deck, and within three minutes the ship's bow reared up and the ship sank stern first.
>
> Everybody was reported to have been on deck before the ship sank, but we were not able to get any boats away. The port boat was washed back on deck but three rafts floated off as the ship sank. There were two men on one raft, four men on another, but there was nobody on the third raft. The rescue ship Toward came along almost immediately and was amongst the survivors within a few minutes.
>
> The captain of Toward afterwards told me that he saw about forty red life Jacket lights in the water, but owing to the inadequacy of the boat and boat's crew, they were unable to get round to the men in the water very quickly. It was very cold and I was very nearly exhausted when picked up after 90-minutes in the water. I was unable to get into the boar on my own, and three of the five members of the boat's crew had to lift me into the boat. There were only eleven other survivors rescued. I was taken on board Toward and we continued to Halifax where we arrived on 1 March.

Post-war records show that U-155 must have missed the second tanker that it had targeted. The rest of the boats in the pack attacked the convoy two days later.

It was a full two weeks before the next victim, a Brazilian ship, was torpedoed east of Cape Hatteras off the American coast. She was the 7,874-ton *Arabitan* and became the last ship sunk in the very successful first patrol.

The base allocated for U-155 to return to was Lorient, the base that Kretschmer, Prien and Schepke, who had all failed to return exactly a year earlier, had used and which had become known as 'the base of the aces'. Fittingly Adolf Piening was to fall into the pattern and the boat continued to use the base for the rest of its active patrol life.

The U-boat returned across the Atlantic, charts for the French coast were consulted, the escort boat met and U-155 soon entered the River Scorfe and secured at Lorient – it was 27 March.

The crew spent less than a month ashore as U-155 was ordered to the Caribbean on Hitler's birthday, 20 April. The U-boat reached its patrol area and Adolf Piening, on sighting Trinidad, must have felt the same satisfaction that Columbus did on first discovering the West Indian island in 1498 after his long voyage.

The U-boat laid off Port of Spain for four days; during this time heavy outward and inward-bound traffic along the route to Barbados and other destinations continued day and night. There was a strong, but careless, air patrol but there was no methodical sea patrol and no lights burning. On 14 May, in a night attack off Trinidad, U-155 torpedoed and sank a fast freighter, the 2,483-ton Belgian *Brabant*.

Three days later the fully loaded British tanker *San Victoria*, of 8,136-tons, was left in a sinking condition after two torpedo hits in a night attack and the 7,667-ton American ship *Challenger* followed five hours later.

Adolf Piening sent a signal to U-boat headquarters saying he intended to operate on the tanker route along the north coast of Venezuela during the full moon period. A signal came back ordering him to strictly observe the three mile limit. The U-boat commander also suggested that Port of Spain would be suitable for mining operations, as mine hits would be taken to be torpedo hits.

On 19 May U-155 had a rare double miss on a freighter and for its trouble was chased for two hours by a four-funnelled destroyer and other patrol vessels. The next day the U-boat picked up a large convoy but was driven off when attempting a night attack.

However, using hydrophone data, the Panamanian 7,795-ton tanker *Sylvan Arrow* was torpedoed and sunk in the early afternoon off Trinidad. A torpedo was fired at another tanker but this missed. Success was following success at three day intervals and again, on the 23rd, another Panamanian steamer, *Watsonville* of 2,200-tons, reported it was sinking after a torpedo attack in the darkness by U-155. The U-boat reported that the freighter was on a south-westerly course and at the same time also reported that Kingston Roads, St Vincent, were empty.

Five days later an American ship, *Jack* of 2,622-tons, was sunk in the Caribbean sea after a morning torpedo attack. A similar sized Norwegian ship, *Baghdad*, was torpedoed and sunk in another morning torpedo attack two days later. It was on this day, 30 May, that U-155 headed eastwards for base, where on arrival two weeks later, the 1WO left the boat.

Once again the crew of U-155 had less than a month ashore before setting off again across the Atlantic to operate off British Guiana. There had been some changes of personnel, which included a new 1WO Hermann Steinert taking over after spending the first five months of the year at the U-boat school – he later went on to command U-128.

It was Thursday, 9 July, when Adolf Piening took his boat to sea for its third patrol. Having reached the patrol position safely it was not until the 28th that the first victim came into the sights. It was an armed Brazilian steamer *Barbacona* of 4,772-tons which was torpedoed and sunk at 0715 in the morning. Fifteen hours later another Brazilian ship, *Piave* of 2,347-tons was sunk after being hit by a torpedo and gunfire. The next night it was the turn of a Norwegian steamer, *Bill*, of the same size to be torpedoed and sunk. The following evening a 6,000-ton American steamer *Cranford* was torpedoed and sunk in much the same position. So ended July.

It was only six hours later, again in the same position, that U-155 opened its August account with a night torpedo attack on the Dutch ship *Kentar* of 5,878-tons. This was followed up by the sinking of the British steamer *Clan Macnaughton* of much the same size.

The freighter had sailed from Freetown on 22 July. At midday on 1 August the weather was fine and clear with good visibility but the sea was rough with a north-east wind. *Clan Macnaughton* was 490-miles from its destination, Trinidad, zig-zagging at nearly 11-knots when it was suddenly struck by two torpedoes.

The first torpedo struck No 4 hold on the starboard side and six seconds later a second torpedo struck the ship under the bridge on the starboard side. Both explosions were dull, the cotton cargo accounted for the lack of noise. No flash was seen with either explosion but a column of water was thrown up in both cases. The beams and hatches were blown off No 4 hold, the derricks were blown out of their crutches and crashed onto the marlin gun emplacement. The ship took a heavy list to starboard but as No 4 hold filled she righted herself and settled down. The boats were ordered to be lowered, and the ship was abandoned at 1230. The stern was under water and the poop awash. Later the stern fell off, due to the explosion amidships, and this portion sank, leaving the forward part afloat.

At 1235 U-155 surfaced, someone appeared on the conning-tower and looked at the boats through binoculars but sailed off without closing any of the survivors' boats. The master of *Clan Macnaughton* recalls:

> *I had twenty-eight men in my boat. During the first night the sea was very rough but after 2 August we experienced a fine sailing breeze with a very hot sun. We rigged blankets as awnings and poured salt water on our hands in an endeavour to keep cool. Some of the crew had a swim at midday. The natives did not complain about the pemmican which I gave them spread on biscuits, but the Europeans did not think very much of it. However, after two or three days we became used to it. The chocolate was very sickly and impossible to eat during the heat of the day. On the fifth day we experienced heavy rainfall and were able to increase our water ration and have a really good drink. During 6 August an aircraft passed close to my boat but in spite of our efforts, she did not see us.*
>
> *On the next day I beached the boat on Tobago Island. I had been sailing for Port of Spain, but the current had swept us to the northwards. We arrived at 1530 at Castara Bay and a number of natives came out to meet us. We were given milk to drink; when we had drunk half the milk the coconuts were filled up with rum. I refused to drink this mixture, but several of the crew drank it and much to their regret these men all passed out. The natives looked after us for a few hours until two buses arrived and took us fifteen miles into Scarborough. We spent the night at a small German-managed hotel there where we were very well treated.*
>
> *The chief officer's boat had been picked up on 3 August and the third officer's boat was picked up by an American vessel. Both crews were landed at Port of Spain.*

The day after the sinking U-155 signalled its success toheadquarters and added that there was brisk tanker traffic in the sea area cast of Trinidad but that approach routes changed at least once a week.

On the evening of the 3rd an 8,000-ton tanker had a lucky escape, a torpedo from U-155 struck the hull but did not detonate, it was probably a dud. However, the tanker sent out an SOS which was picked up and relayed on by a ship in convoy E6. Also in this convoy was *Empire Arnold*, a 7,000-ton British ship bound from Trinidad to Capetown with a cargo of 10,000-tons of military stores.

By the morning of 4 August the ship had dispersed from the convoy and the lookout in the crow's nest was enjoying the good weather and visibility was only marred by a few clouds, although he was scouring the smooth sea for U-boats. There was just a slight sea swell when suddenly, at 1025, a torpedo struck the ship.

No one saw the tracks of the torpedo which struck in the engine room on the starboard side. A column of water was thrown up. A second torpedo followed. The funnel was telescoped into the deck and leaning over to starboard. The ship was abandoned. The starboard forward boat was successfully lowered, with the captain and twenty-two men, the port boat had twenty-four men.

Empire Arnold sank stern first, standing vertically out of the water from the funnel, just seven minutes after being torpedoed. The sea was strewn with wreckage and cargo. The chief officer takes up the story:

> As my boat cleared the port quarter of the ship the U-boat surfaced at a range of about 200-yards. The commander beckoned to me to come alongside, and I pulled over to him. He questioned me as to the name of the ship, the gross and net registered tonnage, and the nature of the cargo. He then asked where we were bound for, and I told him Capetown. He also wanted to know the contents of the cases on board the ship, but I said that I could not tell him. In answer to his questions I told him I was the chief officer, and he told me to come on board, and he would take me to Germany, but I made no move to follow his instructions. The second in command then came out of the conning-tower and asked me similar questions in extremely good English. He asked if I had any wounded, and I pointed out one man, who was badly burnt about the eyes and hands. We put him on board the U-boat, where he was given medical attention, and was subsequently put into the other boat. My mouth was bleeding freely, and this officer once again invited me on board, in order to have my injuries attended to, but I said that it was quite unnecessary, and I remained in the boat. The commander enquired if I had enough food and water, and asked if I knew our course. I told him that I did, and he said that we should make land in about five days. He told us not to be afraid, and that we would probably get good weather. The commander told us that he had torpedoed two tankers on our starboard bow during that morning, and that he intended to sink another ship on our port side, that he was going back to Germany. He said that he had done very well, and had been trailing our convoy for two days.
>
> The commander apologised for sinking the ship, saying, 'It is war', and I said that it was a bad business, and wished it was all over, and he replied, 'So do I, George.' The morale of the U-boat's crew seemed very good, as everyone was laughing and seemed very jolly. The commander pointed out one of our crew who was on a packing case, and said that he would take him off for us. I asked if he had any cigarettes, although I did not expect to be given any, but one man rushed into the conning-tower and threw us a packet. The U-boat went over to the packing case; the commander told the boy to jump into the sea, and one of the crew from the U-boat, who appeared to be an unofficial lifesaver, dived in and brought the boy safely to the U-boat. The commander treated him very kindly, and asked him if he was all right; and where he came from. The boy said that he came from Jarrow, and the commander said that he knew it quite well. He questioned him as to how many torpedoes had hit the ship; the boy said he thought only one, and the men in the conning-tower argued about it for a while. The U-boat then returned this boy to the other boat, and asked similar questions, and took the Captain on board, as prisoner.
>
> The U-boat commander was only aged about twenty-four, and was clean-shaven. All

the crew wore bathing trunks and were very brown. The whole of the time I was being questioned four men stood back to back and scanned the horizon and sky with large binoculars, ignoring us completely. There was a quartered shield on the conning-tower, painted red, white and green, and outlined in black.

After the U-boat had gone, I took the food and water from the two rafts which were floating close to, and instructed the second officer who was then in charge of the starboard boat to put half his crew on to one of these rafts until he could get his boat squared up and organised, and we towed this raft for about six hours with half a dozen men on it. At 1800 I instructed the second officer to take his men from the raft into his boat, and gave him the course, and told him to follow me. I decided to set my course for Trinidad. We had fine weather, with a light north-east wind. The boats kept together for about five days.

On Monday, 10 August, at 0745 we sighted a plane, so I dropped a smoke float, but no notice was taken. At about 0915 we heard the drone of a plane again, and when we spotted it we dropped another smoke float. This plane sighted us, and came down exceptionally low. All the men cheered; he did not ask whether we were short of food, or whether we required assistance but flew up and down in the line of our course, and then flew' away to the east. The next day, at approximately 1600, another plane was sighted. I thought that he could not help seeing us, and I was surprised when he took no notice, either of us or the smoke floats we dropped. At 1900 this same day we sighted a steamer, burned several red flares, and were picked up by a Norwegian steamer. It was 1930 on 11 August and we had been adrift for 8-days and 9-hours and sailed some 480-miles. We were landed in Georgetown on 14 August.

Meanwhile, out at sea, U-155 sank the small Dutch ship *Draco* by gunfire on the morning of 5 August. Three days later U-155 claimed to have sunk an easterly-bound 9,000-ton tanker. It was the *San Emiliano* of 8,071-tons, registered in London. The tanker was bound for Capetown with a cargo of 12,500-tons of aviation spirit. Earlier in the day the tanker had dispersed from a convoy, two days out of Trinidad, and was sailing independently. It had proceeded at 8-knots until 1930 when a hospital ship crossed its bows. As this ship had all her lights blazing the tanker ceased zig-zagging, altered course to the northward, and continued at full speed to get away from her lights and two hours later, then steaming at 13-knots it was struck by two torpedoes.

The first torpedo struck under the bridge on the starboard side, followed about 20-seconds later by another torpedo which struck the pump room about sixty feet abaft the bridge.

The chief officer takes up the story:

I was in my cabin at the time and heard a loud humming noise just before the first torpedo exploded, I thought we were being dive bombed, but on hearing the second explosion I realised we had been torpedoed. Both explosions were very noisy but I am unable to say whether any water was thrown up or if there was a flash. The first torpedo appeared to strike deep down, splitting the ship open and covering the decks with gasoline, while the second one set fire to the ship, and within half a minute the vessel was a blazing inferno from the bridge aft; the crew abaft the bridge had no hope of surviving. I managed to climb through the port on to the fore deck and a few of the crew succeeded in following me. I saw No 2 forward lifeboat was undamaged and the wireless operator volunteered to release this boat. This man crawled on his hands and knees through the flames and released the falls, jumping into the boat as she fell upright into the water. Seven of us bundled into this boat which was still made fast to the ship by the forward painter. I was unable to release the painter but managed to swing the boat off from the ship. Actually it was lucky for me that the painter had jammed because, as the ship still had weigh on her, on releasing the painter we should have drifted into the flames.

Just as we managed to swing clear of the ship the seams opened and burning gasoline poured out over the water. I heard one man shouting from the fo'c'sle head and looking back I could see a member of the crew leaping from the deck into the burning water without an earthly chance of escape, and I was powerless to help them. Four of the crew, including the apprentice, immediately took the oars and rowed away from the ship, but even so the flames gradually crept nearer and nearer the boat. I took one of the oars and pulled like grim death, and as the ship lost her weigh we managed to get about half a mile from her, where we stood by in the hope of sighting further survivors. We picked up four men from the water, there were now twelve of us in the lifeboat. Apprentice Clarke had been badly burnt and was almost unrecognisable; at the time we did not realise how badly he was injured, but when he ceased rowing I found he had been rowing with the bones of his hands, the flesh had been burnt off, I could not get his hands off the oars and finally had to use a knife to do so.

Half an hour after leaving the ship's side a flickering light was observed on the port quarter of the ship. Thinking this was probably the U-boat I flashed an SOS message with the torch, whereupon the flashing ceased and we saw nothing more. One of the wireless operators stated that he saw the U-boat for a few seconds whilst running forward to abandon ship. We stood by the ship all night and at 0700 on the following morning, the vessel appeared to melt amidships and break in two, the after end sank in a mass of smoke and flames, while the bow up-ended and remained afloat and blazing for another hour. The apprentice and the Second Officer both died in agonizing pain during the morning and during the afternoon two other men died from burns and injuries.

At 1100 on 9 August we sighted an aircraft, which circled the burning wreckage several times. We signalled to him, he did not appear to understand, but finally came over and dropped a barrel of water which unfortunately broke on hitting the sea. Throughout that Saturday the aircraft kept in contact with us and at 1830 one of them dropped a parachute with water, rations, medical supplies, cigarettes and instructions to proceed to Dutch Guiana lightship, approximate ninety miles distant. At 1900 the next day we sighted a US Army

transport which picked up we eight survivors and landed us at Paramaribo the next morning.
One of the forty crew members who died, 17-year-old apprentice Donald
Owen Clarke was awarded a posthumous George Cross.
The story of his ordeal in the lifeboat was reported:

> He boarded the only lifeboat that was left intact, which was full of burnt and wounded
> men. He himself was severely burnt on his face, hands and legs. When the painter was cast
> off the lifeboat started to drift back on to the flaming tanker and it was evident that it would
> require a tremendous effort to pull it out of danger. Most of the occupants of the lifeboat,
> however, were so badly burnt that they were unable to man an oar. Despite his own fearful
> injuries apprentice Clarke took an oar and pulled heartily for two hours without a groan or
> murmur of complaint. Only when the boat was well clear did he collapse and then his burnt
> hands had to be cut away from the oar. Although life was ebbing out of his tortured body he
> lay in the bottom of the boat singing gay and cheerful songs to keep up the spirits of his
> injured shipmates. Next day he died.

In two months seventy-eight ships had been sunk and nearly half of them
were oil tankers.

The day after the *San Emiliano* was sunk there was a gun battle with a
small Dutch freighter that was on the same course as U-155 and eventually
the 383-ton *Strabo* was sunk. It was the tenth and last victim of U-155's
third patrol and three days later the award of the Knight's Cross to Adolf
Piening was promulgated. Then things started to go wrong.

Six days after the news of the award, off the hot and steamy Guianas, U-
155 was bombed twice and one rating was lost overboard. The next day, 20
August, U-155 reported that its ability to dive was reduced due to damage
to its battery. It requested a rendezvous with U-510 to take over a bridging
cable as further cells had become defective and it was still unable to dive.
The U-boat was ordered to return home with U-510 and was told that
spare parts were being brought by a boat putting to sea. The two U-boats
met and commenced the eastward return passage. On 4 September they
were ordered to rendezvous with the supply boat U-460 on the evening of
7 September, in mid-Atlantic. After the meeting with the Type XIV boat
and the handing over of parts U-155 was still unable to crash dive and had
to be escorted the rest of the way back to base by U-704, relying on that
boat's radar. The boats eventually reached Lorient on 15 September.

As the boat was obviously to spend some time in port it was brought into
the safety of the U-boat bunker, with its thick roof, for repairs. However,
as it turned out the extra protection from air raids was not necessary as
during the seven weeks the boat was in port, and the crew were ashore, the
sirens only wailed out their warnings three times and this was for aircraft

minelaying off the port; no bombs were dropped.

While the U-boat was being repaired and the crew were taking well deserved leave. Allied ships were assembling for Operation *Torch*, the invasion of North Africa.

The pilotage parties 'Koodoo' and 'Inhuman', detailed to reconnoitre the beaches and lead in the landing forces at Algiers and Oran, reached Gibraltar in September and October. By 3 November the Eighth Army fought the battle of El Alamein and the next day Rommel was in full retreat. On the 6th General Montgomery announced that the battle had ended in complete and absolute victory.

So the way was clear for a second front landing and on Sunday 8 November three powerful Allied task forces landed over 100,000 troops near Casablanca, Oran and Algiers. The force was escorted by five aircraft carriers, one of them HMS *Avenger*. This carrier was the second, of six, to be converted, in America, into an escort carrier from the hull of a merchant ship, in this case the *Rio Hudson*. The 'Woolworth' aircraft carrier with the pine-planked deck had already proved its worth two months earlier with the Arctic convoy PQ18. Her twelve Sea Hurricanes succeeded in shooting down six enemy aircraft and contributed greatly to the protection of the convoy which still lost ten merchantmen sunk.

Also taking part in escorting the landing force was Michael Irwin, in HMS *Ulster Monarch*, whom we met earlier in HMS *Lowestoft* hunting U-boats. He was to have the same job again, now two years on.

It is stated in many history books that Hitler was taken by surprise by the North African landings; this is difficult to understand as the 29th Flotilla U-boats in the Mediterranean were sent to the western end, as is shown in this book. Admiral Dönitz, knowing of the transports off the Straits of Gibraltar, also dispersed U-155, U-515, U-103, U-108, U-411, U-572, U-173 and U-130 to make up Group Schlagtet. On 7 November, U-155 sailed from Lorient and by 9 November U-572 commanded by Heinz Hirsacker, was the first boat in position but was too late to stop the landings.

A year earlier, in the same area, the U-boats had had to remain submerged during the day, but now in November 1942 they were having to remain submerged during the night as well as day, such was the improvement of the Allies' radar. The U-boats' liberty of action was thus considerably curtailed.

Once the troops and supplies were landed their transports had to clear the area as they were vulnerable to U-boat attack. Among these ships were USS *Almaack* and SS *Ettrick* – both listed as LSI's. *Ettrick* was well armed and had forty-one Navy and Army gunners aboard to operate the guns. She also carried a balloon. *Almaack*, which had carried fourteen landing craft and service and anti-tank companies, had been with *Leedstown* at Algiers and among the protecting force here was HMS *Avenger*.

On 12 November, USS *Samuel Chase*, with the *Leedstown* survivors on board, and USS *Almaack* were routed to Gibraltar and arrived in the morning two days later. *Ettrick* was already at the Rock and was waiting to sail at dusk. The master of *Ettrick* recorded that he thought it would have been better had he sailed after dark, thus not making it easy for an observer to see in which direction the ship had sailed – in fact it, together with *Almaack* was routed to the Clyde. Both ships were due to be part of convoy MKF1Y, a fast one from the Mediterranean to the United Kingdom, which was due to form up south of Cape Camarinal.

The ships from Gibraltar arrived at the rendezvous on time but as several of the other merchant ships were late and as the aircraft carrier *Argus* did not arrive until after dark the convoy did not form up until much later. It finally formed into four columns with *Almaack* leading the first with a merchantman and HMS *Ulster Monarch* astern of her. The second column was headed by *Ettrick* as Vice Commodore with HMS *Avenger* and another merchantmen astern. The commodore's ship *Samuel Chase* led the third column with HMS *Argus* astern and there were two merchantmen in the fourth column. The column was escorted by five destroyers and steamed north towards Cape Trafalgar. Just south of Cape Trafalgar it altered course due west. Adolf Piening and his crew in U-155 were awaiting its arrival.

Twelve hours before the convoy set sail the U-boat had been informed exactly what the composition of the convoy would be and what time it was due to leave. The worry of the master of the *Ettrick* about an observer seeing his ship leave Gibraltar was unfounded – the Germans did not need an observer, they were reading naval signals.

At 2030 the convoy changed course and commenced zig-zagging. The weather was clear, the sea calm, bright moonlight and a wind force three. The moon set at 2330, the convoy ceased zig-zagging fifteen minutes later and at midnight it changed course.

Just after 0300 tracer bullets were fired on the port beam of the convoy. A frigate had opened fire on decoy radar balloons that had been released from U-155. Adolf Piening had seen the convoy at a distance of between 4,000 and 5,000-yards, as it was a clear night. The firing had occurred five minutes after the U-boat had sighted the convoy and an emergency turn to starboard was executed. Before this two frigates had raced past U-155 at a speed of between 15 and 18-knots but had not picked it up.

The emergency turn put the U-boat commander at a disadvantage and the four torpedoes, from the bow tubes, were fired at a distance of some 3,000-yards. As soon as they were fired, the U-boat went to 200 metres. The U-boat heard three torpedo detonations and later sent a short signal with this news.

On the surface there was carnage. The ships executed their emergency turn to starboard at a speed of thirteen-and-a-half knots and it was while making the 40-degree turn that the torpedoes struck. The first to be hit was *Almaack*, followed a few seconds later by *Ettrick*. Then almost immediately *Avenger* was hit. *Ettrick* had been five cables away from *Almaack*, and *Avenger* was three cables astern.

When the escort carrier was struck there was a brilliant flash which lit up the whole convoy as she blew up. One of the few observers was Lieutenant Michael Irwin, on middle watch duty, in HMS *Ulster Monarch*, just astern of the carrier. In fact a torpedo was sighted passing just ahead of his ship. It is almost certain that a torpedo hit the *Avenger*'s fuel tanks and the aviation spirit ignited, the pine-planking deck caught alight. In that moment sixty-seven officers and 446 ratings perished.

Of the happenings in *Ettrick* the master recorded:

It was a very noisy explosion and a brilliant flash was seen but no water was thrown up. The torpedo struck the stern tube bracket on the port side and exploded either in No 7 compartment or in the engine room tunnel underneath. This compartment immediately flooded and water entered the engine room through the tunnel. The tunnel watertight doors were open and the water flooded rapidly into the engine room and the engines stopped. The after troop deck was completely wrecked by blast and eighteen naval ratings were lost there. All the lights went out but we had a number of lamps and small torches so were not in complete darkness. The ship did not list but settled down by the stern on an even keel. I sounded the alarm bells and the boats were prepared for lowering. The ship carried six lifeboats of ninety-nine capacity, two motor boats of thirty-four capacity, two accident boats of forty-three capacity and ten LACs. The explosion had caused the belly band of one of the LACs to jam so we were unable to get it away. Also one of the accident boats was lowered in a hurry by the native crew and got jammed in the davits. As we had plenty of boats this one was left. At 0350 I gave the order to abandon ship and by 0400 all boats were in the water.

The watertight door into the engine room had been opened at 0300 on account of the refrigerating engine and was still open when the explosion occurred. The third engineer and the fifth engineer tried to close this watertight door but were unable to fully close it. The third engineer had been badly cut in the leg and finding they were unable to do anything further with this door the fifth engineer assisted his colleague up on deck. The fifth engineer then went to the upper platform with the fourth engineer and attempted to close the door from there with the hand gear but again they were unsuccessful. I think the door must have been bent by the explosion. By this time the water was pouring along the tunnel and flooding the engine room.

At 0430, after a final inspection, I abandoned the ship with the chief officer, SNO, OC Troops and two naval ratings who had remained behind after the rest of the crew had abandoned ship. At 0530 the Norwegian destroyer Glaisdale steamed over after picking up the crew of two of the boats, came over to my boat and took us on board. We then picked up survivors from one or two other boats and then received orders to make a search for the U-boat. She signalled to the other boats that she was off to hunt 'Jerry' and would be back for them shortly. She was joined by another destroyer and together they searched the area.

Down below U-155 heard a number of depth charge explosions in the distance but there was nothing for the crew to worry about.

At 0830 *Glaisdale* turned back to pick up the remainder of the men in the water. The master of *Ettrick* continues:

Dawn had just broken and I could see Ettrick still afloat in the distance. She was listing heavily to port and I watched the list gradually increasing as she quietly settled by the stern until the base of the funnel was awash – then she appeared to right herself for a second, and her bow rose out of the water until the ship was vertical when she slipped slowly under.

When HMS Avenger was torpedoed we saw a brilliant flash which lit up the whole convoy for a few seconds and she blew up. There were only twelve survivors from this vessel and they were picked up by the crew of my boats. The Glaisdale cruised around the wreckage of HMS Avenger looking for survivors, she could find nothing larger than a broken Carley float and numerous small pieces of hatch covers. She then proceeded to pick up the remainder of the men from my boats. The crew of Almaack were still on board so the Glaisdale attempted to go alongside to take them off, but as there was such a heavy swell running she gave it up. One of my LACs was in the water in charge of two naval reserve officers and men of the United States Navy. The Glaisdale then proceeded with all survivors to Gibraltar where we arrived at midnight and anchored the following morning, 16 November, at 0900.

The following morning the master from *Ettrick* boarded the *Moultan* for the passage back to the United Kingdom and at this time he recorded the events of the previous few days.

During the passage a Lascar crew member from his ship told him that a few minutes before *Ettrick* was torpedoed he had heard a noise like an electric drill. The engineers told the master there was nothing unusual about the engines that would account for this noise. The Lascar was above the waterline when he claimed to have heard the noise. The master had said, 'I do not think it could have been the torpedo approaching.' He had been wrong. The attack on the convoy carried out by U-155 was one of the first electronic attacks carried out. The Lascar had indeed heard the torpedo approaching.

In a later, amplifying, signal to U-boat headquarters, Adolf Piening said that in his attack, 30-miles west of Gibraltar, he had fired at three merchantmen, two of 10,000-tons and one of 15,000, Torpedo detonations were heard at 3-minutes 20-seconds, 3-minutes 24-seconds and 3-minutes 25-seconds after firing.

Almaack, of 6,736-tons was towed back to Gibraltar, *Ettrick*, of 11,279-tons, sank, as did HMS *Avenger* of 13,785-tons. However, despite being able to read British signals, it was a considerable time before the Germans learned of the loss of *Avenger*, and then it was not known it was sunk by a U-boat. Adolf Piening himself did not know during the war that he had sunk an escort carrier. He writes of the incident, in English:

> I received at that time, about twelve hours before the convoy left Gibraltar, a signal informing me that a convoy consisting of one carrier and seven to eight big merchant ships would leave Gibraltar at 1900 with westerly course. My position with U-155 was west of Gibraltar Strait all alone, and I took action after the receipt of the signal to attack the convoy.
>
> My intention was to deceive the convoy by starting balloons as radar echoes, and by doing so – to keep my position secret, and I was successful, as one frigate was firing with star shells at these balloon targets. I saw the convoy at a distance of about 4,000 to 5,000-yards in a clear good visible night, about half-an-hour before two frigates as hunters had passed me with a speed of 15 to 18-knots. About five minutes after the first sight of the convoy one frigate was firing with shells at my wood of balloons on my starboard side, and unfortunately the convoy changed its course at this time to starboard, so that I had to fire with a distance of 3,000-yards with my torpedoes. After firing I had to go down to a depth of 200-metres where I heard three explosions of torpedoes without knowing of any success. In my sonar I heard a big number of depth charges in some distance, but I was not discovered.
>
> Next morning I sent a short signal to my U-boat authority informing it that I had succeeded in hitting three torpedoes against ships of the convoy, but I had not seen any result.

A further signal from U-155 on 17 November reported strong air patrols with all types of aircraft in the area around Gibraltar. Single trawlers and destroyers were reported and during the night heavy air and surface searches were carried out with depth charges being dropped at random. Piening said there were small prospects for attacking ships which were well protected at night; he requested freedom of movement. Three days later U-155 sailed for a rendezvous, to the west of Gibraltar, with U-118. This

U-boat was one of only eight Type XB boats purpose-built for minelaying but which were more often used as supply U-boats. The meeting took place on the 21st when the oil pump on the Junkers compressor was replaced and U-155 then took up the position of the returning U-91 in that same area.

Three days later U-155 reported that it had seen nothing except for patrol craft and was picking up radar signals. The U-boat had been forced to submerge during the day and had been subject to radar by night. Piening considered that he had to operate outside a 500 mile radius from Gibraltar, he said this was essential to carry out successful attacks and not to be harried by air patrols.

Permission was given for U-155 to patrol further afield and on the evening of 6 December the Dutch ship *Serooakery* was torpedoed and sunk in mid-Atlantic. The 8,456 ton steamer had dispersed from the outward-bound convoy ON149. As it happened, this was the last success of the patrol but the crew were resigned to spending Christmas at sea. The U-boat, with four victory pennants fluttering, finally returned to the 10th Flotilla base at Lorient, on 30 December, in time to have a bath and be spruced up for New Year's Eve the following day.

On this day Admiral Dönitz recorded in his war diary:

> *The tonnage war is the main task of the U-boats, probably the decisive contribution of the U-boats to the issue of the war. It must be carried on where the greatest successes can be achieved with the smallest losses. It is necessary to draw the firmest conclusions from a clear recognition of this situation, namely the concentration of all possible forces on the main task while knowingly accepting the gaps and disadvantages this will cause elsewhere.*

Exactly a month later, while U-155 was still in port, the 51-year-old Karl Dönitz took over from Raeder as commander-in-chief of the whole *Kriegsmarine* with the rank of *Grossadmiral*. He was still in charge of the U-boat arm and kept very close to his commanders.

It was on 8 February that U-155 set off on its fifth patrol, across the Atlantic again, to the Florida Strait. Unfortunately for U-155 the 'happy time' when they were last at the American seaboard a year earlier was no more.

Ironically, for U-155 they were sent to an area away from where the main U-boat strike of the war was about to be enacted, for in March B-Dienst had exact information about Atlantic convoys and 630,000 tons of Allied shipping was sunk in the month while U-155 was on patrol with not one victory to report. The good news for U-155 came on 1 April when Adolf Piening was promoted to *Korvettenkapitän*. The commander had so far sunk twenty-three ships and damaged another.

In darkness the morning following the news of the promotion the unsuspecting Norwegian steamer *Lysefjord* was sunk off northern Cuba, in the Gulf of Mexico. The victim, of just over 1,000-tons, was much smaller than the commander's estimate, but the next day a more acceptable target hove into view. The U-boat had moved to the north-west, into the Florida Strait, and it was here that the 6,882-ton American tanker *Gulfstate* was torpedoed and sunk.

This fifth patrol had been the least successful to date and when Adolf Piening returned to Lorient on 30 April and learned of other U-boats' successes he was disappointed that he had not had a chance to participate. However, the timing of his arrival was fortuitous. It meant that U-155 would not be called upon to put to sea in May and this fifth month of 1943 was the one in which forty-one U-boats failed to return – the worst month of the war for U-boat losses. At the Casablanca conference in January Churchill and Roosevelt had agreed that 1943 was to be the year when the defeat of the U-boats was to be the first priority.

Following the huge losses Admiral Dönitz withdrew his Atlantic U-boats from the battle towards the end of May and having been in port for six weeks U-155 was due to commence its sixth patrol in mid-June. By this time the British had seized the initiative and began the Bay of Biscay offensive. Practically every operational U-boat had to pass through the Bay en route to and from its patrol area and this became the focal point of the conflict. By mid-June U-boats were putting to sea in small groups, remaining on the surface so that their combined gun-power would hopefully drive off any attacking aircraft. By this ploy the U-boats sacrificed their fundamental advantage and became just a surface vessel. The Allies soon overcame this tactic. An independent aircraft spotting a group of U-boats would keep out of range of the U-boats' fire until reinforcements arrived and they would then all attack from different directions and thus dissipate the defensive fire – that was the theory anyway.

This then was the situation when U-155 was ordered to sea on 12 June. The crew were a little apprehensive as they knew that for the past fortnight Allied aircraft had been actively laying mines in the waters outside the Biscay bases.

Several boats put to sea on this Saturday. A group of three from La Pallice crossed the Bay without loss. Those from Lorient and Brest were not so fortunate; U-68 was also a Lorient boat and U-159, U-415 and U-634 made up the group of five. The group successfully repulsed individual attacks until it reached a position north of Cape Ortegal on the Monday morning.

Four Mosquitos, led by a Polish squadron leader of No 307 Squadron from Predannack, saw the U-boats which immediately formed themselves into a defensive formation as they awaited the inevitable attack. The squadron leader ordered his formation into a line astern attack and it was U-68 and U-155 that became the targets. As the leader began the attack he was met with an intense barrage of fire from the U-boats. The Polish airman saw his cannon shells striking the conning-towers of both U-boats and then his Mosquito's port engine was hit by return fire and immediately seized – he had to withdraw. The second Mosquito roared into the attack but at the fatal moment its guns failed to fire; the other two Mosquitos did not attack.

Both the Lorient-based U-boats turned back to base for repairs and to land the many casualties among their crews; U-155 arrived back on 16 June and for the first time the U-boat was not flying any victory pennants.

It took only a fortnight for the shipyard workers to repair U-155 and during this time the drafting office had made good the crew losses. The U-boat was to put to sea again on 30 June, but the night before sailing a force of Wellingtons laid mines off the base and a passage had to be cleared to allow the U-boat to leave on schedule.

This patrol was its seventh, the aborted one had counted as a full patrol. Ostensibly the patrol was to be to the Caribbean but events overtook the intention.

While ashore Adolf Piening devised a new theory to enter the Atlantic without being attacked and decided to put it into practice. He would use Spanish coastal waters, being very careful to remain just outside the three mile limit. The thinking was that aircraft radar would not pick up his U-boat because of the proximity of the Pyrenees and the background of other hills and cliffs on the north coast of Spain that ran down to Finisterre. More sea miles were covered this way but the U-boat did not have to cross the Bay of Biscay where the Allied aircraft were finding and attacking U-boats without too much difficulty at this time. The U-boat would be entering the Atlantic at a point far removed from the bases of hunting aircraft from the United Kingdom and Gibraltar. The theory worked out well in practice and this route became known as the 'Piening route' by U-boat headquarters and other U-boat commanders.

However, on this occasion, when U-155 reached the Atlantic safely in early July events had been happening further out to sea which put out all U-boat headquarters' planning.

Out in the Atlantic, U-boats were waiting to be refuelled and the Type XIV replenishment U-462, which was to have proceeded in convoy to refuel Group Monsun comprising nine Type IXC and two Type IXD boats failed in two attempts to break through the Biscay blockade; on 2 July this milch-cow was damaged by an air attack shortly after leaving Bordeaux and had to return. Already at sea U-487 was ordered to take the place of U-462 and be ready to refuel the Group by 14 July in a position 700-miles south of the Azores. But U-487 had replenished eight Type VIIC boats since 6 July and was 120-tons of fuel short of the requirement necessary to provide each boat in Group Monsun with 40-tons. An outward-bound Type IXC boat, U-360, was therefore directed to transfer the bulk of its fuel to the tanker, leaving only enough on board to return to base. Once more things did not work out according to plan, for on 13 July aircraft from USS *Core* sank U-487 and the following day U-160 was sunk, with all its crew, by aircraft from USS *Santee*. On 15 July U-159, whom U-155 had originally been due to relieve, was sunk, also with the loss of all the crew, in the Caribbean by a USN patrol squadron.

Meanwhile, two of the transitting U-boats had also been sunk by aircraft while proceeding independently through the Bay of Biscay. The refuelling was eventually carried out by U-155 and U-516 some 600-miles west of the Cape Verde Islands; but of the eleven boats of Group Monsun only five remained to continue their passage through the South Atlantic to the Indian Ocean.

Within a week the U-boat arm suffered a fatal blow with the loss of three U-tankers. Two, U-461 and U-462 were sunk in the Bay on 30 July and on 4 August U-489 was sunk to the west of the Faeroes. It is a matter of fact that all nine of the milch-cows weresunk by aircraft attacks.

However, there was some consolation for U-boat headquarters. The 'Piening route' was being used successfully. Late on in the evening of 2 August, as heavy air and surface patrols were sweeping north-west of Cape Ortegal in search of fresh victims, Dönitz ordered four U-boats on their way home to proceed through Spanish coastal waters without regard for the three mile limit. Later U-155 used this route to return to Lorient.

The Allies were not quite sure what was happening. From 7 August until the end of the month only three U-boats were sighted in the Bay. This figure was disappointingly low after the large number in the previous few months – U-boat headquarters had good reason to thank U-155 for initiating this route. There were, however, some serious disadvantages for U-boats using this narrow channel, such as liberty of manoeuvre and the prevalence of fishing craft in the coastal waters.

It was on 11 August that U-155 returned to Lorient, the second successive patrol with no sinkings to report. However, the U-boat moved north, to Brest, before commencing its eighth patrol the following month.

This patrol was to be the last with Adolf Piening as commander, it was also the longest patrol, lasting from 21 September until 1 January 1944. The patrol area was to be the north-east coast of South America. Even though U-155 had changed its leaving base, the RAF's minelayers followed the U-boat and laid mines off Brest during the night of 20/21 September.

Only one ship was sunk on this patrol, and that was on the Equator, to the north of the Guianas, on 24 October. The Norwegian motorship *Stranger* of 5,393-tons, was torpedoed and sunk. There were no longer the easy pickings there had been in the previous months.

Adolf Piening stayed with U-155 until February when, as a *Korvettenkapitän*, he was appointed to be in charge of the 7th U-boat Flotilla at St Nazaire, a position he held until the end.

When a list of the top U-boat commanders was published after the war Adolf Piening was credited with sinking twenty-five ships with a total of 127,645-tons – this put him 21st in the table of successful U-boat commanders in the Second World War. In fact, as is shown in this chapter, he sank twenty-six ships and severely damaged *Almaack*. The ship not included in the German list was obviously HMS *Avenger* of 13,785-tons. Had the escort carrier been included it would have taken his total above the 140,000-ton mark and put him in the top twenty, actually in sixteenth place in the successful U-boat commanders' table.

However his inclusion as a U-boat ace in this book is certainly merited, by his sinking of an escort carrier, of which five altogether were sunk during the war.

After 30 hard months of operations U-155 was still fit for underwater action and *Oberleutnant* Johannes Rudolph of the second officers' class of 1937 was appointed to command the boat for its next patrol.

This patrol, which commenced at Lorient on 11 March, was to the coast of West Africa. It was unsuccessful, for no ships were sunk, and, to make matters worse, on 23 June as the U-boat was nearing Lorient on its return it was attacked and damaged by a Portreath-based Mosquito of No 248 Squadron. It managed to reach port later in the day.

By the time the U-boat returned events had taken a turn for the worse for the Germans. The Allies had landed, and had more than a foothold, in France.

In August the new commander was himself replaced by the 26-year-old *Oberleutnant* Ludwig von Friedeburg from the pool at Lorient. He had previously been 1WO in U-548, another Type IXC boat.

On 6 August Bomber Command were diverted from what their

Commander-in-Chief claimed was their legitimate target of bombing Germany. Twelve Lancasters and three Mosquitos of the famous Dambusting No 617 Squadron bombed the U-boat pens at Lorient. Two Tallboys hit and penetrated the concrete roof covering the U-boat pens. The very next day the American 4th Armoured Division were on the outskirts of the town. Most of the civilians and dockyard workers had already left the area and it was time for the U-boats to move. The last U-boat to leave from the French base was U-155; it had been fitted with a schnorkel which came in useful for the transfer to Kristiansand in southern Norway. The passage commenced on 9 September and the new commander successfully negotiated the many patrols and other hazards and entered the *Kriegsmarine* base on 17 October.

The following day the boat continued through the Kattegat to Flensburg and later Kiel, which it reached on 22 October. Here, at a proper German shipbuilding yard, the U-boat was given a long refit.

At this point Ludwig-Ferdinand von Friedeburg was appointed to another U-boat then under construction. *Kapitänleutnant* Erwin Witte was nominally commander during most of the refit, but in March *Oberleutnant* Friedrich Altmeier, former commander of U-1227, took over command. His task was not arduous.

On 6 May Admiral Dönitz ordered all U-boats to cease hostilities. On this day Friedrich Altmeier conned the U-boat from Kiel up the Little Belt to Fredricia.

The U-boat, U-155, that had served the *Kriegsmarine* so well and had always brought its crew back to base, was ignominiously sunk, about 30-miles north of Malin Head with many other anonymous U-boats, in 'Operation *Deadlight*', the destruction of all surviving U-boats at the end of the war.

CHAPTER ELEVEN

WHAT MIGHT HAVE BEEN

During 1941 Blohm and Voss at Hamburg built 52 Type VIIC U-boats, U-559 to U-610 inclusive. Not one of them survived the war as a *Kriegsmarine* boat. All except one were sunk; U-573 was interned by the Spanish in May 1942 after putting into Cartagena following a depth charge attack north-west of Algiers by aircraft from No 233 Squadron. This U-boat later served in the Spanish Navy.

The U-boat featured in this chapter, U-562, was amongst those lost. During its career, its success rate was not high and its record would still probably languish amongst those of other undistinguished U-boats, had it not been for its last success; even this was not for what it achieved, but more for what it might have achieved. Its success could have caused the largest loss of life at any one strike. But back to the beginning.

The Blohm and Voss yard at Hamburg was earmarked for special attention while the batch of U-boats were being laid down. During the night of 15/16 November, 1940, a force of sixty-seven twin-engined bombers raided the shipyard; heavy damage was caused and there were many casualties in what was the most successful Bomber Command raid carried out up to this time. Two nights later there was another raid, followed by another a week later. There was then a comparative lull in raids on the German city and U-562 was launched on Tuesday, 24 January.

In March *Oberleutnant* Herwig Collmann was appointed as the U-boat's first commander. He had been born in Posen in 1915 and served as 1WO in U-56 and joined his new command from U-17.

After the Baltic sea trials the boat was brought to Kiel and it was from the *Tirpitz* pier jetty that U-562 left Germany, never to return, on 19 June. The course was due north, through the Little Belt into the Kattegat and Skagerrak, over the Rosengarten, to patrol in the North Atlantic. The patrol lasted six weeks and ended at Lorient on 30 July. There were no successes to report to Admiral Dönitz.

For most of the crew it was their first visit to the west of France and once they had found their land legs and had a bath they donned their best blues and explored the town. The boat was in port for a month before putting out to the Bay of Biscay on 25 August. However, something was wrong and U-562 put into Brest where it stayed for eight days before putting to sea again on 11 September. It was at this time that *Kapitänleutnant* Horst Hamm became commander of U-562. He had spent six months as 1WO aboard U-96 and then six months as commander of the Type IIA boat U-58 at Kiel. The 25-year-old Düsseldorf-born commander was to spend the last seventeen months of his life in the boat when for him, and the rest of the crew, it was to become an iron coffin.

It was more than six weeks after sailing on the North Atlantic patrol that the first victim was sunk, when in a night attack, the small British steamer *Erna III* was sunk by torpedo. The U-boat then moved south where it trapped its second victim on 2 October. The British steamer *Empire Wave*, of 7,463-tons, travelling in convoy, had reached half-way across the Atlantic, westbound from the United Kingdom, when it was struck by a torpedo from U-562 just before 0700. The ship sank and the U-boat escaped and returned to base on 15 October. This was the only occasion that U-562 would be able to fly two victory pennants on its return.

A new 1WO, Walter Huth, joined the boat for its fifth patrol. The U-boat sailed after a month but was recalled, to Lorient, two days later. Plans had been changed and on the following day, 20 November, U-562 set off for the Mediterranean. This was at a time when the British were reinforcing their troops in North Africa and there were capital ships available as prime targets. As has already been recorded, *Ark Royal* had just been sunk and *Barham* suffered the same fate before the U-boat reached the Mediterranean.

The U-boat forged through the narrow waters that separated Europe from Africa on the night of 27/28 November to join the Mediterranean's 29th U-boat Flotilla.

There was an auspicious start for U-562 in its new surroundings for, in the dark hours on 2 December, just two miles north of Point Magri, Morocco, it torpedoed and sank the 4,274-ton British steamer *Grelhead*.

Three weeks later, on the next patrol at the other end of the Mediterranean, off Tobruk, an 8,000-ton ship was the target of the night of 23 December. A detonation was heard after seven and a half minutes but no Allied loss resulted.

The first quarter of 1942 was completely blank for U-562 and in April its minelaying only accounted for two small boats off Famagusta. The next torpedo attack was on a Dutch motor tanker *Adinda* in the early hours of 14 July off the south coast of Lebanon. However, the ship was only damaged.

On 9 December, following the North African landings, U-562 fired at a destroyer, one detonation was heard, but the Allies did not report any losses.

Following this singular lack of success the 29th Flotilla headquarters must have been pleased to receive a short signal from U-562 on 21 December:

> *At 0220 two hits after 61-seconds on a large transport, eastern area. Sinking noises. The steamer is presumed sunk.*

However, the contents of this signal were not quite correct – but, to begin the story of *Strathallan*, for that was the ship attacked, it is necessary to go back a decade.

The *Strathallan*, of 23,722-tons, was the last pre-war addition to the P&O Company's fleet. This splendid ship made up to five the 'Straths', as they were known to the rich and fortunate tourists in the golden age of cruising. These stylish ships were decked out in a livery of all-white hull and upperworks, buff yellow funnels and masts and contrasted greatly with the sombre tones of the rest of the Peninsular and Oriental fleet. In the carefree days of the thirties, the rich and titled dined and danced their way across the Mediterranean.

In 1942, the converted and now grey-painted Strathallan was classified as a troop transport and on 11 December it left the Clyde, as part of a convoy bound for Oran. Aboard there were 5,122 persons, comprising 296 Army officers and 4,112 soldiers, 248 nurses and 466 crew. The ship was well armed with guns and machine-guns and even carried a small number of depth charges. Bags of mail were carried in the bullion room in the hold.

The convoy proceeded south without incident, except for bad weather during which a number of ships were damaged, turned into the Mediterranean and early on 21 December had reached the end of the Oran swept channel. It was just seventy miles from its destination.

There was a full moon, good visibility, the weather was fine and the sea smooth. Ideal conditions, in fact, for a surprise U-boat attack, and 17-562 was on hand. At 0223 Horst Hamm fired at what he thought was a 14,000 ton troop transport and claimed to have heard two hits.

Strathallan was travelling at 14-knots when she was hit by a torpedo on the port side in the engine room. The explosion was very loud and it shook the whole ship. There was no flash but a huge column of water was thrown up right over the ship; a large hole was made on the port side, damage was caused to the bulkhead between the engine room and the boiler room, and also to the port after settling tanks. The boilers were not damaged, but the settling tank was, and the oil ran out into the boiler room. All lights and power failed, and the vessel listed 15-degrees to port immediately. The emergency dynamo was started, emergency lighting throughout the ship was switched on, power was put on to the steering gear and the emergency pumps were put on to the engine room.

'Boat Stations' was sounded on the alarm gongs. *Strathallan* carried four motor boats, sixteen lifeboats all fitted out to hold roughly 1,600 people, and enough rafts to take the remainder with some to spare. Troops and crew mustered quickly by means of megaphones and messengers, and boats were manned. Everybody remained very steady and behaved extremely well, but several men did jump overboard.

The sea being smooth, and the possibility of being hit again by a second or third torpedo being probable orders were given to lower the boats. They all got away except two. The rafts were then cleared away and some were launched with their painters fast on board in readiness. The list of the ship at this time was 10-degrees, but gradually increased to 12-degrees as the water gained in the engine room.

The chief engineer reported that the after engine room bulkhead was intact and the carpenter reported that all compartments except the engine room and the boiler room were nearly dry. All remaining troops were ordered to keep to the starboard side of the vessel to ease the list. Later, feeling that the ship would remain afloat for some time, the master recalled many of the ship's company from the boats. He told them there was no immediate danger, and many of the troops climbed to the higher part of the ship and went to sleep.

At 0400 HMS *Laforey* asked if the ship could be towed and towing commenced about two hours later, the ship being steered from the bridge with the emergency power. At daybreak a second 9-inch manilla rope was passed to the destroyer, and towing continued at a speed of about five to six knots. At 0630 the emergency bilge pumps were reported to be gaining on the water in the stokehold.

At 1030 a destroyer nosed in on the starboard quarter of *Strathallan* and embarked about 1,200 troops. *Laforey* was then signalled with the suggestion that the remainder of the troops be disembarked. At 1115 HMS *Verity* passed and signalled she had picked up 1,179 troops and nurses. At 1230 HMS *Panther* left full of troops and ten minutes later another destroyer arrived. By 1400 all the troops had been disembarked.

An hour earlier it had appeared very probable that *Strathallan* would get in to Oran, but an emergency bilge pump which had pumped much oil over the side was failing and could not cope with the leak. The tug *Restive* approached to assist in pumping, but at 1315 flames shot high out of the funnel and continued burning fiercely and paint on the funnel and ventilators burnt and dropped off.

It appeared now that oil had reached the still very hot brickwork in the boilers and heated and ignited the oil fuel from the settling tanks or bunkers. Going below the master examined the bulkheads in B, C, D and E decks and found them already red-hot and paint and woodwork smouldering. It appeared hopeless, but he ordered the emergency fire pumps to be started up and for fire-hoses to be passed over from the tug, which had arrived alongside. The ammunition from a magazine on A deck was ordered to be thrown overboard. This was done but the fire could not be tackled in so many places, and the centre of the ship was soon ablaze. It was impossible to check the flow of air through the accommodation decks owing to the windows and ship's side scuttles being broken.

The master returned to the bridge through dense smoke and almost immediately flames shot up through the B deck lounge to the officers' quarters. The 18-year-old cadet helmsman remained at the wheel until ordered off and both he and the master had to drop over the foreside of the bridge and run through the smoke to amidships on the starboard side of C deck where the tug was alongside. The master then went aft and ordered 'abandon ship'; all those still on *Strathallan* quickly boarded the tug and *Restive* cast off.

HMS *Laforey*, which had ceased towing at about 1400, was still in the area and the crew members from the troopship transferred to her which allowed *Restive* to return to *Strathallan* where she picked up the tow ropes and continued towing. The chief officers and master from *Strathallan* remained on board *Laforey* in case their knowledge of the ship could be of any assistance.

Towing continued throughout the rest of the day and through to the early hours of 22 December, when at 0400, *Strathallan* rolled over on her port side and sank about twelve miles from Oran.

In the event only two Army officers and six Lascar seamen were lost, and not 5,000. But what might have been. It appears certain that only one torpedo struck *Strathallan* although two detonations were reported by the U-boat commander. Had two torpedoes struck, the ship may well have sunk in a very short time, taking with it some 5,000 British troops. It was attacked at a time when those on board would have been least prepared to save themselves, most of them being asleep. What was a serious loss of a much-loved liner could have been one of the biggest disasters of the war.

After the torpedoing U-562 had been hunted and was damaged by depth charges. A signal was sent to the 29th Flotilla headquarters saying the U-boat was returning and because of a breakdown of the periscope it requested permission to put in to Pola. As the U-boat did not report any serious faults and could therefore be ready for sea again in a relatively short time, it was ordered to La Spezia in order to avoid the long journey to Pola.

In the early afternoon of 23 December U-562 reported that it had been attacked with depth charges and machine-gun fire that morning by a *Luftwaffe* aircraft, despite giving recognition signals. One crew member had been lost overboard.

The U-boat, unknowingly, was inside the anti-submarine hunt area allotted to *Luftflotte* III east of the Spanish and south of the French coast. The boat did not know that this was a forbidden area. A quick investigation revealed that the Captain U-boats was to blame; for some obscure reason the U-boats at sea were not informed, as had been the intention, of the anti-submarine hunt area created at the end of November. The hunt area limited the U-boats' inward and outward routes too narrowly. The route north of the Balearic Islands could not be abandoned and so a new ruling was given. The unfortunate U-562, attacked by friend and foe, was then ordered to leave the area. Group West was informed of the U-boat's position and was requested to forbid any more anti-submarine hunts.

That evening all the U-boats were informed of the limits of the anti-submarine hunt area. At 1907, U-562 was requested for a position report, and this was received at 1944 showing the U-boat to be south of the Riviera and west of Corsica. The next morning U-562 put in to La Spezia.

A later full investigation of attacks by *Luftwaffe* aircraft revealed that U-562 had fired an incorrect recognition signal. On this occasion the U-boat had been questionably fortunate, it was not to have the same fortune the next time, when it was seen by British aircraft.

The U-boat crew were pleased to be able to spend Christmas ashore, even although they were unable to spend it in Germany. By February of 1943 their U-boat was ready for sea again and the area they were to patrol was off the coast of Cyrenaica.

By the afternoon of 19 February, U-562 had reached a position about 70-miles from the coast, north-east of Benghazi. Here the U-boat was sighted on the surface by a Wellington of No 38 Squadron of the Mediterranean Air Command at 1325. This information was sent by W/T to the escort commander of a convoy which was escorting ships from Alexandria to Tripoli. Obviously the U-boat was stalking the convoy as it only took the escorts an hour to locate the position once they started the search – which in turn says volumes for the correct position given by the aircraft's navigator.

At 1420 HM destroyers *Derwent* and *Isis* were ordered to join *Hursley* to search for the U-boat. At 1515 *Hursley*, a Hunt-class destroyer, obtained a firm asdic contact at a mile distant and notified the others.

Conditions for an attack were ideal, visibility was good, the sea calm with only a light north-east wind. *Hursley* pointed towards the target, which had been identified as a U-boat, and the echo was held. Obviously the hydrophones in U-562 had picked up the sound of the destroyer, because as it drew near Horst Hamm ordered a burst of speed which took it rapidly to the left of the destroyer bearing in at 15-knots and contact was lost at 80 yards. A five charge pattern, set to 50-feet, was dropped. The shallow setting was in case the U-boat was at periscope-depth observing the convoy. Contact was lost after this first salvo was released at 1530.

Isis attacked at 1550 and again an hour later. After that second attempt *Isis* reported her asdics were temporarily out of action. A square search was continued round the estimated position of the U-boat and at 1705 *Hursley* again picked up a contact, confirmed as a U-boat, a mile away. The contact faded at 1,300-yards, but at 1710 *Isis*, whose equipment was now back in action again, attacked and she made two more attacks, estimating U-562 to be deep. As soon as *Isis* had made her attack *Hursley* picked up the target at 1,200-yards and swept in at 15-knots. At half-a-mile slight movement right by the U-boat was noted and the throw-off made accordingly. At 200 yards the U-boat gave a burst of speed to get across the destroyer's bow. Course was altered accordingly with the ship steadying up just before a 10-charge pattern, set to 100 and 225-feet, was fired. To everyone's astonishment, the U-boat surfaced on the starboard side of the destroyer, only about a hundred feet away. This was as the pattern was being fired and before any of the charges had exploded. Charges from the starboard thrower exploded just 20-feet away from its after deck gratings and about the same distance abaft the conning-tower. These charges either straddled the U-boat or both landed on its starboard side. It was fortunate for U-562 that shallow settings had not been used.

The U-boat surfaced on an even keel and remained awash for about half-a-minute and then submerged again. Orders were given to open fire but the depression was too great. In the short time that U-562 was visible it was seen to be damaged; the conning-tower was buckled and tangled wire was seen round it. The two stern tubes were clearly discernible. One opinion was that the conning-tower 'was split open' but obviously this could not be so.

The destroyer captain launched a further snap attack as soon as the charges had exploded to further demoralise the U-boat's crew. *Hursley* turned hard-a-starboard; the range was only 500-yards when the ship was on the attacking course. The bearing drew right in the last stages of the attack. Four charges were dropped from the traps as the throwers were not ready due to the difficulty in reloading them caused by the ship heeling over. Contact was held down to 50-yards. It was now 1732.

Five minutes later *Isis* attacked and then *Hursley* came in again and at half-a-mile it was considered that U-562 was lying stopped. A 10-charge pattern was fired five minutes after *Isis*'s last attack and a large bubble of air came to the surface on the starboard beam after the pattern was fired, a charge from one of the starboard throwers having landed a few feet ahead of it.

After the attack contact was regained, showing the target to be in the same position and was held out to a thousand yards, when it gradually faded away. *Hursley* was turned at 1,300-yards and swept back through the position, but no further contact could be obtained, not even after a second sweep through this position, *Isis* lost contact at the same time. A search was then carried out in the vicinity but there were no signs of wreckage or oil and no contacts were obtained.

The captain of *Hursley* thought that the second attack was instrumental in causing U-562 to submerge again and that the fourth and last attack of the day probably sank it, as both ships lost a good contact at the same time and for no apparent reason.

At this time *Hursley* was ordered back to the convoy, but later in the evening the Commander-in-Chief despatched a signal ordering both *Hursley* and *Isis* to return and continue the hunt. *Hursley* immediately turned round, increased to 22-knots and made back to the position. Very early the next morning *Hursley* ran in to a very large patch of light diesel type oil. This was reported by signal at 0100. *Hursley* then returned but later in the forenoon a striking force entered an enormous patch of diesel oil at least five or six miles in extent and ships searched the area independently for signs of bodies or wreckage but without result. At 0930 one of the ships found diesel and lubricating oil gushing up and considered that the U-boat had been destroyed. The sinking of U-562 has been officially credited to *Hursley*, *Isis* and to the Wellington who first sighted it.

The U-boat had operated in busy waters for two years but went for long periods without any successes to report. Its last attack, on *Strathallan*, could have dealt the Allies a severe setback. The loss of 5,000 troops might possibly have delayed the invasion of Sicily. Had the second torpedo struck the troop transport and the ship had sunk immediately, or exploded like *Barham*, Horst Hamm would have made the world's headlines the next day. His last success, sinking the 23,722-ton liner *Strathallan* qualifies his inclusion, but the sinking of the *Viceroy of India* and *Strathallan* were just two of the losses of the P&O fleet. By the time the war ended half of their fleet, 1.2 million tons, had been sunk.

CHAPTER TWELVE

U-Boat Postscript

The stories in previous chapters, while complete in themselves have often produced interesting additional snippets of relevant information on subsequent events, and these merit a chapter on their own.

As for example the story of *Courageous* given in Chapter I. It seems incredible that men in their fifties were recalled to serve aboard *Courageous*. It was their age that cost them their lives, for many did not survive in the sea, as did the younger men. It was indeed fortunate that the fuel tanks or tanks of aviation spirit did not catch fire as a result of U-29's torpedoes, for the casualty list would then probably have been much higher.

It will be remembered that Lord Louis Mountbatten in *Kelly* had picked up many of the carrier's crew. While taking them to Devonport a signal was received on board giving the position of *Kensington Court* which had just been sunk by U-32. The captain ascertained that the condition of the survivors was not critical and, never one to opt out of a fight, headed at full speed to the position given hoping to find the U-boat. The hunt was kept up all night but all that was found was wreckage – the survivors had, of course, been rescued by the Sunderland flying boats and U-32 was miles away. The next morning *Kelly* continued its journey to Devonport where survivors from *Courageous* were off-loaded on to waiting ambulances to take them to hospital.

Otto Schuhart wrote, in reply, to a survivor from *Courageous*: 'I think in

September 1939 you will have been very angry at me; but I did only my duty, and it was not so easy to do so.'

San Florentino, which escaped torpedoing by U-29 on 4 March 1940 was later sunk by U-94 on 1 October 1941.

Otto Schuhart later served under Paul Büchel who was then commander of the 21st U-boat Flotilla based on Pillau. Hans Jenisch had succeeded Paul Büchel as commander of U-32.

The supernumerary, potential U-boat commander, carried in U-32 on its last patrol was Fritz Wentzel. He was captured, and later helped *Lieutenant* Franz von Werra make the only known successful escape, back to Germany, from Canada. He says Hans Jenisch was known as 'Excellency' and was one of Germany's best men. He also says that *Balzac*, the convoy straggler that U-32 was stalking when attacked, was thought to have been a large steamer of the P&O line! On 22 June 1941 it took 190 rounds from the secret raider *Atlantis* to sink *Balzac*, but in the long running fight *Balzac* had plenty of time to transmit her RRR signal and it was accordingly necessary for *Atlantis* to disappear from the western side of the South Atlantic.

In his book *Single or Return*, published by William Kimber and Co Limited, as are all other books mentioned in this chapter, Fritz Wentzel writes: 'Before leaving Lorient I had been kitted out afresh and some of the things had come from captured British stores. In those days all our submariners were going around in British Army battledress and underpants.' This explains why survivors from various ships described the U-boat personnel as wearing khaki.

On the day after the sinking of *Empress of Britain* there was a general broadcast which said: 'To all, tugs are also worthwhile targets'. Fritz Wentzel writes, 'The implied reproach was for us... we could have polished off the two tugs without the slightest difficulty.'

At a post-war U-boat reunion gathering in Germany, Gus Britton of the Submarine Museum was introduced to Hans Jenisch and said to him, 'You're the bugger who tried to kill me when you torpedoed *Fiji*. 'Never mind that now,' said Hans Jenisch, 'let's go and have a drink!'

Incidentally the captain of *Fiji* was Captain William Gordon Benn, who had been captain of *Royal Oak*, earlier sunk in Scapa Flow by U-47.

It may be of interest to some to know that one of the Wellingtons that bombed Wilhelmshaven on 18 December 1939 while U-32 was on trials, remains today as one of only two of the 18,461 Vickers' twin-engined bombers. Two weeks after returning from the raid N2980, while on a training flight over Scotland, developed engine trouble and the crew were ordered to bale out. The pilot then landed the bomber on Loch Ness and released himself before it sank. There the Wellington remained, from 31 December, 1939, until September 1985, when it was recovered with some difficulty. The aircraft is now being restored at the Brooklands Museum at Weybridge in Surrey, where it was built.

The reason that Reschke and Guggenberger were asked to report their observations on the sinking of *Ark Royal* was that U-205 claimed to have attacked the carrier earlier in the morning and heard detonations. When U-83 attacked in the afternoon and heard explosions it claimed to have attacked *Malaya!* No wonder there was confusion. There is no doubt, however, that it was the afternoon attack by Guggenburger in U-81 that accounted for the famous old ship.

Friedrich Guggenberger became a prisoner-of-war when his later charge, U-513, was sunk off Santos. Post-war he was a distinguished West German Admiral. One of the watch officers also aboard U-81 Hans Speidel joined him 'in the bag' after he took command of U-643 and the story of that boat can be read in my book *Autumn of the U-Boats*. Georg-Werner Fraatz who, with his crew, was rescued by U-81 from U-652, had been attacked by carrier aircraft from No 203 Squadron off Sollum. His experience of sinking his own U-boat with a torpedo fired by himself from another U-boat must surely be unique. He and his crew in the new boat U-529 were all lost on 15 February, 1943, when depth charged by a Liberator aircraft of the RAF's 120 Squadron, off Cape Farewell.

Ark Royal had a very full life which is outside the scope of this book. Her full story is described in *Ark Royal* by Kenneth Poolman and The *Four Ark Royals* by Michael Apps.

I corresponded with Hans Dietrich von Tiesenhausen and Squadron Leader Ian Patterson who first attacked U-331. The airman said he later spoke to the German commander when he was being interrogated in London, although the commander does not recall this. He was rightly very upset about his crew being machine-gunned although the U-boat had surrendered and he adds 'one thing was certain, my boat would have gone down before any uninvited person would have been able to come aboard – however, the torpedo fired from the plane solved that problem.'

The full story of *Barham*, until the day she was torpedoed by U-331 can be found in my book *Battleship Barham*. A few extracts from this and my other books are included here, and further information has been added to them.

In the chapter on *Eagle*, an outline of Operation *Pedestal* has been given. Several books have been written on this subject, but probably the best is by

Peter C Smith, with whom I worked for many years. His *Pedestal* has been recently re-published, with many new photographs.

In the story of U-178, which sank *Duchess of Atholl*, it is strange that the commander should have claimed the sinking of *Mendoza* as *Laurentic*, an armed merchant cruiser that was ten thousand tons larger. Also, U-178 torpedoed *Adviser* an hour after midnight but the commander says he did not see the sinking 'because of air patrols' – this seems strange at night, and *Adviser* did not sink anyway. Moving on, the last commander of U-178 *Kapitänleutnant* Wilhelm Spahr had been a chief quartermaster in U-47 at the time of the sinking of *Royal Oak* and had worked his way up to command a U-cruiser.

The big mystery is why *Orcades* was allowed to sail when a U-boat was known to be operating on its route. Not only was U-172 sinking ships, it also used its wireless which was obviously being picked up in South Africa. Perhaps a clue lies in the speed of the liner. The 'Queens' and other large liners were able to outrun U-boats, and the master of *Orcades* says:

> I had been given orders to proceed at 15-knots until I reached latitude 10-degrees South and then to increase to 17-knots and to continue at that speed until I reached the United Kingdom in order to have four days' fuel on arrival. My maximum speed was 20-knots but I could not have maintained that speed for more than seventeen days and as my orders were not to stop on route I was forced to reduce to 15-knots in order to reduce fuel consumption.

Possibly there was a misunderstanding, perhaps *Orcades* should have steamed at full speed through the danger area and reduced speed later to economise on fuel. In the event the liner was hit while making an economical 15-knots.

The reporting of mis-spelt ship's names by U-172 is not surprising even though Carl Emmermann was seen consulting his identity book. Many an English person hearing the name *Llandilo* would probably think it was spelt with a Cl not an Ll and Germans unused to seeing double letters at the beginning of a name would be much more prone to an error of this type.

Moving on to the one survivor from *Benlomond*: it was indeed fortunate that he was floating up and down the coast of Brazil. My encyclopedia says the magnitude of the discharge from the Amazon is so vast that the salinity of the Atlantic Ocean is altered for a distance of 200-miles from the river's mouth. So it is very probable that the Chinese survivor was floating in fresh water and did not suffer quite so much as he perhaps might have done elsewhere.

Oberleutnant Herbertus Korndörfer, the second commander of U-413, was the former 1WO in U-593 and the story of this successful boat can be found in my book *Defeat of the Wolf Packs*.

Oberleutnant Dietrich Sachse in U-413, had been as unfortunate as Captain Benn in losing two U-boats in five months he suffered the ultimate fate in U-413.

In the space of a couple of days two letters arrived for the author from previous correspondents, Captain William H R Armstrong in Barbados and Lieutenant-Commander Michael Irwin RN (Rtd) of Gosforth. The former suggested writing a book about the activities of U-boats in the Caribbean and the latter was on the subject of the escort carrier *Avenger*. The common denominator is U-155, hence the chapter on Adolf Piening, who, appears to have been an outstanding U-boat commander.

Piening rightly says that the attack on HMS *Avenger* and the convoy was one of the first electronic attacks in the war, but as we have seen earlier, it was not the first. In a letter Adolf Piening wrote: 'Nobody on the German side knew during the war that your escort carrier *Avenger* was sunk by a U-boat. I did not get this information until after the war, in 1948, when a special group was comparing the War Diaries of your Admiralty, with my diary.' I just hope that if this book is read in the right quarters he will be moved five places up the U-boat Commanders' list from 21 to 16.

So, on to U-562, a U-boat that up until its last success had achieved very little in a long time. When *Strathallan* was attacked the U-boat commander fired two torpedoes, and claimed two hits sinking a 14,000-ton troopship. In fact the liner was 10,000-tons more and only one torpedo was believed to have struck her. After being depth-charged the commander requested to put in to Pola, in the north Adriatic sea. This to me suggests that what little enthusiasm there might have been in the boat was now beginning to wane – for Pola was the most distant port in which a U-boat could receive attention and it would effectively have been out of commission for some time and the facilities at the Yugoslav port could not match those in Italy and Greece. Then there was the incident of U-562 being attacked by a *Luftwaffe* aircraft. This cannot be blamed on the commander, but the 2WO, as signals officer, should certainly have known what the correct recognition signals of the day were.

The last moments of the U-boat were also bizarre. The fact that it was forced to the surface, seen to be badly damaged, and then submerging for the last time perhaps suggests it was out of control. Surely, once it was on the surface it should have stayed there, either attempting to escape at full surface speed, or to have allowed the crew a chance to escape before a scuttling charge was activated.

Walter Huth, who had been 1WO in U-562 before taking over command of U-414, brought his new charge to the Mediterranean. He survived just three months longer than his old colleagues, suffering the same fate from surface forces, on 24 May.

It is fifty years since plans to put Type VII U-boats into mass production were made. Much has happened to under-water strategic thinking in the past half-century. Torpedoes are now fired by computer and indeed each submarine launching is an occasion. It is safe to say there will be no more *U-Boat Aces*.

Glossary

ACL's	Boats built to carry forty full equipped soldiers (Assault Landing Craft)
Asdic	Device for detecting submerged U-boats. From initials Allied Submarine Detection Investigation Committee
B. Dienst	*Beobachtungsdienst* – German intelligence service
Capt. D	Captain of destroyers
CET	Central European time
D/F	Direction finding
ETA	Estimated time of arrival
FAT	*Federapparat Torpedo* – a torpedo with a pre-set course
Gnat	Accoustic or homing torpedo fired from a U-boat
GRT	Gross registered tonnage
GSR	German search receiver
HA	High angle (gun)
LAC's	See ACL's above
OC	Officer commanding
ORP	*Okret Rzeczypospolites Polskies* (warship of the Republic of Poland)
RRR	(or RRRR by Europeans) - being attacked by a surface raider
R/T	Radio Telephony
SOS	Save our Souls - international distress call
Sparky	Telegraphist
SNO	Senior Naval Officer
SSS	(or SSSS by Europeans) – being attacked by a U-boat
ULD	*U-Boote Lehr Division* – U-boat training division
VLF	Very low frequency
W/T	Wireless telegraphy
1WO	First watch officer
2WO	Second watch officer

Ships of approximately 20,000-tons, and more, sunk at sea by German U-boats during World War Two.

Date	Ship	U-boat
17 September 1939	HMS *Courageous*	U–29
4 July 1940	*Carinthia*	U–46
21 July 1940	*Champlain*	U–65
28 October 1940	*Empress of Britain*	U–32
7 March 1941	*Terje Viken*	U–99
13 November 1941	HMS *Ark Royal*	U–81
25 November 1941	HMS *Barham*	U–331
11 August 1942	HMS *Eagle*	U–73
10 October 1942	*Duchess of Atholl*	U–178
10 October 1942	*Orcades*	U–372
11 November 1942	*Viceroy of India*	U–407
14 November 1942	*Warwick Castle*	U–413
21 December 1942	*Strathallan*	U–562

Escort carrier sunk at sea by a U-boat

14 November 1942	HMS *Avenger*	U–155

INDEX